LOOK EAST POLICY AND NORTH-EAST INDIA

About the Editor

Utpal Kumar De, Ph.D. in Economics from the University of Burdwan, is now holding the post of Professor of Economics at North-Eastern Hill University, Shillong, India. Currently he is the Head of the Department of Economics. Previously he held the positions of Lecturer in Analytical and Applied Economics at Tripura University, Agartala, Tripura from 1994 to 2001.

Professor De has thus been engaged in teaching various aspects of economics at post-graduate level for over 21 years. He mainly teaches Micro-economics, Econometrics, Environmental and Resource Economics and Development Economics. His research interest is in Agricultural Economics, Issues on Environmental and Natural Resource Management, Empowerment of Women.

Professor De has visited a number of countries in Asia and Europe and delivered lectures in a number of conference and symposium. He has presented over sixty research papers in various international and national seminars and conferences. Besides completing a number of research projects, he has published over seventy five research articles in various reputed international and national journals.

LOOK EAST POLICY AND NORTH-EAST INDIA
Achievements and Constraints

Editor

Utpal Kumar De

Professor and Head

Department of Economics

North-Eastern Hill University, Shillong

Published on behalf of

North-East India Council for Social Science Research

SHILLONG

CONCEPT PUBLISHING COMPANY PVT. LTD.

NEW DELHI-110059

ISBN-13: 978-93-5125-192-7

First Published 2016

Published and Printed by

Concept Since 1974

Concept Publishing Company Pvt. Ltd.
A/15-16, Commercial Block, Mohan Garden
New Delhi-110059 (India)
T: 25351460, 25351794, *F*: 091-11-25357109
E: publishing@conceptpub.com, W: www.conceptpub.com
Editorial Office: H-13, Bali Nagar, New Delhi-110 015, India.

Cataloging in Publication Data--Courtesy: D.K. Agencies (P) Ltd. <docinfo@dkagencies.com>

National Seminar on Look East Policy and North-East India: Achievements and Constraints (2010 : Shillong, India)
Look East policy and North-East India : achievements and constraints / editor, Utpal Kumar De.
pages cm
"Published on behalf of North-East India Council for Social Science Research, Shillong." Papers presented at the National Seminar on Look East Policy and North-East India: Achievements and Constraints conducted in Shillong by North-East India Council for Social Science Research during 26-27 March, 2010.

Includes bibliographical references and index.
ISBN 9789351251927

1. India, Northeastern--Economic policy--Congresses. 2. India, Northeastern--Foreign economic relations--Southeast Asia--Congresses. 3. Southeast Asia--Foreign economic relations--India, Northeastern--Congresses. I. De, Utpal Kumar, 1968- editor. II. North-East India Council for Social Science Research.organizer. III. Title.

HC437.N67N38 2010 DDC 338.9541 23

PREFACE

The Look East Policy announced by the Government of India is an outcome of the thought of increasing trade relations through various sub-regional cooperations with the South-East and East Asian countries in the age of rapid globalisation. The cooperation has been based on the social, economic and political as well as strategic reasons. In this globalisation phase countries, across the world have been trying to achieve their export led growth in the international market depending upon their competitive strength with reduced barriers on import and export and accelerated trade in goods as well as services. The move is supposed to accelerate the overall growth process, reduce poverty and inequality, facilitate movement of human resources faster and help in acquiring technology and knowledge, etc.

Till 1990, India's major trade was with the Western world inherited from its colonial stage and necessities of fossil fuel import as well as technology and its trade relations with the Eastern nations that were in the pre-colonial time came down to a very low level. Because of its technological backwardness compared to the Western countries its export never increased significantly as against the rising import and negative trade balance. Despite the recognition of the role of international trade in economic development India's share in international export and import has been barely one per cent despite being the second largest populist country in the world. Proportion of this trade with the Eastern countries was very low which may be because of the political, institutional and infrastructural barriers. Whatever trade has been observed with the Eastern neighbours, has been taking place mainly through the land custom stations and porous borders despite having poor transport infrastructure. After realising the potential of trade expansion accelerate the growth process India announced its "Look East" policy in 1991 in an attempt to increase its engagement with the East Asian countries. It tried to enter into a sub-regional agreement and have regional free trade area in the phase of globalisation practice in order to protect the interest of the whole region and the individual countries as well. Consequently, in 1992, it became a sectoral dialogue partner of the Association of South-East Asian Nations (ASEAN).

ASEAN, which is a geo-political and economic organisation with 10-member countries, was formed in August 1967 by Indonesia, Malaysia, the Philippines, Singapore and Thailand. Since then, the membership has expanded to include Brunei Darussalam, Cambodia, the Lao People's Democratic Republic, Myanmar and Vietnam. ASEAN's objectives are to accelerate economic growth, social progress and cultural development among its members, protect peace and stability of the region, and provide opportunities for the member countries to discuss their differences peacefully. India enter into the full-fledged dialogue with the ASEAN in 2003 and thereafter India's export as well as import has increased with these countries substantially. Also India engaged itself with her neighbouring countries like Bangladesh, Myanmar, Nepal, Bhutan, Thailand, etc. to reduce the trade barriers, import duties and allow various commodities to be sold in the respective countries and *vice versa*. The objective is also to encourage exchange of ideas, technologies, manpower and construction of trade routes in order to facilitate the cooperation in the field of technology, idea, trade and mutually benefit the engaged countries in terms of income and employment opportunities. For India, as most of the trade is supposed to occur through the North-Eastern region, the region is supposed to be benefited most in terms of employment generation and expansion of tourism that has not so far contributed much to its progress.

The policy of Look East from its hitherto Look West on every aspect has increased India's share of trade to these nations in its total external trade and accelerated growth process. But, the policy also raised doubt about several questions including security, border situations, flooding of imported cheap items from the neighbours especially in North-Eastern part of the country that has very little industrial product to export, except its raw mineral resources and thus its employment and income impact. Unless the region becomes competitive and capable of producing exportable industrial products it would only act as a transit instead of being benefited economically and reduce poverty or inequality.

The present book is a compilation of 21 research papers presented in the National Seminar on ***Look East Policy and North-East India: Achievements and Constraints*** conducted in Shillong by ***North-East India Council for Social Science Research during 26-27 March, 2010***; that addressed on various aspects related to Look East Policy in the phase of globalisation or its previous regimes. The outcome of those papers highlighted the prospects of trade opportunities, possible threats, development and other issues with special emphasis on the North-Eastern region of the country. Mostly, the papers are descriptive and exploratory in nature and with empirical investigations. The papers as chapters are grouped into three categories. Chapters of the first part "Regional Integration and Development" mostly describe the issues of East and South-East Asian integration and development. The very first chapter by U.K. De on "Emerging Trends of India-ASEAN Trade and India's Look East Policy" examined how far India could integrate itself with other Asian nations, particularly with ASEAN, through the expansion of export to the ASEAN member countries and import from these countries. The results revealed a mixed outcome. The analysis shows that India's share in both export and import of ASEAN has gone up during the previous decade. Also, proportions of India's total export and import occurred with ASEAN have increased during the previous decade, i.e. after India became a full-fledged dialogue member of ASEAN. Though its trade (both export and import) with these countries has increased, there has been rising trade deficits with ASEAN, especially after the adoption of Look East Policy. P.K. Adhaypok, H. Saikia and D. Phukan in their chapter entitled "South-East Asian Economic Integration and Look East Policy of India" examined the nature and extent of South-East Asian regional economic cooperation and its prospect as well as the challenges it posed to India. They also analysed the direction and growth of India's international trade with various regions in the world. They observed the Look East as a vehicle for Asian economic integration and equity based domestic progress of India. Chapter by S. Gogoi and B. Baruah on "Look East Policy: An Opportunity or Uncertainty", however, did not show much progress of North-East India after the adoption of such policy. They also pointed out the issue of corelational linkage between policies and ground realities of social and economic situations of the region in general which in their opinion has not been addressed adequately before adopting such policies. The opening of traditional Stilwell Road and the potential opportunities as well as threats have been highlighted by K. Kalita and M. Gogoi in their Chapter. Potential of trade as well as its impediments are discussed in relation to economic integration by Saikia, Kachari and Bhattacherjee in their chapter on "India-ASEAN Economic Relation: A Study of North-East India". The chapter provided more stress on the development of infrastructure for the promotion of regional integration as well as trade. M. Goswami also highlighted the security dynamics in the light of Look East Policy of India in a very brief note.

The second part "Look East Policy and North-East Indian Perspective" addressed mostly on the North-East Indian perspective in the light of

Look East Policy of India. Nripen Dhar in his chapter on "Look East Policy and North-East India and Its Political Economic Implications" stressed mostly on the social and political integration of South-East Asian countries for the promotion of trade, transport and tourism for the mutual benefits of the countries in the region. S. Saikia and B. Medhi reviewed the relevance of having a separate Look East Policy in the phase of globalisation. They raised doubt about the impact of promotion of trade through strategic relations of East Asian countries on the North-East region of India. They advocated for greater involvement of the people of the region in the process of production and distribution activities as well as education through industrial progress that may make the region competitive and participate in the process proactively. Chakraborty and Ray provided a historical description of Space and Region Formation from the pre-colonial to colonial to post-independence period and how the process affected the region from social, economic and political point of view. So, the relevance of Look East Policy for the region is highlighted. Tarun Dutta is his chapter described the potential of North-Eastern region and then tried to examine how the region can be benefited once the Stilwell Road is reopened in the ambit of Look East Policy. He also described the importance of this Road from the point of view of military strategy and trade for India. A.K. Mishra in his chapter "Look East Policy and North-East India: The Growing Prospects" also described the prospect of the region in the light of growing integration and opening up of various trade routes, especially the traditional Silk Road. He also apprehended about the security issues and the military problems because of the important strategic position of the region. Development opportunities and the challenges of the sub-regional cooperation under the initiative of Look East Policy have also been discussed by D.D. Mali and A. Banerjee in their Chapters. P.J. Goswami and H.N. Das also described India's trade performance in recent past with the East Asian countries and addressed various infrastructure requirements for the promotion of trade relations in the region.

A major part of the trade with East Asian neighbours and also with other Asian countries takes place through the transit parts of Manipur and many people of the state are involved in this trade for their survival. Thus, a number of chapters in third part "Look East Policy and Manipur" addressed the issues of Manipur in connection with the Look East Policy of the Government of India. K. Bimola Devi in her chapter on "Look East Policy and Manipur" described the involvement of men and women of Manipur in border trade with Myanmar as well as various social and cultural programmes in the neighbouring countries and its benefit. She also mentioned the ill effects of drugs imported illegally from China, Thailand, Malaysia, etc. that affect the health of youth and even children of the state. L. Seityabati Devi and K. Kunjani Devi analysed the pattern and composition of border trade that takes place through Manipur with Myanmar in their respective chapters. The chapter of latter author also described how the handloom and small entrepreneurs of the state are benefited due to Look East Policy. T.N. Zimik highlighted the illicit plantation and trade of opium and informal trade of narcotics through illicit transit routes and simultaneous diversification of these trades with the opening up of trade routes under Look East Policy. O. Sareeta Devi in her chapter entitled "Look East Policy and Its Impact in Manipur" also described how border trade picked up after the adoption of the Policy and suggested the need to gear up the institutional mechanism along with infrastructure for the empowerment of people. Binarani Devi in her chapter, however, mentioned the trafficking of women and children along with illegal trade in drugs due to social degeneration in Myanmar that needs to be controlled if the beneficial effects of Look East Policy are to be reached to the mass population for their welfare.

This book thus addressed a number of issues related to Look East Policy, regional and sub-regional cooperation in social, economic and political front and development of trade, technology, manpower, tourism and the overall economy of India and other Asian countries and the creation of opportunities and associated problems of North-East India in particular. A wide number of issues like illegal trade, drug trafficking and trafficking of women and children along with the expansion of cultural exchange have also been discussed. The book provides a lot of information on trade and development as well as other relevant matters pertaining to the welfare of the country and North-East India. It may, therefore, be a good acquisition by the teachers, students, researchers and policy makers.

(UTPAL KUMAR DE)

CONTENTS

PART III
Look East Policy and Manipur

LIST OF TABLES

LIST OF FIGURES

CONTRIBUTORS

Dr. Adhyapok, Prodip Kumar: Associate Professor, Department of Economics, Cotton College, Guwahati, Assam.
Email: padhyapok@hotmail.com

Dr. Banerjee, Amalesh: Institute of Business Management and Research, Kolkata, Retired Professor of Economic, Rabindra Bharati University, Kolkata, West Bengal.

Mrs. Bhattacharjee, Deepali: Ph.D. Scholar, Department of Economics, Dibrugarh University, Dibrugarh, Assam.

Dr. Boruah, Bubu: Department of Geography, North Lakhimpur College, North Lakhimpur, Assam: Email: bububoruahrgu@gmail.com

Dr. Chakraborty, Gorky: Doom Dooma College, Doom Dooma, Assam, Email: gorky8bob@gmail.com

Mr. Das, H.N., I.A.S. (Retd.): Former Chief Secretary, Government of Assam, Adelaide, 281 Zoo Narengi Road, Guwahati-781024, Assam.

Dr. De, Utpal Kumar: Head, Department of Economics, North-Eastern Hill University, Shillong, Meghalaya, Email: utpalkde@gmail.com

Ms. Devi, L. Seityabati: Department of Political Science, Kamakhya Pemton College, Hiyangthang, Manipur. Email: info@manipuruniv.ac.in

Dr. Devi, Ksh. Bimola: Professor, Department of Political Science, Manipur University, Imphal, Manipur. Email: info@manipuruniv.ac.in

Dr. Devi, K. Kunjani: Associate Professor, Department of Political Science, Lilong Haorcibi College, Thoubal-795130, Manipur.

Dr. Devi, O. Sareeta: Associate Professor, Department of Home Science, Kackching Khunou College, Kackching Khunou, Umathel, Thoubal Distt.-795103, Manipur.

Dr. Devi, Th. Binarani: Associate Professor, Department of Political Science, G.P. Women's College, Imphal, Manipur.

Dr. Dhar, Nripen: Retired RD, NSO, West Bengal Region, MOF, Government of India, Kolkata-700059, West Bengal. Email: nripendhar_cal@yahoo.in

Dr. Dutta, Tarun: Assistant Professor, Department of History, Assam University, Silchar, Assam. Email: duttaarun796@gmail.com

Dr. Gogoi, Mouchumi: Assistant Professor, Department of Economics, Moran College, Sivasagar-785670, Assam.

Gogoi, Swapnali: Department of Geography, North Lakhimpur College, North Lakhimpur, Assam. Email: swapnaligogoi77@yahoo.com

Mr. Goswami, Manoranjan: Retired Colonel, Guwahati, Assam.

Dr. Goswami, Pranay Jyoti: Professor, Department of Commerce, Assam University, Silchar, Assam. Email: pranay.jyoti.goswami@aus.ac.in

Kachari, Sri Khagen: Professor and Head, Department of Economics, Dhemaji Commerce College, Dhemaji, Assam.

Dr. Kalita, Kamalesh: Assistant Professor, Department of Economic, Tinsukia College, Kachujan, Tinsukia-786125, Assam. Email: tinsukiacollege1956@gmail.com

Prof. Mali, D.D.: Former Director, Indian Institute of Entrepreneurship, Guwahati, Assam. Email: wranji@yahoo.com

Mr. Medhi, Bishmita: Research Scholar, Department of Geography, North-Eastern Hill University, Shillong, Meghalaya. Email: bishmita.elsa@gmail.com

Dr. Mishra, Ajay Kumar: Assistant Professor, Department of Political Science, Wngcha Rajkumar Government College, Deomali, Arunachal Pradesh.

Dr. Phukan, Devojit: Associate Professor, Department of Economics, D.R. College, Golaghat, Assam. Email: d_phukan@debrajroycollege.org

Dr. Ray, Asok Kumar: Rajiv Gandhi Foundation, Rajendra Bhawan, Rajender Road, New Delhi.

Mr. Saikia, Biren: Research Scholar, Department of Economics, Dibrugarh University, Dibrugarh, Assam. Email: birensaikia38@yahoo.co.in

Dr. Saikia, Hemanta: Assistant Professor, Department of Economics, H.P.B. College, Golaghat, Assam. Email: hemantaassam@yahoo.com

Mr. Saikia, Sailajananda: Assistant Professor, M.C. College, Barpeta, Assam. Email: s.sailajananda@gmail.com

Dr. Zimik, T. Ninghorla: Associate Professor, Department of Political Science, Pettigrew College, Ukhrul, Manipur.

PART I

Regional Integration and Development

1

EMERGING TRENDS OF INDIA-ASEAN TRADE AND INDIA'S LOOK EAST POLICY

Utpal Kumar De

Introduction

India's Look East Policy is an important aspect of sub-regional cooperation to extend the free trade area among the eastern nations in the ambit of overall globalisation. The integration of India with these Eastern countries to form a block has been in order to gain competitive advantage with other blocks in the world. This Eastern block controls over approximately one-fourth of the overall world trade. However, India's share of total world trade despite increase after the structural reform and liberalisation, privatisation and globalisation policy adopted in 1991, is yet very small as compared to its size of the economy and population. The Framework Agreement for trade in goods between India and broadly ASEAN, which was the basis of trade negotiations, envisaged a substantial reduction in applied tariff rates and non-tariff barriers. India-ASEAN free trade agreement (FTA) has aimed at enhancing trade gains and provides potential trade opportunities for both India and ASEAN (Raju, 2010). During previous few years, after it became full-fledged member of ASEAN, India's export to ASEAN countries increased along with its import from those nations and slowly India's trade deficit declined in recent past. But there remains a threat of rising import even of many agricultural products (particularly from Indonesia and Malaysia) which was also rising during pre-free trade agreement period. The primary reason has been the access to duty free channel imports for value-added exports. This would mean that these products are being imported (from ASEAN and other countries) under duty free channel for exporting value-added products in the pre-FTA years and are likely to continue in the post-FTA period.

However, the region witnessed vigorous efforts during 1990s towards formation of regional trade agreements (RTAs) by South Asian countries. Seven South Asian countries (Bangladesh, Bhutan, India, Maldives, Nepal, Pakistan and Sri Lanka) formed the South Asian Association of Regional Cooperation (SAARC) in 1985 as a first step towards regional cooperation and Afghanistan also became member of it afterwards. In 1995, the SAARC launched the South Asian Preferential Trading Agreement (SAPTA) as the second step towards regional cooperation. Also the South Asian Free Trade Agreement (SAFTA) came into effect in July 2006, as the third step towards regional integration. In addition to being SAFTA members, some countries in the region (Bangladesh, Bhutan, India, Nepal and Sri Lanka) are also members of the Bay of Bengal Initiative for Multi-Sectoral Technical and Economic Cooperation (BIMSTEC) along with two Association of South-East Asian Nations (ASEAN) members (Myanmar and Thailand). Also, there exist bilateral trade agreements, such as the Indo-Lanka Free Trade Agreement (ILFTA) and the Pakistan-Sri Lanka Free Trade Agreement (PSLFTA). Bangladesh, India and Sri Lanka are also members of the Indian Ocean Rim Association of Regional Cooperation (IOR-ARC) formed in 1997.

Studies on the impact of such regional integration in East, South and South-East Asia and India's participation in ASEAN on the growth of inter- and intra-regional trade, reducing inequality, poverty in the participating countries especially in India show contradictory results (Hassan, 2001; Hirantha, 2004; Batra, 2004; Moktan, 2008; ADB and UNCTAD, 2008; Bandara, 2009).

This chapter thus tried to examine the changes in trend of India's foreign trade with the ASEAN nations in the pre- and post-Look East Policy period.

Materials and Methods

Secondary data on international trade have been mainly collected from the UN-COMTRADE Statistics of one digit level at Standard International Trade Classification. Data are also collected from ASEAN Merchandise Trade Statistics Database, Statistical Yearbook or World Trade Organization, International Trade Statistics, 2013. Also, information on India's export and import has been collected from the exim databank of Ministry of Commerce and Industry, Government of India. From their over time variation in composition and trend of India's export and import with these ASEAN countries have been computed and compared.

Also, India's trade volume with ASEAN is compared with her overall international trade.

For the purpose, the whole period of 1980 to 2013 is divided into 1980-90 (pre-structural reform and pre-globalisation), 1991-2001 (globalisation, privatisation) and 2002-2013 (post-Look East) sub-periods. Growths of India's export, import, trade balance etc. in these sub-periods are compared. Both graphical and mathematical description is given to understand changing India's position in the international trade with ASEAN. Growth of export or import has been examined by fitting a semi-log linear equation of the type

$$LnY_t = a + b \cdot t + u_t$$

where Y_t is the value of independent variable at time t (year),

u_t is the standard random disturbance term with usual classical linear regression properties, and

b represents the annual exponential rate of growth.

Time series pattern of India's export and import has also been examined for stationarity to understand whether the growth of trade follows a stationary pattern. It is examined by using Augmented Dickey Fuller (ADF) test (Green, 2003; Dickey and Fuller, 1979). The following regression is run on the time series observations of the variable.

$$\Delta Y_{it} = \alpha_i + \beta_i \cdot t + \gamma_{i0} Y_{i,t-1} + \sum_{j=1}^{pi} \delta_{i,j} \Delta Y_{i,t-j} + \varepsilon_{it} \text{ where } t = 1, \ldots, T \ldots$$

Here, Y_{it} is the value of export or import at time t. The inference is based on the usual Dickey-Fuller τ-statistic of γ_{i0}, which has a non-standard distribution. If the value of the coefficient γ_{i0} is found to be less than zero and is statistically significant then the series is stationary. The Akaike information criterion has been used to determine the lag length parameter p_i. This equation has been estimated taking the time trend into consideration. After unit root test we observed both the series to be integrated of order 2 and thus cointegrated pattern has been checked between export and import (Engle and Granger, 1987; Johansen, 1988).

Observation

Growth of India's Export and Import vis-à-vis Its Share with ASEAN

India's external trade has grown proportionately over the years. Since, 1980 though both the exports and imports increased, growth of overall import increasingly outpaced the growth of overall export, particularly after 2002 (Figure 1.1). India's export increased from 7529.14 million USD in 1980 to 17940.18 million USD in 1990; while it jumped to 43878.49 million USD in 2001 and steadily reached a figure of 336611.39 million USD in 2013. On the other hand, her import increased from 13818.7 million USD in 1980 to 23799.15 million USD in 1990; and then grew to 50671.11 million USD in 2001 and then steadily jumped to a figure of 466045.57 million USD in 2013. It thus appeared that though overall export achieved an annual exponential growth of about 11.6 per cent, import grew at an annual exponential rate of about 11.4 per cent.

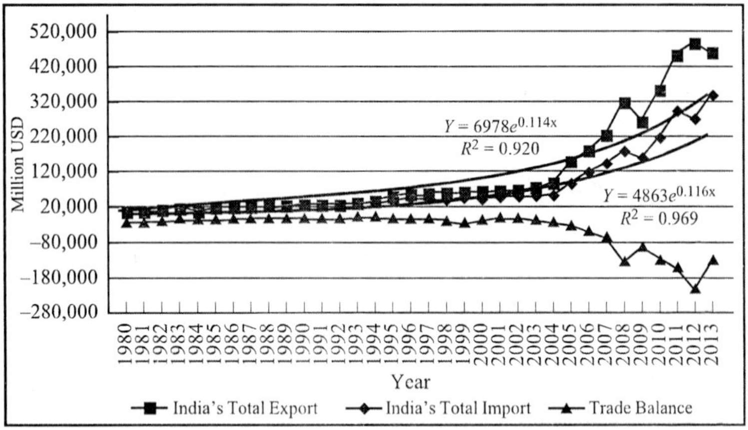

Figure 1.1: Growth of India's Total Export and Import during 1980 to 2013

Table 1.1 revealed that though during 1980s export grew at a relatively faster rate, during 1990s, with the privatisation and globalisation, due to opening up of the domestic market, relaxation of barriers and rising import of capital goods; growth of import became much faster than that of export and that has been accelerated after the adoption of Look East policy. It is noticeable that both the export and import increased in the latter periods. But acceleration of import has been much higher than that of export. Annual exponential growth rates of total export and import of India in percentage term for the period 1980-90 were 8.53 and 5.1 respectively and that increased to 8.55 and 10.04 during 1991-2001. These figures registered 17.5 and about 20 during 2002-13. Thus, trade deficit is found to show a rising trend. The deficit came down from 6289.56 million USD in 1980 to 1609.53 million USD in 1990 and increased again to 6792.62 million USD in 2001 and further after its integration with the eastern neighbours to about 129434 million USD in 2013.

Table 1.1: Annual Exponential Growth of Overall Export and Import of India as Estimated from Semi-Log Linear Equation in Different Sub-periods

Category	*Period*	*Coefficient*	*t-value*	*Adj R^2*	*F*
Export	1980-1990	0.0853*	8.63	0.88	74.49*
	1991-2001	0.0855*	11.17	0.925	124.76*
	2002-2013	0.175*	20.51	0.974	420.60*
	1980-2013	0.1167*	31.95	0.969	1020.99*
Import	1980-1990	0.051*	7.20	0.84	51.78*
	1991-2001	0.1004*	11.39	0.928	129.69*
	2002-2013	0.1998*	13.40	0.942	179.60*
	1980-2013	0.1146*	19.28	0.918	371.84*

Note: * Indicates that the coefficient is significant at one per cent level of significance.

Sources: *UN COMTRADE Database*, United Nations Statistical Division and *ASEAN Yearbooks* 2012, 2013.

Growth of proportion of India's overall export to ASEAN (10) and proportion of total import coming from ASEAN (10) is presented in Figure 1.2. Though export and import to ASEAN in absolute sense has increased continuously and got momentum after India's globalisation move and more particularly after integration policy switch over towards her eastern neighbours (Figure 1.3), the proportion of total India's external trade happening with ASEAN does not follow a smooth path (Figure 1.2). In percentage share, however, proportion of India's total export moved towards ASEAN increased faster than that of import. But the overall export despite its growth increasingly falls short of import in the latter periods and thus its movement towards look east did not yield any

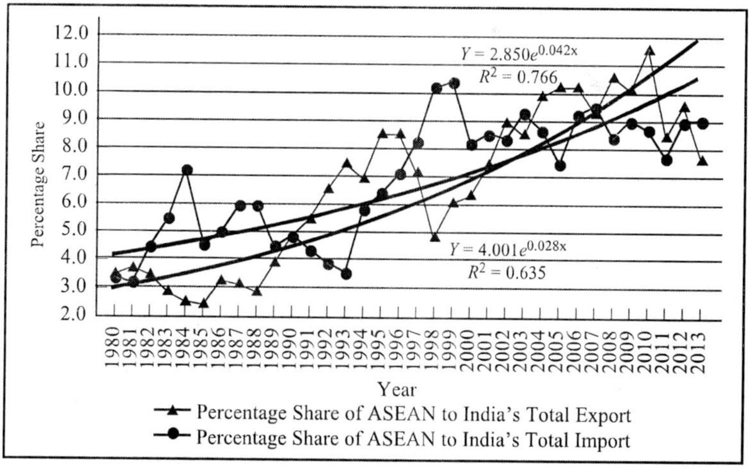

Figure 1.2: Growth in Percentage Share of ASEAN to India's Total Export and Import

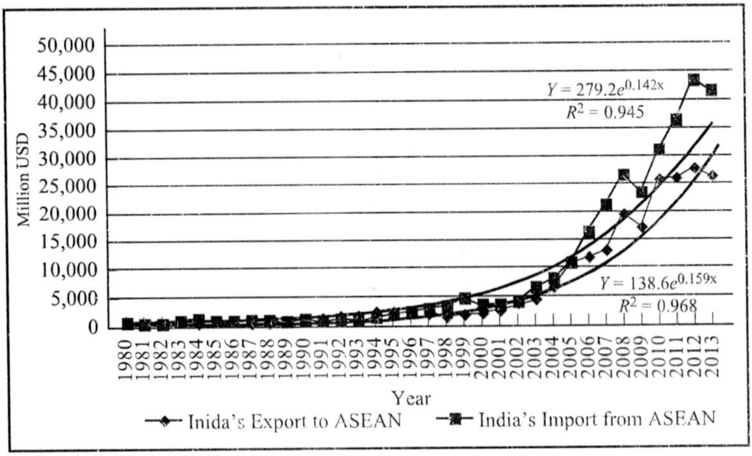

Figure 1.3: Growth of India's Export to ASEAN (10) and India's Import from AEASN (10)

result in correcting the balance of payment deficit. Table 1.2 revealed that annual exponential growth rate of India's absolute export and import to ASEAN in percentage term was 10.5 and 9.06 for the period 1980-1990. These values were 8.35 and 19.8 during 1991-2001 and recorded 17.2 and 20.12 during 2002 to 2013 sub-periods. These results also show that growth of exports to ASEAN has been less than that of imports from ASEAN since 1991, though both the values increased remarkably after 1991. For the overall 1980-2013 period, however, annual exponential growth rate of export was marginally higher than that of import.

Table 1.2: Annual Exponential Growth of India's Export to ASEAN and Import from ASEAN as Estimated from Semi-Log Linear Equation in Different Sub-periods

Category	*Period*	*Coefficient*	*t-value*	*Adj R^2*	*F*
Export	1980-1990	0.105*	3.742	0.565	14.00*
	1991-2001	0.0835*	3.57	0.54	12.723*
	2002-2013	0.172*	11.201	0.919	125.46*
	1980-2013	0.16*	31.39	0.968	985.12*
Import	1980-1990	0.0906*	5.334	0.732	28.45*
	1991-2001	0.198*	8.34	0.873	69.50*
	2002-2013	0.2012*	13.53	0.943	183.15*
	1980-2013	0.143*	23.48	0.943	551.15*

Note: * Indicates that the coefficient is significant at one per cent level of significance.
Sources: *UN COMTRADE Database*, United Nations Statistical Division and *ASEAN Yearbooks* 2012, 2013.

It is to be noted that after the GATT Accord in 1990 followed by the formation of WTO to provide institutional framework for the promotion of trade in goods and services among the countries, India also liberalised its trade through the relaxation of barriers, reduction in tariff and forming various free trade agreements bilaterally and multilaterally. The volume of trade has also increased rapidly after 1990. Also, India became a full-fledged dialogue member of ASEAN in 2002 and in October 2003 signed a Free Trade Agreement between these two regions, where India committed to design its peak tariffs and upgraded its trade relations with each member of ASEAN. However, as we observed import from ASEAN increased disproportionately afterwards as compared to the exports to these region raising trade deficits. On the other hand, proportion of overall export of commodities by ASEAN members imported by India grew after 2001 along with its share of ASEAN import from India to its overall import. It appeared a certain amount of divergence of overall trade of ASEAN towards India. But, after 2005, percentage of ASEAN export towards India increased faster than the proportion of ASEAN import to India and in the last two years both showed a declining trend (Figure 1.4). Though proportion of ASEAN countries' import exported by India increased gradually up to 2010, proportion of ASEAN countries' export imported by India had a set back during 1988 to 1993 and it has been associated with more fluctuations due to the foreign exchange crisis and restrictive import policies followed due to political turmoil in India at that time.

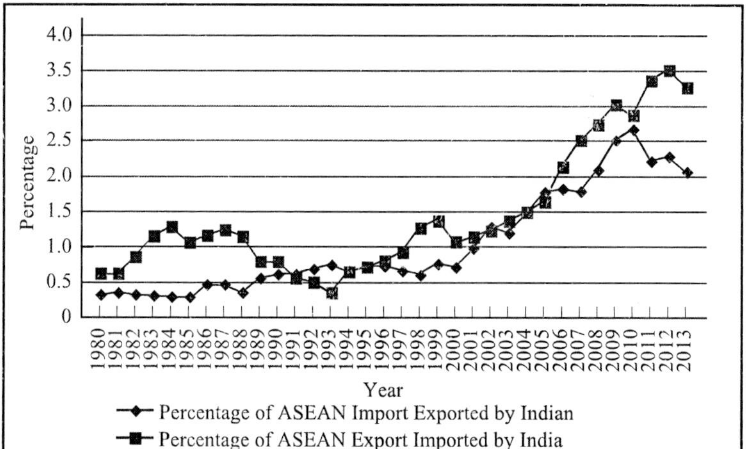

Figure 1.4: Growth of Proportion of ASEAN Import Exported by India *vis-à-vis* Proportion of ASEAN Export Imported by India

Stationarity of India's Overall Export and Import and Trade with ASEAN and their Interrelations

Table 1.3 reveals that both the series of export and import of India are non-stationary and integrated of order 2. Thus, there should be a cointegrating relation between the two. The testing of cointegrating relation is examined by Johansen's test including trend and intercept. Also, it is tested by Augmented Engel-Granger (AEG) test. The significance of the coefficients indicates a strong cointegration between the two (Table 1.4). The cointegrated relationship is shown by estimated equation-1, where a unit change in import is associated with the 0.635 unit variation in export.

Table 1.3: Unit Root Test for Stationarity of Growth of Overall Export and Import of India Using ADF Criterion (1980-2013)

Category		*Coeff.*	τ	*Trend*	*t Value*	*Adj R^2*	*F*	*Log Likelihood*
Export	Level	0.25	2.08	366.7	0.95	0.784	17.95	–301.37
	1st Diff	0.105	0.35	512.75	1.44	0.856	44.21	–314.36
	2nd Diff	–3.55***	–18.06	615.29***	3.03	0.952	191.41	–314.43
Import	Level	4.515	3.012	–2955.7	–1.52	0.679	6.078	–276.14
	1st Diff	–0.373	–0.786	1761.0*	1.852	0.696	13.82	–330.48
	2nd Diff	–5.48***	–8.872	1173.6**	2.014	0.892	58.80	–330.87

Note: ***, ** and * indicate that the coefficient is significant at 1, 5 and 10 per cent level of significance respectively.

Sources: *UN COMTRADE Database*, United Nations Statistical Division and *ASEAN Yearbooks* 2012, 2013.

Table 1.4: Testing Cointegration between Overall Export and Import of India

(a) Unrestricted Cointegration Rank Test (Trace)

Hypothesized No. of CE(s)	*Eigen Value*	*Trace Statistic*	*0.05 Critical Value*	*Prob.***
None*	0.611603	34.54801	15.49471	0.0000
At most 1*	0.125321	4.284751	3.841466	0.0384

Note: Trace test indicates 2 cointegrating eqn(s) at the 0.05 level.
* denotes rejection of the hypothesis at the 0.05 level.
** MacKinnon-Haug-Michelis (1999) *p*-values.

(b) Unrestricted Cointegration Rank Test (Maximum Eigen Value)

Hypothesized No. of CE(s)	*Eigen Value*	*Max-Eigen Statistic*	*0.05 Critical Value*	*Prob.***
None*	0.611603	30.26326	14.26460	0.0001
At most 1*	0.125321	4.284751	3.841466	0.0384

Note: Max-eigenvalue test indicates 2 cointegrating equations at the 0.05 level.
* denotes rejection of the hypothesis at the 0.05 level.
** MacKinnon-Haug-Michelis (1999) *p*-values.

On the other hand, though we observed some growth in export to and import from ASEAN, the unit root test revealed that the growth of export to ASEAN is not a consistently stationary growth at all and subject to high fluctuations over time, while the temporal variation in import from ASEAN is integrated of order 2 (Table 1.5). It indicates that there is inconsistency in the growth of export despite a continuous growth of import from those nations. However, Granger causality test suggests that there exists a both-way causal linkage between the import from ASEAN and the export to ASEAN (Table 1.6). But, uncertain fluctuation of export to ASEAN makes it difficult to predict the future trade deficit and to plan for meeting the emerging trade deficit with the ASEAN countries.

$$\begin{aligned} \text{Total Export} &= 4932.15^{**} + 0.6354^{***}\ \text{Total Import} \\ &\quad\ (2.29) \qquad\qquad (53.07) \\ \text{Adj } R^2 &= 0.988, \quad F = 2816.47, \\ DW &= 1.95, \quad \text{Log Likelihood} = -360.32 \end{aligned}$$

Table 1.5: Unit Root Test for Stationarity of Growth of India's Export to and Import from ASEAN using ADF Criterion (1980-2013)

Category	*Criteria*	*Coeff.*	τ	*Trend*	*t Value*	*Adj R^2*	*F*	*Log Likelihood*
Export	Level	0.228	0.623	107.18	1.38	0.723	7.274	–202.69
	1st Diff	–1.37	1.80	121.78*	1.73	0.897	21.023	–193.41
	2nd Diff	–4.35	–1.90	24.81	0.51	0.97	74.36	–196.08
Import	Level	2.271	4.471	5.785	0.108	0.918	27.79	–195.26
	1st Diff	1.716	2.038	83.52	1.16	0.913	24.97	–193.77
	2nd Diff	–7.70**	–3.61	175.99**	2.84	0.96	59.10	–197.10

Note: ***, ** and * indicate that the coefficient is significant at 1, 5 and 10 per cent level of significance respectively.

Sources: *UN COMTRADE Database*, United Nations Statistical Division and *ASEAN Yearbooks* 2012, 2013.

Table 1.6: Test of Granger Causality between India's Export to ASEAN and Import from ASEAN

Null Hypothesis:	*F-Statistic*	*Prob.*
Export to ASEAN does not Granger Cause Import from ASEAN	26.444	4.E-07
Import from ASEAN does not Granger Cause Export to ASEAN	5.109	0.0131

Table 1.7 shows the rising trade deficit with high fluctuations over the years after India became a full-fledged dialogue member of ASEAN. Except a limited trade surplus with Vietnam, Cambodia, the Philippines

and Singapore, India has dwindling trade deficit with other ASEAN nations. Overall, India has growing trade deficit with the ASEAN countries after it followed the path of Look East Policy. The Figure 1.5 reveals the rising deficit over the years, especially after 2002. Along with that the reduction in tariff to zero level by India on a number of items that these countries export to India (including some agricultural products where the domestic producers may face uncertain price competition) may increase the trade deficit further and occupy the markets of many domestic consumer products. Viswanathan and Shah (2008) already demonstrated the adverse impact of trade liberalisation on the India plantation sector,

Table 1.7: India's Balance of Trade with ASEAN Countries, 1995-2011

(million USD)

Country	*1995*	*2002*	*2005*	*2007*	*2008*	*2010*	*2011*
Singapore	45.5	46.7	2268.1	–511.5	549.1	532.50	1436.03
Indonesia	200.3	–493.6	–1628.9	–2962.2	–3772.0	–2640.42	–1674.86
Thailand	302.2	376.1	–137.3	–519.0	–659.5	–566.09	–677.78
Malaysia	–504.9	–587.7	–1292.2	–3875.3	–4427.0	–1099.01	–1167.93
Vietnam	108.5	276.4	506.1	1088.3	1441.0	621.49	723.47
Philippines	122.4	334.5	278.9	397.9	527.4	205.32	206.19
Myanmar	–131.9	–278.9	–371.9	–646.3	–668.9	–512.32	–312.94
Cambodia	1.8	16.3	20.9	43.6	49.6	19.15	25.48
Brunei Darussalam	7.2	4.3	3.6	–225.3	–308.7	–-191.25	–94.96
Lao PDR	NA	NA	NA	NA	NA	–1.10	6.27
ASEAN (10) Total	151.1	–306.0	–352.7	–7209.8	–7269.1	–3631.73	-1531.03

Source: Based on *UN Comtrade Database*, Francis (2011).

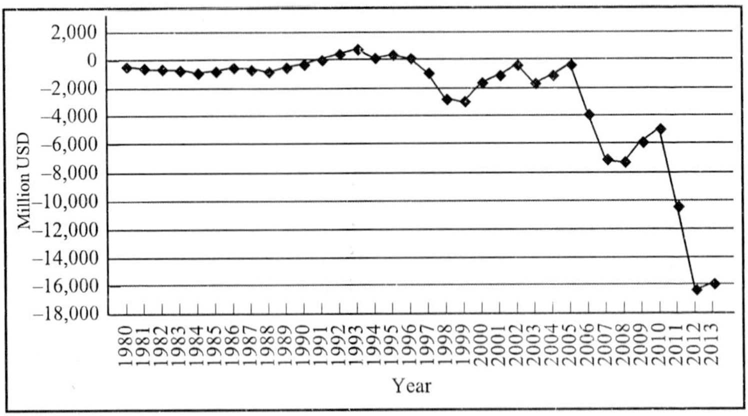

Figure 1.5: Trend of India's Balance of Trade with ASEAN

especially tea and rubber production. Among these nations India major export and imports occurs with Singapore, Malaysia, Indonesia and Thailand though the share has declined in recent past. However, it is also interesting to note that India's imports from its closed neighbour Myanmar, Lao PDR, Brunei Darussalam and Vietnam have declined during last few years though the export has increased.

Growth of Foreign Direct Investment in India

During the period 1990s, India entered into several regional or sub-regional co-dialogues in order to promote export, acquire technology and achieve overall economic growth. Various concessions have been given to attract foreign capital especially in the manufacturing sector to boost up the economy and meet the aforesaid objectives. Though foreign direct investment coming to India has increased significantly from 0.075 billion dollar to 36.5 billion dollar during 1991 to 2011, FDI of India in other countries has also increased from 0.011 billion dollar to 12.6 billion dollar during the same period (De, 2014). It indicates that India is now capable of entering the markets of outside world, not only through export promotion but also through expansion of industrial and service sector activities by its multinational companies in other countries depending on their capability to compete. However, it is yet to catch the fast growing Asian nations like China in terms of attracting foreign capital or foreign direct investment and progress in manufacturing activities and expand its export.

Figure 1.6 indicates the rising gap of proportion of world inflow and outflow of FDI shared by India since 1991 that got a boost after 2007. Rising inflow of foreign capital for the purpose of investment came in the form of capital goods and also reflected in the rising import over and above the export.

Concluding Remarks

The onslaught of globalisation and involvement of India in the formation of several regional and sub-regional cooperation, and free trade area with various eastern nations *vide* its Look East Policy could not bring India significantly closer to the emerging Asian nations. Despite, the fact that there was a notable crisis in these fast growing Asian countries in late nineteen nineties and recovery afterwards, India could access more markets of ASEAN countries. Thus, export to those countries has increased over time. Also, import from ASEAN has increased more rapidly during

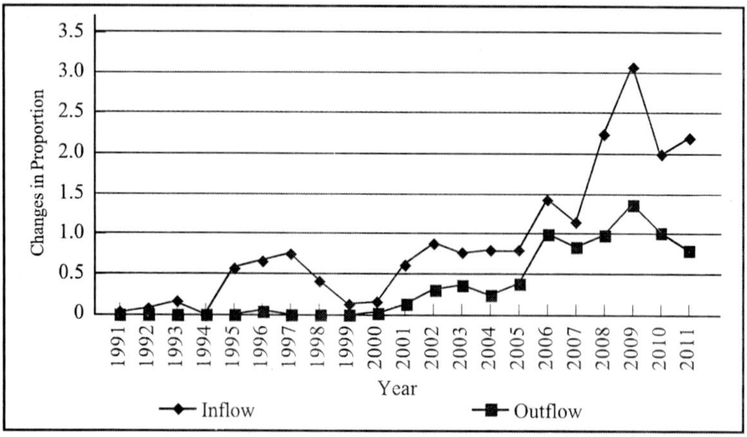

Figure 1.6: Changes in Proportion of World Inflows and Outflows of FDI for India during 1991 to 2011

the last decade. Not only that, proportion of ASEAN import and export shared by India has increased. But share of India's total export and import occurred with these nations increased with high fluctuations. Moreover, the trade deficit with major ASEAN countries has increased in the last decade. We find strong causality between India's export and import and export-import share with ASEAN are highly cointegrated.

In spite of all those movements, India has to go a long way especially to improve its manufacturing base with best possible technological update, especially in its North-Eastern states for which the Look East policy was initiated. If the production base is not improved in these states, this region will remain a supplier of only the raw materials and not of the finished product and face competition and thus will be flooded with the cheap products imported from these eastern neighbours as has been going on until now.

REFERENCES

ADB and UNCTAD (2008): *Quantification of Benefits from Economic Cooperation in South Asia*, MacMillan India Ltd., New Delhi.

Bandara, J.S. (2009): "Playing with Numbers: Critical Evaluation of Quantitative Assessments of South Asian Regional Integration", *Economic and Political Weekly*, Vol. xliv (48), November 28, pp. 67-75.

Batra, A. (2004): "India's Global Trade Potential: The Gravity Model Approach", *ICRIER Working Paper No 151*, Indian Council for Research on International Economic Relations, New Delhi.

De, U.K. (2014): "India's Look East for Integration with East Asia: Step Towards Progress", *Journal of International Economics*, 5(1), January-June, pp. 105-21.

Dickey, D. and W. Fuller (1979): "Distribution of the Estimators for Autoregressive Time Series with a Unit Root", *Journal of the American Statistical Association*, 74, pp. 427-31.

Engle, R.F. and C.W. Granger (1987): "Co-integration and Error Correction: Representation, Estimation and Testing", *Econometrica*, 55, pp. 251-76.

Green, W. H., (2003): *Econometric Analysis*, Pearson Education. Singapore.

Hassan, M.K. (2001): "Is SAARC a Viable Economic Bloc? Evidence from Gravity Model", *Journal of Asian Economics*, 12(2), pp. 263-90.

Hirantha, S.W. (2004): "From SAPTA to SAFTA: Gravity Analysis of South Asian Free Trade", University of Nottingham, U.K., unpublished paper.

Johansen, S., (1988): "Statistical Analysis of Cointegration Vectors", *Journal of Economic Dynamics and Control*, 12, pp. 231-54.

Moktan, S. (2008): "Evaluating the Intra-regional Exports and Trade Creation and Trade Diversion Effects of Trade Agreements in SAARC Countries", *South Asian Economic Journal*, 9(2), pp. 233-60.

Raju, S. (2010): "ASEAN-India FTA: Emerging Issues for Trade in Agriculture", paper presented at the Seminar on "ASEAN-India FTA and Way Forward", February 5-6, 2010, Centre for Development Studies, Thiruvananthapuram.

Viswanathan, P.K. and Shah, A. (2008): "Trade Reforms and Crisis in India's Plantation Agriculture: Case Studies of Tea and Rubber Plantation Sectors", Paper presented at the Fourth Annual South Asia Conference on Trade and Development 2008 organised by CENTAD, New Delhi, during 17-18 December.

2

SOUTH-EAST ASIAN ECONOMIC INTEGRATION AND LOOK EAST POLICY OF INDIA

Prodip Kumar Adhyapok, Hemanta Saikia and *Devojit Phukan*

Introduction

South-East Asia has been the faster growing region in the world for the past three decades where the economy of Japan and the newly industrialising economies of South-East Asia have been formed as the models of accomplishment for other emerging economies. After the shadow of the 1997 crisis, they appear to be a mounting identification of larger economic harmonisation and cooperation among the major Asian countries to augment Asia's role in world affairs. Over the years, regional economic integration has been adopted as a strategy for development in different parts of the world in 1990s, following the formation of single market by the European Union and North American Free Trade Agreement (NAFTA). With the rising esteem of regional economic integration worldwide, more than half of the world trade is now conducted between members of regional trading arrangements of preferential basis. In the past few years, South-East Asian countries have also recognised this potential of regional economic integration which is clear from numerous free trade arrangements (FTAs), especially Association of South-East Asian Nations (ASEAN). At the same time, the economic reorganisation and liberalisation have paved India's rapid economic future growth and international economic relations. Looking these, India has adopted 'Look East Policy' (LEP) to promote economic integration with East Asia which provide an opportunity to economic transformation and growth to its lagging regions particularly the North-Eastern states which can help India to shape an Asian economic community. India is negotiating bilateral free trade agreements (FTAs) with East Asian economic authorities which cover trade in goods and services as well as investment, as a template for FTAs hoping that bilateral FTA negotiations will eventually lead to a regional FTA that covers all of East Asia and India. India has accepted ASEAN+6 (ASEAN member countries plus China, Japan, South Korea, India, Australia and New Zealand) as the regional framework for an Asian economic community, with its inclusion as a inaugural member in the East Asia Summit held in Kuala Lumpur in December 2005. In this background, the Look East Policy (LEP) followed by India since 1991 has made the East Asian region, the country's largest trade partner which bring several economic problems and prospects to India in general and North-Eastern region in particular. This chapter has attempted to examine, the way for regional economic cooperation in South-East Asia that could become the third pole of the world economy. It also discusses the environment of the trade of Asian countries and the extent to which he negotiation approach will help India to foster economic growth.

Objectives

The main objectives of the chapter are to:

1. Examine the nature and extent of regional economic cooperation in South Asia and Indian trade relation with other countries.
2. Examine future prospect of regional cooperation by India on the eve of Look East Policy (LEO).
3. Analyse the prospects and challenges for LEP from an Indian viewpoint.

Methodology

This study is based on mainly secondary data collected from the publications of various organisations, viz. Ministry of Commerce, Statistical Department, Government of India, UNDP, IMF, World Bank, Directorate of Economics and Statistics of various State governments, Research publications of individuals, etc.

Results and Discussion

1. *Economic Reform and Regional Foreign Trade of India*

India's effort to gather speed of industrialisation and improve international competitiveness received a boost up with the declaration of the New

Industrial Policy in July 1991. The Policy changes were planned to draw sustained capital inflows into India, which provided opportunities for growing weight abroad, setting up the basis for a distorted relationship with East Asia. India is one of the fast rising countries in the world, growing rate of about 8 per cent in past few years. Large population of India provides market to the countries of the world. So, India's foreign trade should also replicate its potentials to materialise as a super power. The total volume of India's foreign trade has gone up from ₹ 1,250 crore in 1950-51 to ₹ 6,30,80,109 crore in 2003-04. At the same time, the value of India's imports has increased because of rapid industrialisation, policy of import liberalisation, within the country. However, the exports have not grown significantly due to primary product base, increased domestic consumption, inadequate export promotion measures, etc.

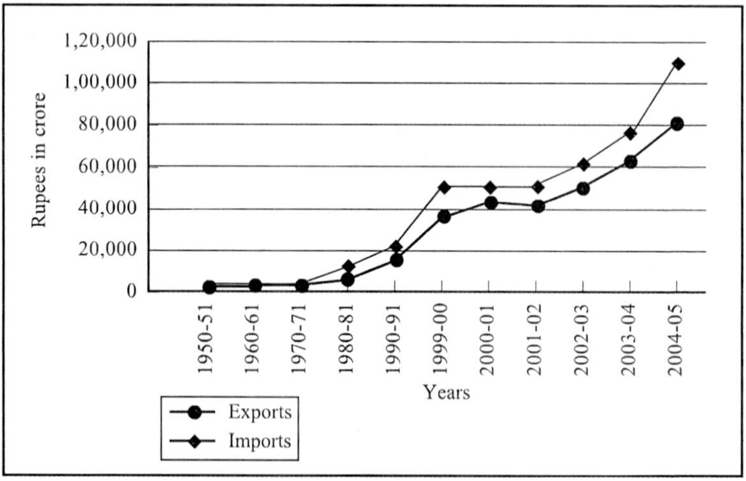

Source: Ministry of Commerce, Government of India.

Figure 2.1: India's Foreign Trade

Comparing the growth rate in exports and imports during 1950-51 to 2004-05, sharp increase in both, export and import, is observed after 1970-71. During this period imports have grown at faster rate than exports, and the trade balance shows sharp increase after 2001-02 which is negative. So, this increasing trade deficit has been a cause of concern for all associated with the policy making in the context of Look East Policy (LEP).

In case of the direction of India's foreign trade, other Asian countries and Oceania are major trading partners for India as far as exports are concerned. 55 per cent of total exports from India are made to this region and followed by West Europe, and America. Major destinations for Indian products within Asia and Oceania region include Hong Kong, Japan, Singapore, followed by China and Singapore. Major export destinations for Indian goods in West Europe are U.K. (18.80%), Germany (14.02%), Belgium (12.95%), and Italy (11.46%). Exports made to American regions are mainly concentrated in North America (87.04%). India's exports to East Europe and C.I.S. and Baltic States show very low figure of 0.22 per cent and 1.31 per cent of the total exports respectively.

Table 2.1: Trade Situation of India

Region	*Export (Values in ₹ crore)*			*Import (Value in ₹ crore)*		
	2007-08	*2008-09*	*% Growth*	*2007-08*	*2008-09*	*% Growth*
East Asia	5,67,316	7,99,238	40.88	33,72,658	53,65,367	59.08
ASEAN	65,93,187	86,52,513	31.23	91,24,477	1,19,42,145	30.88
South Asia	38,71,968	38,82,302	0.27	8,50,063	8,26,445	–2.78
EU Countries (27)	1,38,85,979	1,79,21,442	29.06	1,54,65,618	1,94,43,488	25.72
East Europe	42,702	58,339	36.62	14,397	14,345	–0.36
Southern Africa	14,52,388	14,28,376	–1.65	19,45,810	32,91,746	69.17

Source: Department of Commerce, Export Import Data Bank.

Recent trend of direction (India's foreign trade) reflects that the main trade destination of India is the European countries and followed by the other Asian countries. However, the growths in export and import both during 2007-08 to 2008-09 were highest for East Asian countries and India's trade with ASEAN also showed as significantly higher growth.

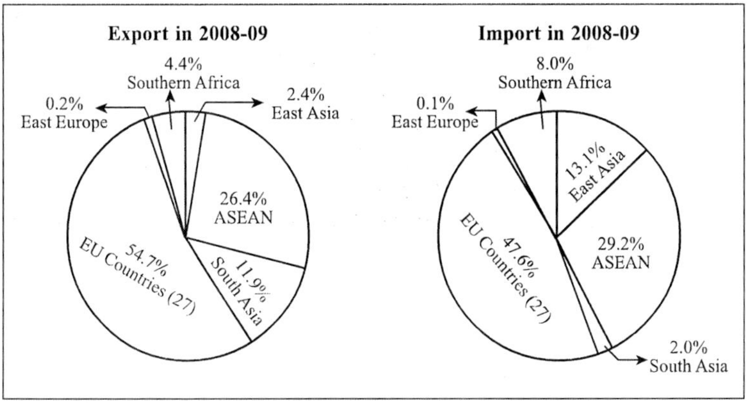

Figure 2.2: Percentage Distribution of India's Export and Import in 2008-09

Table 2.2: Total Trade of India with Top 20 Trading Partner Countries
Year: 2008-09 (*Values in ₹ crore*)

Rank	*Country*	*Export*	*Import*	*Total Trade*
1.	U. Arab Emts.	1,10,229.08	1,05,926.43	2,16,155.51
2.	China P Rp.	42,661.33	1,47,605.60	1,90,266.93
3.	USA	96,458.42	84,818.28	181,276.70
4.	Saudi Arab	22,940.14	89,747.04	112,687.18
5.	Germany	29,194.75	54,922.42	84,117.17
6.	Singapore	37,756.88	34,561.42	72,318.30
7.	Iran	11,565.17	55,821.84	67,387.02
8.	Hong Kong	30,390.69	29,732.54	60,123.23
9.	Korea Rp.	18,353.59	39,658.19	58,011.78
10.	U.K.	30,344.58	26,767.71	57,112.29
11.	Australia	6,576.33	50,496.52	57,072.85
12.	Switzerland	3,525.26	52,703.21	56,228.47
13.	Japan	13,807.71	35,832.82	49,640.54
14.	Malaysia	15,780.36	32,591.56	48,371.93
15.	Nigeria	7,065.31	39,995.48	47,371.93
16.	Kuwait	3,628.41	43,199.45	46,827.85
17.	Belgium	20,309.40	26,057.89	46,367.28
18.	Indonesia	11,577.83	30,751.29	42,329.12
19.	Netherlands	28,889.96	8,669.62	37,559.58
20.	Italy	17,364.88	19,983.56	37,348.44
	India's Total	8,40,755.05	13,74,435.37	22,15,145.96

Source: Ministry of Commerce, Government of India.

Among the top 20 trading partner countries of India, five Asian countries share 23.52 per cent India's total external trade. The direction of India's foreign trade shows concentration of exports and imports to the countries of Europe, Asia and Oceania regions, especially China, USA, Japan, and Singapore, etc. So, there is the opportunity for India of strengthening the trade relation with South Asian countries. But before going for strengthening the trade relation there is a need to have closer look on the trade deficit, direction and diversification of the foreign trade of India.

2. *Foreign Direct Investment in India*

Foreign Direct Investment (FDI) is considered to be the most attractive type of capital flow for emerging economies as it is expected to bring latest technology. However, India has only very recently emerged as a destination for FDI since the pre-reform years were marked with a sharp antipathy towards foreign capital. Over the period 1991-2000 FDI approvals varied considerably over the geographical span of India. Four states (Karnataka, Maharashtra, Tamil Nadu and Gujarat) accounted for over one-third of total FDI approvals. The shares of these individual states were 7.6, 13.7, 6.7 and 5.3 per cent respectively. The shares of Kerala, Haryana, Punjab and Rajasthan were comparatively smaller whereas the flow of FDI into populous states such as Bihar and Uttar Pradesh and in the North-Eastern States has been virtually negligible.

Country-wise FDI inflows to India are dominated by Mauritius (34.49%), followed by the United States (17.08%) and Japan (7.33%). As per the United Nations Conference on Trade and Development (UNCTAD) report titled "Assessing the Impact of the Current Financial and Economic Crisis on Global FDI Flows" India achieved a growth of 85.1 per cent in FDI inflows during 2007-08, which was the highest globally. The total flows increased from US $25.1 billion in 2007 to US $46.5 billion in 2008. This is despite 14.5 per cent decline in global FDI inflows from US $1,940.9 billion in 2007 to US $1,658.5 billion in 2008. India also ranked 9th in global FDI inflows in 2008.

Table 2.3: FDI Inflows to India (US $)

Rank	*Country*	*August 1991 to March 2000*	*2000-01*	*2001-02*	*2002-03*	*2003-04*	*2004-05 (up to Nov.)*	*Total Inflows*
1.	Mauritius	13,272 (3,608)	4,111 (942)	10,063 (2,182)	3,766 (788)	2,609 (567)	3,730 (811)	37,551 (8,898)
2.	USA	8,956 (2,450)	1,544 (356)	1,748 (382)	1,504 (319)	1,658 (360)	2,401 (522)	17,811 (4,389)
3.	Japan	3,314 (898)	977 (224)	809 (178)	1,971 (412)	360 (78)	466 (101)	7,897 (1,891)
4.	Netherlands	2,260 (628)	706 (162)	890 (196)	836 (176)	2,247 (489)	906 (197)	7,845 (1,847)
5.	UK	2,286 (670)	303 (70)	1,673 (366)	1,617 (340)	769 (167)	361 (78)	7,009 (1,692)
6.	Germany	2,396 (672)	540 (123)	519 (113)	684 (144)	373 (81)	553 (120)	5,066 (1,254)
7.	France	1,002 (280)	455 (104)	499 (108)	534 (112)	176 (38)	165 (36)	2,822 (679)
8.	South Korea	2,094 (572)	90 (21)	5 (1)	188 (39)	110 (24)	115 (25)	2,601 (682)
9.	Singapore	1,244 (344)	502 (117)	251 (54)	180 (38)	172 (37)	225 (49)	2,573 (639)
10.	Switzerland	948 (269)	71 (16)	180 (40)	437 (93)	207 (45)	287 (62)	2,130 (525)
Total FDI Inflows		60,604 (16,701)	12,645 (2,908)	19,361 (4,222)	14,932 (3,134)	12,117 (2,634)	11,728 (2,549)	1,31,385 (32,290)

Source: Economic Survey of India, 2006-2007.

In terms of *UNCTAD Survey 2008-10*, China is the most preferred investment destination, followed by India, the United States, the Russian Federation and Brazil respectively. Similarly, *AT Kearney's 2007* FDI Confidence Index shows China, India and USA as the most preferred locations in that order. For long-term prospects, *JBIC Survey* of Japanese manufacturing Transnational Corporations (TNCs) showed India replacing China as the most promising country for business operations of Japanese TNCs. Robust economic growth, an improved investment environment and opening up of critical sectors like telecommunications, civil aviation, refineries, construction, etc. facilitated FDI inflows into India. So, there is the prospect of heavy FDI inflow to India through the opening up of the East Corridor of India in the eve of the Look East Policy.

3. *Sustainability and Competitiveness of Indian Economy*

Unremitting growth also requires improved government capability, including transparency in service delivery. It also entails reform of the institutional framework that governs business and investment activities. Despite strong economic performance of India, that has lifted many out of poverty, poverty rates have not come down substantially. Poverty is still widespread in India, with 260 million people living on less than US $1 dollar a day. Economic growth has also not led to a lower unemployment rate. Continuing widespread poverty and high unemployment will likely erode support for the pro-reform political parties in the coalition government. Currently, India's trade liberalisation is credited with contributing to only a part of India's economic growth. There have been high expectations that further reforms to India's investment regime will lead to a significant rise in foreign direct investment, which in turn will have a positive impact on India's economic growth. In spite of that, free trade and more foreign investment have a close association with India's effort to reform its political, institutional and economic institutions. India's reforms and domestic development offer the background as well as the overall framework within which its international economic policies can be understood. The LEP is an integral part of India's reform package, and its implementation has resulted in the reorientation of India's foreign economic policy. The policy has had a significant impact on the country's domestic development, including the reform process. India's reforms and domestic development provide the background as well as the overall framework within which its international economic policies can be understood.

Look East Policy and Economic Development of North-East India

For the past 15 years India has pursued a foreign economic policy that facilitates closer economic and institutional ties with East Asia. In 1992, former Prime Minister P.V. Narasimha Rao launched the "Look East Policy" (LEP) with the objective of establishing closer economic integration with the South-East Asian states. In the past, India's engagement with much of Asia, including South-East and East-Asia, was built on an idealistic conception of Asian brotherhood, based on common experiences of colonialism and of cultural ties. The pace of development of the North-Eastern Region of India (NER) is determined, however, as much by trade, investment and production as by history and culture, which motivates Look East policy. Thus, the LEP signalled the end of India's previous pursuit of self-reliant economic development, and the start of an era in which India strived to take advantage of new opportunities from international trade and investment. The LEP also sent a strong signal that East Asia would be integral to India's economic opening. The region would no longer be overlooked, as it had been by India's previous foreign economic policy, but would now be regarded as a source of new business opportunity and inspiration for economic development. Since 1997 when Myanmar was admitted into ASEAN as a full member, India's North-East assumed importance in its LEP. This policy undoubtedly facilitated India's economic and strategic relations with South-East Asia but the share of the North-East in this policy remained insignificant. Former Prime Minister Manmohan Singh referred to India's North-East as the gateway to the 'South-East Asian Countries' in November 2004. This policy holds the potential to make NER the commercial corridor of India linking the ASEAN nations enabling its people to harvest economic well-being through trade, transit and tourism. NER then will no longer be in isolation and remoteness, but prosper with business opportunities knocking at the door. For example, redefining of Asian Highways — AH-1, AH-2 and AH-4 to provide India easier road connectivity with the neighbouring countries. restoring Stilwell Road connecting Arunachal Pradesh with Myanmar, holding of Thailand and India Ministerial level North-East Business Summit followed by Thailand Ministerial visits to NER and showcasing North-East India Trade and Investment Opportunity Week at Bangkok in October 2009, setting up of Tourism Desk at the Embassy of Thailand and India Desk at Board of Investment, Thailand, etc. are moves towards achieving the declared objectives.

India spends huge amount in transporting food items like pulses, poultry products, grains, etc. to NER for which the people have to pay more to meet the cost of transportation. Likewise, prices of all other items that come from our hinterland are higher in the region reducing the affordability of its people. Countries like Myanmar and Thailand — next door to NER — can provide many of the items at much cheaper price because of saving in the cost of carriage. Even a poor neighbour like Bangladesh can supplement our requirement of fish, which is a staple food item of this region. It always makes sense to trade goods with the neighbours. At the same time, India-ASEAN economic relations improved over the years, leading to multifaceted institutional arrangements being developed by the two sides. India was accepted by ASEAN as a sectoral dialogue partner in 1992, a full dialogue partner in 1995, a member of the Asia Regional Forum in 1996, and a summit partner in 2002. Since 2003, India, ASEAN and its individual member countries have agreed to, and begun negotiations on FTAs after signing the Framework Agreement on Comprehensive Economic Cooperation. India has concluded the Comprehensive Economic Cooperation Agreement with Singapore (2005). India's East Asia strategies have gradually moved away from solely focusing on ASEAN since the early 2000, with its warming relations with other East Asian economic powers, particularly China and Japan.

Problems of Look East Policy

(a) India currently has limited economic integration with East Asia. India has yet to become a significant market for most East Asian economies.

(b) The insurgency problem has left the region unchanging in all respect.

(c) Delayed infrastructural development deferred the spectrum of growth for the region.

(d) Inefficient bureaucratic processes are perceived to limit India's commitment to engage with East Asia.

(e) Lack of work incentive to grasp the global opportunities leads India back foot.

(f) Complex socio-cultural and ethnic frameworks in NER make hardship for rapid socio-economic development of the region.

Strategic Suggestions for Regional Cooperation

(a) *Reorganisation and Transformation*

Closer economic ties with East Asia require greater effort on India's part to liberalise trade and investment. The economic reform and liberalisation supports India's effort to lower trade barriers and liberalisation and investment regimes.

(b) *Sustainable Growth*

India has increasingly turned its focus to sustaining its rapid growth. Strong economic ties with East Asia would help India for accessing growth opportunities in Asia.

(c) *Inclusive Equity Based Development*

The Look East Policy is seemed as influential in dealing with internal disparity in India's development, and fostering more equity-based growth. The economic development of India's seven north-eastern states in particular lags behind the nation's development. Trade with South-East Asia also has the potential to turn the region from land-locked to land-linked, providing India with land routes to South-East Asian countries.

(d) *Area Focus*

In approaching East Asia, India initially chose to focus on ASEAN. This was because ASEAN members were the first ones to respond favourably to the LEP.

Conclusion

A broader regional economic integration in Asia within the Indian framework could be an engine of growth for not only the participating countries, but also has the potential to enhance the welfare of the rest of the world by unleashing the synergies of Asian countries for trade creation. India and East Asian countries need to deepen their ongoing cooperation further and cooperate in shaping towards creation of an integrated or seamless Asian market which could emerge as the third pole of the world economy after NAFTA and the EU. The rise of India has introduced new dynamism in the process of South East Asia's economic integration and in moving towards an Asian economic integration, China, India and Japan economic weights make them dominant players. However, ASEAN also sees India's involvement as an opportunity to poise the influence of either China or Japan, and help ASEAN. In this aspect the LEP has facilitated East Asia's growing share of India's worldwide trade and made the region more important to India's development. By looking East, India has used the LEP to support economic reforms and liberalisation, sustain its rapid growth, facilitate its economic integration with East Asia, and promote equity-based domestic development. While initially used to send a strong signal to the world of India's economic liberalisation, the LEP has increasingly become a vehicle to push for India's participation in Asia's economic integration. But India needs to keep on eye the relative gain and lose and future prospects of LEP and it needs to develop policy framework for looking at the sustainability of inclusive growth and development of human resource of the North-East India.

REFERENCES

Agarwala, Ramgopal (2004): "Reserve Bank of India: An Institutional Framework for Regional and Monetary Cooperation in Asia" in Nagesh Kumar (ed.), *Towards an Asian Economic Community: Vision of a New Asia*, New Delhi and Singapore, pp. 177-203.

Kumar, Nagesh (ed.) (2004): *Towards an Asian Economic Community: Vision of a New Asia*, New Delhi and Singapore.

——— (2005): "A Broader Asian Community and a Possible Roadmap", *Economic and Political Weekly*, Vol. XL (36), pp. 392-31.

——— (2005): "Towards a Broader Asian Community: Agenda for the East Asia Summit", RIS Discussion Paper No. 100, New Delhi.

Job, Brian (1999): "ASEAN Stalled: Dilemmas and Tensions Over Conflicting Norms", Paper presented to the 1999 Annual Meeting of the American Political Science Association, Atlanta, USA, 2-5 September.

Jomo Kwame Sundaram (1988): *A Question of Class: Capital, the State, and Uneven Development in Malaya*, New York: Monthly Review Press.

Jovanovic, Miroslav N. (1998): *International Economic Integration: Limits and Prospects*, London: Routledge.

Karras, Georgios (1997): "Economic Integration and Convergence: Lessons from Asia, Europe and Latin America", *Journal of Economic Integration*, 12(4), December.

3

LOOK EAST POLICY
An Opportunity or Uncertainty

Swapnali Gogoi and *Babu Boruah*

Introduction

To quote the Nobel Prize-winning economist Joseph E. Stiglitz, "The most successful developing countries in the world have achieved their success through trade, through exports". Tremendous economic development has taken place in the last six decades since the end of the Second World War. It has been noticed that International trade has fostered the wealth of various nations. It is only because of international trade the poor fishing island Taiwan transformed into a prosperous country of the world without any natural resources. Korea, Thailand, Singapore, Hong Kong and others also followed a more or less similar growth path and became prosperous.

North-East India is a land-locked area. No doubt, it had trade connectivity with the outside world in the historic past, but after the British conquest over the region, they put barriers on the trade between Bhutan and Assam and treated Myanmar as a strategic frontier. They built a major transportation infrastructure primarily for taking tea and other resources through Kolkata and disrupted the old trade routes. Again, after partition of India in 1947, North-East India lost its natural trade routes through Bangladesh. Its land connectivity with the rest of India or outside India remained limited to the 22 km 'chicken's neck' through northern West Bengal. Formerly, North-East India was on the southern trails of the Silk Road and through this road the region had connectivity with the world outside in the ancient times. Reopening of the 1,736 km Stilwell Road at Ledo leading to Kunming in the Yunnan province of China *via* Myanmar would go a long way in boosting up the volume of cross-border trade between the North-Eastern states and the South-East Asian countries. Increased trade will, in turn, contribute immensely to the strengthening of the economy of the North-Eastern states, especially that of Assam.

Look East Policy — Genesis

India's Look East Policy (LEP) first enunciated in 1991, had its genesis in the end of the Cold War, following the collapse of Soviet Union. Having lost of Soviet's economic and political support, India began to look for alternate energy sources among its immediate neighbours. After the start of liberalisation, it was a very strategic policy decision taken by the Government of India in the foreign policy.

The policy was developed and enacted during the government of former Prime Minister P.V. Narasimha Rao and rigorously pursued by the successive former governments of Atal Bihari Vajpayee and Manmohan Singh. Ex-Prime Minister Dr. Manmohan Singh described India's Look East Policy as 'a strategic shift in our perspective' and further clarified that "the age-old India-ASEAN linkages have given a renewed thrust with the impressive growth of connecting and the ever increasing flows of trade and tourism between India and ASEAN". Dr. Singh also said that the North-East India could be a gateway for the ASEAN and East Asia.

Look East Policy — Objectives

The primary objective of the policy is to take advantage of the new opportunities in trade and investment by improving socio-economic and political relationship with the so-called economic 'tigers' of South-East Asia. Under the Look East Policy of the Central Government, Moreh an Indian town in Chandel district of Manipur bordering Myanmar was projected as one of the Land Custom Stations (LCS) in the North-East region and was bustling with trading activities worth crores of rupees. Besides, the land routes connecting Myanmar could give a boost in the development of the region and the country at large was also the hope of the millions of Indians. In the initial stage, the focus of the Look East Policy was much on ASEAN. India's conscious efforts to forge closer economic ties with ASEAN members improve rapidly. India become a sectoral dialogue partner in March 1993 in the three areas, namely trade, investment and tourism and finally became a full dialogue partner in

1995. India became member of the ASEAN Regional Forum (ARF) in July 1996 and finally, to a Summit Level Partner in 2002.

Look East Policy —Milestones

The first phase of India's Look East Policy was ASEAN-centred and focused primarily on trade and investment linkages. The second phase, which began in 2003, was more comprehensive in its coverage, extending from Australia to East Asia, with ASEAN as its core. The new phase marks a shift in focus from trade to wider economic and security cooperation, political partnerships, physical connectivity through road and rail links. India-ASEAN cooperation now covers a wide field, including trade and investment, science and technology, tourism, human resource development, transportation and infrastructure, and health and pharmaceuticals. India signed "Long Term Cooperative Partnership for Peace and Prosperity" with ASEAN, which was the corner-stone of India's Look East Policy. India preferred to use the Comprehensive Economic Cooperation Agreement as a template for Free Trade Agreements (FTAs), because of its comprehensive coverage of trade in goods and services as well as investment.

The very first agreement in this field was the Indo-Myanmar Trade Agreement signed on January 31, 1994. The agreement provided for establishment of trade on the basis of equality and mutual benefit. As the Myanmar has a common border of 1,643 kms with four of India's states, viz. Arunachal Pradesh, Nagaland, Manipur and Mizoram and for trade with China and other South-East Asian countries by the land route, all movements have to be through Myanmar. It is true that Myanmar itself is poor and brings lot of smuggled precious stones, gold bars, teak wood, arms and drugs each year. But its strategic geographical location cannot be ignored. Thus India proposed to build a Trans-Asian railway network through Myanmar to Singapore. The Asian road highway is already under construction through Myanmar. The ultimate idea is to link up the Indian Ocean with the South China Sea.

Regional cooperation has been given a boost ever since the first BIMSTEC (Bay of Bengal Initiative of Multi-Sectoral Technical and Economic Cooperation) summit in July 2004. The countries concerned in this summit were Bangladesh, India, Sri Lanka, Thailand and Myanmar.

Again, the Thailand's Mekong Ganga Cooperation Project aims at revitalisation and development of overland trade, tourism, communication and transport. The countries involved are India, Myanmar, Thailand,

Laos, Cambodia and Vietnam. The following agreements have been entered into India-ASEAN relationship:

- Framework Agreement on Comprehensive Economic Cooperation (for establishing a FTA in a time-frame of 10 years) was concluded in Bali in 2003.
- An ASEAN-India Joint Declaration for Cooperation to Combat International Terrorism has been adopted.
- India has acceded to the Treaty of Amity and Cooperation (TAC) in 2003, on which ASEAN was formed initially (in 1967).
- Agreement on "India-ASEAN Partnership for Peace, Progress and Shared Prosperity" was signed at the 3rd ASEAN-India Summit in November 2004.
- Setting up of Entrepreneurship Development Centres in ASEAN member states like Cambodia, Myanmar, Laos and Vietnam (one in Laos is already functional).

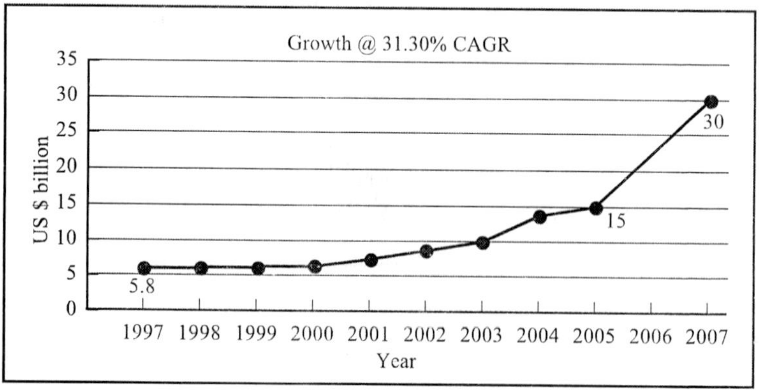

Figure 3.1: Trend in India-ASEAN Trade

These are the developments which will advance the Look East Policy and enhance India's economic and diplomatic relation with these countries. Earlier India and Thailand had signed two agreements: one to enhance cooperation on renewable energy and the other on cultural exchanges. The conference of Bangkok in October 2007, might result in some investment in North-East by Thailand.

Areas of Interest

It is found that the legal and formal arrangements of the policy are now more or less complete. But, which of the areas would be more benefited by it? The thrust areas would obviously be the agriculture and its allied sector, handloom and handicrafts (including processed bamboo products) and service sectors, like tourism, education and health-care. All the export potential studies have laid emphasis on a common item, namely agro-horticulture. A wide range of products under this sector have a potential market across the borders. Handloom products contribute 21 per cent of India's textile exports. Nearly, 64 per cent of the country's total looms operating in the North-East India (nearly 15 lakh units), while the region's share of fabric production is only 20 per cent and, consequently its share of textile export is hardly 5 per cent. So, North-East could be a leading handloom product exporter if this sector was developed into an organised one. Similarly, with a rich tradition of handicrafts and being a repository of arts and crafts, this region produces a variety of handicraft items which are eco-friendly as well as unique in craftsmanship and should, therefore, lead the country a new light in export of such products.

Look East Policy and the North-East — Is It Ready for This?

There is a big question regarding the success of Look East Policy in North-East.

North-East India is not yet economically as developed as the rest of India. Because of low investment, the whole of North-East India has only 166 medium and major industries and some of them have been already declared sick. It is not because of lack of qualified personnel or standard of education. In reality the region has been treated as a supplier of raw materials and a buyer of finished products from 'Mainland India'. As a result, unemployment is high in the region. About 25 per cent of the active workforce is unemployed in North-East India. It creates serious insurgency mindset among the educated youth. Industrial products of North-East India are also very limited. Agricultural products also need proper processing and packaging before the same can be exported. The quality of service sector is also very low. Even tourism has not been so attractive because of the various facilities not up to the mark and also because of the projection of the security environment in very bad light. An extremely concentrated endeavour would be required to achieve economic development of the region and make it competitive and ready for participation in the Look East Policy. Processing industries of agricultural products have to be set up to manufacture quality goods which can be offered in international markets at acceptable prices. The entire infrastructure of roads, railways, communication and air transport need to be completely revamped. Similarly, hotels, restaurants and resorts will have to be built for the sophisticated tourists to meet their demands. Again, in order to achieve closer trade relations, it is expected that India's peak tariff rates would be reviewed to make these at per with the rates in the ASEAN countries for which a Free Tread Agreement was also signed. If that cannot be achieved, Look East Policy will not benefit the region. In that case, it would remain like a bridge between the rest of India and South East Asia.

Situations on the Ground — Uncertainties

However, the actual ground scenarios seem to differ from the nation's projection. The trade between the ASEAN countries and Assam or other states in the North-Eastern region has not yet been picked up in spite of the Centre's announcement of Look East Policy. Reopening of the trade between Sikkim and China's Tibet on July 6, 2006 happened due to the opening of business route through Nathula Pass. But the Sikkimese traders have not gained much from it because of the imposition of some trade restrictions from the Indian side. It is encouraging that the Union Commerce Ministry is seriously considering to reopen the Stillwell Road for increased interest in trade and the resultant prospects of business along it. But, NH-39 still remains unsafe both for passengers and transportation. The highway is abundant with pit-holes, un-repaired culverts and bridges and landslides, being left unattended by the concerned authorities. Moreover, various militant groups active in the region are levying illegal heavy taxes for passing through the hills. Despite the deployment of Assam Rifle troops for every 10 kms from Palel (36 km) to Moreh, with another two posts of Assam Regiment, the insurgents groups pose a big threat to the vehicles plying on the highway. In addition, the police and the customs post also charge equally. They allow transportation of any kind of goods (both legal and illegal) after payment of specific amount laid down personally by the officer whosoever is in charge of the post. Furthermore, Moreh is famous for all kinds of illegal arms and drug consignment deals meant to enter India's North-Eastern region, destined for various parts of the country. Since the Indo-Myanmar border area is unfenced and porous with thick forest and unmanned, drugs coming from the old Golden Triangle of South-East Asia have their easy entrance. Contraband drugs are brought in by Burmese smugglers and transshipped to inner-part of Manipur by the various militant groups after deducting their percentage share. However, they allow the purchaser to resell outside the state only. Proliferation of small arms in the area is an open secret and there is no lack of contacts at the Moreh market for illegal deals, though problem lies with further trans-shipment. Again, a section of business tycoons in Guwahati has expressed serious doubt about its early opening citing the menace of several insurgent groups across the Indo-Myanmar border and the country's security, as reasons. If the route is kept open and the trade made absolutely decontrolled in an unfriendly atmosphere that prevails across the international border due to the movements of the militants, some of them may cross over to this side of the border in the name of business and indulge in violent activities posing a serious threat to internal peace.

Conclusion

Indian External Affairs Minister has visited Indonesia and Singapore. After that the Prime Minister of Thailand, Vietnam and Cambodia have visited India. A Thai business delegation visited the North-East Region of India some time ago. But, it has not yet borne any positive results in terms of trade and investment. In short, the Look East Policy of India through the North-East still remains stagnant under the limits of documents only. The need of the hour is the corelational linkage between the policies with the ground realities so as to give a boost to the development activities in the country at large. It is time that concrete steps were taken in the field for the full operation of the policy by creating conditions conducive to the growth of Trans-Border trade in North-Eastern region. Involving the local people in various stages of implementation of the Look East Policy is of utmost importance for its ultimate success.

REFERENCES

Bhattacharjee, Shibdas (2010): "India's Look East Policy on Right Path", *The Assam Tribune*, January 29, p. 6.

Das, H.N. (2007): "Preparing North East for Look East Policy", *The Assam Tribune*, November 7, p. 6.

4

THE STILWELL ROAD
Opportunities and Threats

Kamalesh Kalita and *Mouchumi Gogoi*

Introduction

India's North-East is comprised of the states — Assam, Arunachal Pradesh, Meghalaya, Manipur, Tripura, Nagaland, Mizoram and Sikkim. The region has been witnessed of unity in the diversity and a unique geophysical unit. It has an area of about 2,62,185 sq km with a population of 38.98 million in 2001. The region has more than 220 ethnic groups (tribes) with about 250 languages and dialects. All the ethnic tribes have their own distinctive unique and rich cultures. In spite of blessed with nature's bounty, the region is facing with the problems of economic development. North-East India shares a land boundary of 1,643 km with South-East Asia through the states of Kachin, Sagain and chin in Myanmar. Indeed, in the time of globalisation and liberalisation no country is developing without regional cooperation. Thus, of late India's Look East Policy (LEP) has given due attention to explore the potentialities of economic growth in the Sub-Region with proper trade, treaties and platform. The enhancement of cross border trade with the ASEAN countries, particularly Thailand through Myanmar could easily boost up the economy of North-East India. Because, the cross border point Tamu (Myanmar) is only 5 km away from Moreh (India). The Trilateral Highway (1,360 km), which was initiated under the Meckong-Ganga Cooperation in 2005 was a bold step of India's LEP towards the promotion of trade and commerce among South-East countries. This highway runs from Moreh to Maw Sot in Thailand through Myanmar. Realising the importance of topographic domain in North-East India, India's LEP has given more importance on land connectivity (road and rail links) with neighbouring countries, particularly with Myanmar in recent years. For instance, the ASEAN-India Car rally which was flagged off by Ex-Prime Minister of India Dr. Manmohan Singh in Guwahati in 2004. In this connection, the Tamu-Kalewa (160 km) India-Myanmar Friendship Road built in 2001 by Border Road Organisation (BRO) could also be mentioned. However, reopening of old trade route viz. *Stilwell Road* (Ledo Road) could also boost up and rejuvenate the economy and regional cooperation among the ASEAN countries. The Stilwell road was constructed under the supervision of General Joseph Warren Stilwell during Second World War from Ledo to Kunming in Yunnan province of China to support the allied soldiers who were fighting in the war. This 1,726 km long highway was once used as a major trade route to carry goods and services to China. However, due to some strategic and diplomatic reasons it is not still fully utilised for free trade between India, Myanmar and China. Of course, some sections of the roads are needed to be repaired before it recognised internationally. If the readymade Stilwell Road is reopened as a part of India's LEP in near future, it will enhance and increase the rapid economic growth in the Sub-region. Further, it will also deepen the economic integration and progress among the ASEAN countries by subduing the anti-social activities. Therefore, in the present discussion an attempt has been made to highlight the chances and threats of reopening of the old trade route, i.e. Stilwell Road to promote the faster economic development of the region.

The Stilwell Road and the Look East Policy

The economy of the India's North-East is predominantly based on agriculture. More than 65 per cent of population of the region is mainly engaged in agricultural activities. The traditional mode and limited use of modern tools and technologies in the agricultural activities of the region has always led to low production and low agricultural growth rate. It is important to note that the physiography of the region is mainly comprises plain and valleys (Brahmaputra, Barak, Tripura and Manipur), plateau (Meghalaya), and hills and mountains. About 70 per cent area of the region comes under undulating topography. Which is why, it is difficult to practice the large scale agricultural activities and establishment of heavy industries on that. Besides, different types of natural and social disasters are also hampering the economy of the region. However, to boost-up the development processes of the region Government of India has taking some serious steps in past few years. For example, the provision of a separate ministry, i.e. DONER for north-east reveals this fact.

India's Look East policy is also a part of Central Government's policy to push-up the region. Of course, some critics feel that India's Look East Policy was not primarily adopted only for the development of North-East India, but for some other reasons. As Rajib Sikri pointed that there is a strong economic rationale to India's LEP. A combination of factors — the collapse of its valued economic partner, the Soviet Union, the financial crisis that hits India, and the ineluctable logic of globalisation compelled India to embark on its economic reforms in the early 1990s. Realising that it has missed some openings in the past because of its autarkic path of development, India is now keen to plugging into the dynamic ASEAN region that was rapidly evolving into a critical mass of global economic strength. However, it is already mentioned that India's Look East Policy has given due attention to explore the potentialities of economic growth in the Sub-Region with proper trade, treaties and platform. The enhancement of cross border trade and links with the ASEAN countries, especially Thailand through Myanmar could easily boost up the economy of North-East in particular and the country as a whole. Therefore, observing the geophysical constrains of the region only land connectivity is a suitable option to look at the East. Mr. Pranab Mukherjee once stated at a seminar on LEP at Shillong on 16th June, 2007 that *geography is opportunity* and, therefore, region like the North-East India have enormous possibilities to exploit their geographical contests and bring significant benefits to population residing in those regions in a much direct and participative manner than before.

Transport and communication, i.e. *connectivity* is an epitome to the cultural relationships that exists between the physical environment, patterns of social and political activity and level of economic development. In advanced and developing countries, investment in transport is a matter of political negotiation, economic calculation and environmental consideration (Adams, 1981). As in the developed world, land transport (road and railway) is now the dominant and universal mode of transport in less developed and developing countries. Hence, the development of transport and communication system is very urgent needs for the development of this region. It is a fact that Myanmar located at a crucial location in India's gateway to ASEAN as it is the only ASEAN country which has a land and maritime boundary with India. Therefore, by adopting some realistic and pragmatic policy like Look East could improve our relationship with Myanmar. It is mentionable that our relationship with Myanmar has been gradually improving since 1988. This relationship has been taken a realistic shape after signing the bilateral border trade agreement by both the countries on 21st January, 1994. As a result two important trade points, namely Moreh (India) and Tamu (Myanmar) were opened on 12th April, 1995. Subsequently, India and Myanmar had agreed to open another four check posts, namely Pangsau Pass, Paletwa, Lungwa-Yanyong and Pangsha-Pangnyo between the nations. Opening of these border posts have been enhancing and encouraging the legal and official trade between the countries.

After becoming the member of ASEAN and BIMSTEC (Bay of Bengal Initiative for Multi-Sectoral Technical and Economic Cooperation) region in 1997 Myanmar has also shown keen interest in promotion of trade with its neighbouring countries. Both the countries have been trading now a number of items (22 items). It is said that road is the golden path of the trade and commerce. Hence, opening of old and probable new trade roads between the countries could help both the countries to attain the goal of inclusive growth. Of course, both the countries have already taking a number of projects to develop its accessibility and the connectivity among the ASEAN countries. For example, the 160 km India-Myanmar Friendship Road Project, 1,360 km India-Myanmar-Thailand Trilateral Highway Project, upgradation of Yangon-Mandalay Trunk Line Project, development of Rhi-Tidim and Rhi-Falam road sections in Myanmar and the Kaladan Multimodal Transport Project, etc. The NH-39 which is running through Manipur and also connects the Moreh town is a very important road which can play a very vital role in promoting the speedy development of Indo-Myanmar Trade. Therefore, this road and the town Moreh need special attention and care from both the countries. Moreh a small border town popularly was known as little India once a tribal village. The India origin Myanmarese settlers had contributed to the growth of this business town. They did good business importing goods from Burma and selling them in Moreh. Just opposite to the Indian market there is a market known as *Emplalong*, where vendors are from Myanmar and customers from India. The easy accessibility to this market, people no longer buy imported goods from Indian shops. They buy them from the *Emplalong* market at cheaper rate (Patil, 2010).

The main focus of this chapter is on the old Stilwell Road with reference to India's LEP. Whether reopening of this particular road will success the LEP to a greater extent? It is mentioned already that the Stilwell Road was constructed during Second World War from Ledo through Hokawang valley to Kunming in Yunnan province of China to support the allied soldiers who were fighting in the war and was once used as a major trade route to carry goods and services to China. However, for centuries, the route through Pangchau Pass remained a wild natural path by which Ahoms, Khamtes, Tai-phakes, Shimphos, Tariungs and Taikhamyungs were entered in Grater Assam in different times. And in the time of the Second World War its importance was again rediscovered. Some old official records reveal that the Stilwell Road was the only route through which bulky goods were transported to Myanmar. This road was planned in February 1942 by the General Headquarters and finally started the work in April 1942. Thousands of workers from Burma, Assam and China were engaged for the construction of the road. Miju, Mishinmi, Tangsa, Sema, Aor and Garo people were discharged their labour to construct the Stilwell Road. Initially, Stilwell Road was planned to connect Ledo to Mogeung in Kachin state and finally linked with the old Burma Road. This section of the road (Lashir to Kunming) was constructed in 1938. For the construction of the road an amount of US $15 crore was spent at that time. The road was used as a major trade route up to 15th August, 1945, but with the end of Second World War it was also closed subsequently. During the last 50 years Indo-Myanmar Governments have not given any due attention to resume its activity. However, when Indian government has taken its own LEP, its importance has been again increasing gradually. Hence, Government of India is thinking to open Stilwell Road as a part of its LEP strategy.

Opportunist and Threats of Reopen the Stilwell Road

Some positive aspects we can underline if we reopen the Stilwell Road:

1. It will enhance and improve the quality of people living on both sides of the Indo-Myanmar border. The tribes for example, living on both sides of the Pangchau pass bears same racial, cultural and social traits. By improving people to people contact, the region could easily be developed culturally and economically. It will increase the volume of export in local products of both the countries. It is believed that North-East India is also blessed with numbers of mineral resources. If these mineral resources are explored, mined and export in proper way the, economy of the region will definitely develop in very fast way. It is worth mentioning that the process of development should always be environment friendly and sustainable. Besides, the sentiments of the local people living in the region are also taken into account in this regard.

2. It will increase the flow of goods and services among the ASEAN countries. Exchange of new views and technology will also help the countries a lot. It may open a new vista of relationships with Korea, Japan and Australia. It will also help to strengthen our tie with neighbouring countries that could have brought political and economic advantages.
3. Opening of Stilwell Road will help us to combating terrorism to a certain extent. For example, some tracts of Indo-Myanmar border (i.e., Kachin, Sagain) are using by different insurgent and terrorist groups (ULFA, NSCN, PLA, KIA) of the region. It is known that as many as 14 insurgent groups are very active in this region. Therefore, regional cooperation is very very essential for combating the same. As terrorism is no longer a local but a global phenomenon.
4. It will boost the Tourism industry in the region. Tourism is one of the most important civil industries in the modern world. The region is endowed with diverse tourist attractions with perfect destinations for holiday and adventures. The world famous Kaziranga National Park, World's largest river island 'Majuli', the Mother Goddess Kamakhya Temple, the Brahmaputra River, the Majestic Tea Gardens, Tawang Gumpa, Rumtek Monastery, the Limestone caves in Meghalaya state are a few mentioned only have always been attracting the various categories of tourists from all over the world. Reopening of the Stilwell Road will encourage the tourist's inflow to this region. Geotourism and medical tourism may develop in the region in a special manner.
5. It will also give additional advantages in the time of natural disasters, if any. The regional economic cooperation will foster economic and political stability during the time of disasters.

On the other hand, there are some negative aspects, which is why Stilwell Road should not open up immediately.

1. It is already mentioned that North-East India is a playground of many insurgent and terrorist groups. Geographical isolation, deep jungles, introvert people, etc. may lead to the growth of insurgent activities in the region. It may increase the possibility of supply of arms and ammunitions by the various insurgent groups to the region.
2. Opening up the Stilwell Road may flood with the cheap and non-durable electronic goods in the Indian markets. For example, *Emplalong* market in Indo-Myanmar border.

3. Free and easy communication system may increase the anti-social activities and fatal diseases in the area.
4. Some corner believe that if in near future same ethnic groups (Buddhist circuit) in the region may demand a separate territory like proposed *Greater Monpha* state what will happen in this situation! It will create again turmoil in the region.

Conclusion

In conclusion it may be said that despite of some disadvantages of reopening of the Stilwell Road, the economic cooperation, political goodwill and cordial relationships among ASEAN countries could eliminate all the ills and boost up the region in a prospective way.

REFERENCES

Baruah, S.N. (1991): *Tribes of Indo-Burma Border — A Socio-cultural History of the Inhabitants of the Patkai Range*, Mittal Publication, New Delhi.

Goswami, N. (2009): "Looking East through India's North-East: Identifying Policy Challenges and Outlining the Responses", *IDSA, Occasional Paper*, Vol. 2, New Delhi.

Hilye, B. and K. Richard, eds. (2000). *Modern Transport Geography*, John Wiley & Sons.

Nath, D. (eds.) (2004): "Reopening of the Stilwell Road — Prospect and Problem", *MAKAIAS*, Kolkata.

Sikri, R. (2007): "Debate: India's Look East Policy" in *Indian Foreign Affairs Journal*, Vol. 2, No. 2.

The Week, March 7, 2010.

Souvenir of 24th Biennial Conference NEIGS and National and Human Disaster in NE India and their Management, Tinsukia College (15 and 17 May, 2007).

Proceedings of International Conference on Regional Cooperation, 18-19 January, 2004, Margherita College, Margherita.

5

INDIA-ASEAN ECONOMIC RELATION
A Study of North-East India

Biren Saikia, Khagen Kachari and *Deepali Bhattacharjee*

Introduction

Indian economy is increasingly getting integrated with the world economy through trade and investment flows, both inward and outward. The "Look East Policy" is a part of India's response to the process of globalisation. This has opened up new avenues for Indian exporters, entrepreneurs, businessmen, professionals and consultants to explore new business opportunities abroad, particularly with the neighbouring countries and also South-East Asian countries. The region occupies a very strategically and geo-politically sensitive frontier zone of the country, sharing 98 per cent (4,600 km) with international boundary with the four different countries, i.e. Bangladesh, Myanmar, Bhutan and China, while having only 2 per cent (33 km) of its border with the mainland India. The Look East Policy, initiated in the early 1990s was basically conceived to increase India's economic interactions and linkages with South-East Asian countries. India can learn much from the ASEAN countries as to what items could be exported and as to what export policies and procedures should be followed. This is one aspect of the Look East Policy.

Under this policy, India seeks economic cooperation with the ASEAN and its neighbouring countries through its North-Eastern Region (NER). ASEAN and its neighbouring countries have become the largest market and one of the fastest growing economies in the world at present. Using ASEAN countries as examples, India decided to adopt new strategy to focus on export led economic growth to achieve a major breakthrough in economic development. In the post-Cold War period, and particularly since the latter part of the 1990s, India's relations with all the major powers, especially the US, have shown considerable improvement. There is now greater mutual understanding of inter-linkages between economic, security and strategic interests of India on the one hand and major powers on the other. After India became a Sectoral dialogue partner of the ASEAN in 1992, an ASEAN-India Business Council (AIBC) was established to advance business opportunities and now ASEAN emerged as a major actor in the politics of the Asia Pacific region. It was felt that India needed a long term partnership with the ASEAN countries in the interest of its stability, security and development. In this chapter an attempt has been made to examine the Indo-ASEAN economic relation through NEI. It has also been tried to analyse the potential of NEI in this integration process and to highlight the obstacles that might hinder this integration process.

Objectives of the Study

The objectives of this study are to:

1. Explain the Indo-ASEAN economic integration through the North-Eastern region.
2. Outline the benefits of economic integration of India with ASEAN countries.
3. Highlight the India's present Export-Import Scenario with ASEAN countries.
4. Highlight the potentials of exchange in North-East India with ASEAN countries for socio-economic development of the region.
5. Highlight the obstacles that might come in the way of India's economic integration with the ASEAN countries.

Data and Methodology

The methodology used in this chapter is descriptive and analytical in nature. Important inputs for the study were received from different books, journals, newspapers and various websites. Personal experience and knowledge in the field also helped to make meaningful interpretation.

1. *Indo-ASEAN Economic Integration Through the North-Eastern Region*

Since 1980s, India continues to have buoyant trade relations with South-East Asian countries. During 2003-04, South-East Asia and ASEAN countries taken together accounted for 21.3 per cent of the total volume of India's international trade. India's trade relation with North-East Asian countries like China, Japan, Republic of Korea and Hong Kong has also increased tremendously over the years. China has emerged as India's third largest trading partner after the USA, overtaking countries like UK and Belgium in 2003. To provide physical connectivity with the eastern countries, India has already signed Trans-Asian Highway projects, initiated by United Nations Economic and Social Commission for Asia Pacific (UNESCAP). On the political fronts, India has made efforts to improve relationship with neighbouring countries especially with China, Myanmar and Bangladesh.

India and the ten Member countries of ASEAN signed the India-ASEAN Framework Agreement on Comprehensive Economic Cooperation (CECA) in Bali, on 8th October, 2003. This forward-looking Agreement is aimed at forging a closer economic partnership in the twenty-first century between the ASEAN member countries and the Republic of India by minimising barriers and deepening economic linkages between the trading partners, lowering costs, increasing intra-regional trade, investment and productive efficiency, and carries forward the historical economic and commercial ties established between the peoples of the two regions since time immemorial. The CECA is expected to create a large market of over 1.5 billion people, with a combined current GDP of $1.2 trillion, and would cover agreements in investment and services, in addition to trade in goods. The existing economic relations between India and ASEAN based on some key macro-economic indicators which are highlighted in Table 5.1.

Table 5.1: Macro-Economic Indicators (2003)

Country	*Population (million in 2001)*	*GDP at Current Prices (million US $) (2003)*	*GDP Growth*		*GDP per Capita (US $) (2003)*
			Rate of Growth of GDP (1996-2000) (%)	*Rate of Growth of GDP (2000-03) (%)*	
(1)	*(2)*	*(3)*	*(4)*	*(5)*	*(6)*
India	1033.4	600,658	5.7	8.2	508
ASEAN	459.3	685,981	1.4	5.0	1,266
Brunei	—	4,715	—	3.2	12,971
Cambodia	—	4,215	—	5.0	310
Indonesia	213.6	208,625	–1.0	4.1	973
Laos	—	2,043	—	5.9	362

(*Contd.*)

Table 5.1 (*Contd.*)

(1)	(2)	(3)	(4)	(5)	(6)
Malaysia	23.8	103,737	3.4	5.3	4,198
Myanmar	—	9,605	—	5.1	179
Philippines	77	79,270	3.0	4.7	973
Singapore	4.1	91,355	6.4	1.1	20,987
Thailand	61.2	143.303	–0.9	6.8	2,291
Vietnam	79.6	39,021	6.4	7.2	481

Source: ASEAN Statistical Yearbook, 2005, *RBI Handbook of Statistics*.

ASEAN's population is about half that of India's population of over one billion persons. The most populous country in ASEAN, viz. Indonesia, has about a fifth of India's population. However, ASEAN's per capital income $ 1,240 at current prices is nearly two and a half times that of India. The gap may narrow somewhat over time but is not likely to reverse in the foreseeable future.

As per the World Bank record ASEAN's Gross National Income (GNI) in current dollars in 2001, which stood at $565 billion, was about a fifth higher than that of India. However, measured in purchasing power parity (PPP) terms, ASEAN's GNI of $1,832 billion was about 70 per cent that of India's. The gap in GNI between ASEAN and India in current dollars has been narrowing since the second half of the 1990s. This is because during the 1996-2000 period, while ASEAN as a group exhibited average annual growth rate of 1.4 per cent, the corresponding growth rate for India was 5.7 per cent. ASEAN as a group has grown more rapidly since 2000, but its average growth rate has remained lower than that of India.

2. *Benefits of Indo-ASEAN Economic Integration Through NER*

North-East India (NEI) plays an important role and the region can act as the bridge between the country's economy and the ASEAN due to racial affinity, cultural similarities, social and more importantly geographical location. Since India's NER is a strategic location to link the countries with ASEAN. The North-Eastern Region (NER) comprising eight states — Assam, Arunachal Pradesh, Meghalaya, Mizoram, Nagaland, Manipur, Tripura and Sikkim (since December 2002) is situated at the outskirts of the country with 8.06 per cent of Indian geographical area and 3.79 per cent population. The per capital income of the region has an average of ₹ 12,918 as compared with the national average of ₹ 17,978 (at current prices of 2001-02) and nearly 35 per cent of population is below the poverty line as compared to 22 per cent of national average. The entire North-East region except Sikkim is connected to the rest of the country through a narrow 20 km wide Chicken's neck corridor near Siliguri (West Bengal). Sikkim is also connected with the Indian main land *via* West Bengal, but it remains at a distance from other NE states. Out of six international boundaries touch the whole of India (i.e. China, Pakistan, Bangladesh, Bhutan, Nepal and Myanmar) five of them about 5,000 km touch North-East India (namely, China, Nepal, Bhutan, Myanmar and Bangladesh). Despite being rich in natural resources with fertile land, rich forests and mineral deposits, the region is still very poor.

The geographical isolation of North-East India (NEI) has resulted in its economic backwardness and its alternation from the mainstream India. A time has come to convert its geographical isolation into an economic opportunity. Cross border trade can become an engine to the growth of the economy. To face global competition, trade taking place within the regional arrangement is widely recognised by the developing countries including India. In this situation India's "Look East Policy" is the first step and boon for NE India as a development strategy option for the people. It is apparent that NE India as a whole needs a big push or a kick starts to lunch the economy on the development path. Therefore, Look East Policy provides an opportunity to overcome the problem of distance from big markets.

India's Look East Policy begins with the bilateral trade agreement between India and Myanmar through Moreh in Manipur and Tamu in Myanmar which was signed on 21st January, 1994. The actual follow-up action of trade was formally opened on 12th April, 1995 by the Hon'ble Minister of State of Commerce, Government of India, Shri P. Chidambram along with his Counterpart, Minister of Trade of Myanmar Lt. General Tunkyi. The international trade between ASEAN countries and India through Moreh in Manipur is the first step in India's 'Look East Policy'. More interestingly, by integrating with Myanmar, NEI can easily access to the entire ASEAN market as well as its neighbouring countries. Though it is not legalised by the Centre, there is hardly any family in NEI without commodities from ASEAN and its neighbouring countries. Again most of the commodities coming from Myanmar are of third country origin. So, trade negotiation through Myanmar has opened up opportunities for India to have access even to the non-ASEAN neighbouring countries as well.

India added a new dimension to its foreign policy by linking its North-Eastern states to South-East Asia through road and rail link *via*

Myanmar. It is part of a large project to build up Eurasian land and rail corridors that can connect Singapore to Istanbul and Europe *via* both India and China. The trans-continental highway and railway can lead to ultimate link up to China, Russia and Central Asia (Mero, 2005), and Indian Government has been trying to develop a Train-Highway project under India-Myanmar, Thailand, Transport-Linkage project.

India also needs to deepen its links with the Mekong Ganga Cooperative Forum (MGCF) — a new cooperative forum floated by India with five of its eastern neighbours, namely — Myanmar, Thailand, Cambodia, Vietnam and Laos. This move by the Government of India will surely benefit NEI. Tourism, culture and education are given precedence and priority in the cooperative framework. Indian professionals teaching English and computer skills can raise the standards of education and knowledge base. ASEAN can also get its manpower requirements (technical and managerial) from India which are both competitive and culturally compatible. NEI can contribute immensely to realise this well-deserved goal. English speaking and writing ability of majority of the people from North-East India is definitely considered as strength, and can best be exploited as human resource for better international trade cooperation.

3. *India's Present Export-Import Scenario with ASEAN Countries*

India's main exports to ASEAN include gems, jewellery, meat and meat preparations, cotton yarn, fabrics, made-ups, engineering goods, transport equipment, machinery and instrument, electronic goods, marine products, fruits and vegetables, rice, drugs and pharmaceuticals, and chemicals. Imports are comprised artificial resins, plastic materials, natural rubber, wood and wood products, electronic goods, non-ferrous metals, metal-ferrous ores, metal scrap, organic chemicals, edible oils, coal and fertilizers. ASEAN-India trade in 2001-02 stood at $7.8 billion of which India's exports to ASEAN stood as $3.5 billion which imports stood at $4.3 billion. ASEAN, especially Malaysia, Singapore and Thailand have become a major source of Foreign Direct Investment in India. Though it was a pittance in 1991, the cumulative approved FDI between January 1991 and May 2002 from ASEAN stood at over ₹ 14,000 crore.

It is revealed from Table 5.2 that India's export and import to Asian and ASEAN regions accounts for 48.46 and 35.22 per cent respectively as against 24.06 and 21.17 per cent respectively with Europe and only 20.61 and 7.78 per cent with America. This clearly shows that Indo-ASEAN trade occupies higher status and has become the focal point.

The present export and import scenario with some of the South-East Asian countries is shown in Table 5.3.

Table 5.2: Direction of India's Foreign Trade during 2001-02

Sl.No.	*By Region*	*Percentage Share of Total Exports*	*Percentage Share of Total Imports*
1.	Asia and ASEAN	48.86	35.22
2.	Europe	24.06	21.17
3.	America	20.61	7.78

Source: Chronical, April issue 2008, Vol. XVIII, No. 10.

Table 5.3: India's Export and Imports with South-East Asian Countries (2006-09)

(*US $ millions*)

Sl.No.	*Country*	*2006-07*		*2007-08*		*2008-09*	
		Export	*Import*	*Export*	*Import*	*Export*	*Import*
1.	Singapore	6064.84	5485.86	7371.33	8121.81	8220.07	7443.34
2.	Hong Kong	4677.42	2482.18	6308.46	2700.56	6672.29	6420.75
3.	South Korea	2513.03	4802.78	2853.26	6040.73	3996.86	8605.05
4.	Malaysia	1303.43	5291.25	2568.91	6007.99	3436.30	7032.04
5.	Japan	2860.78	4592.51	3855.76	6326.49	3005.63	7618.72
6.	Thailand	1443.38	1744.73	1808.84	2302.19	1981.36	2660.23
7.	Taiwan	912.87	1677.18	1735.83	2401.58	1455.08	2776.52

Source: Economic Intelligence Service, CMIE, Mumbai, October, 2009.

It is observed from Table 5.3 that Singapore, Hong Kong, South Korea, etc. are the very favourite destinations from the export-import points of view, as these countries import many more goods and services from India. Table 5.4 shows the growth of export and import share between India and ASEAN and other major economies during 2008-09.

Table 5.4: India's Trade with ASEAN and Other Major Economies (2008-09)

(*in $ billion*)

Countries	*Exports*			*Imports*		
	April 08-Feb. 09	*% Growth*	*% share*	*April 08-Feb. 09*	*% Growth*	*% share*
EU	34.9	14.3	21.9	35.5	12.2	13.5
US	18.6	–0.4	11.7	15.7	29.0	6.0
China	8.4	–11.4	5.2	28.1	13.2	10.7
South Korea	2.8	10.8	1.8	7.5	38.8	2.8
Japan	2.7	–14.4	1.7	6.9	21.3	2.6
ASEAN	16.9	2.96	10.6	23.4	2.99	8.9

Source: Pratiyogita Darpan, October 2009.

It is evident from Table 5.4 that both the import and export of India grow with the European Union at a higher rate in comparison to the ASEAN and the other countries during 2008-09. The countries like US, China and Japan show negative rate of growth in India's export during the year. Regarding import, US is in a better place than all the other concerning countries. Despite some slow down in Indo-ASEAN trade as a whole as cleared from Table 5.4, the bilateral trade with some ASEAN countries has grown significantly. The ASEAN country-wise break-up in export and import with India is shown in Table 5.5.

Table 5.5: Share of Export and Import between India and Some ASEAN Countries During 1996-97 to 2008-09

(in $ million)

Countries	*Exports*				*Imports*			
	1996-97	*2005-06*	*2007-08*	*2008-09*	*1996-97*	*2005-06*	*2007-08*	*2008-09*
Indonesia	–6.35	701.8	689.1	1224.2	608.98	1518.4	2017.4	2584.2
Malaysia	41.58	556.2	780.7	1252.9	1030.91	1243.2	2489.3	3434.2
Myanmar	39.30	NA	NA	NA	168.65	NA	NA	NA
Philippines	34.61	253.7	225.7	350.0	16.76	115.0	NA	NA
Singapore	13.44	3196.9	2560.9	4637.3	1080.94	1624.8	2913.5	3663.3
Thailand	–0.31	550.7	624.5	960.9	199.42	634.3	989.4	1165.7
Vietnam	--1.09	301.0	403.5	673.1	1.75	64.8	NA	NA

Source: Centre for Monitoring Indian Economy (CMIE).

From Table 5.5 it is clear that the exports of India are highest with Singapore since 2005-06 than the other South-East Asian countries. Similarly, the import from this country with India also shows an increasing trend.

From Table 5.6, it is seen that among all the ASEAN countries SIngapore shows a better performance in the share of export and import in the recent years as per the available data. Table 5.7 reveals the fact that the export of India to these countries are not in a smooth trend as the imports from these countries.

Table 5.6: Percentage Share in Total Export and Import of India and ASEAN

Countries	*Exports*			*Imports*		
	2005-06	*2007-08*	*2008-09*	*2005-06*	*2007-08*	*2008-09*
Indonesia	1.34	1.13	1.50	1.98	2.12	1.91
Malaysia	1.06	1.28	1.53	1.62	2.62	2.54
Myanmar	NA	NA	NA	NA	NA	NA
Philippines	0.48	0.37	0.43	0.15	NA	NA
Singapore	6.10	4.21	5.69	2.11	3.07	2.71
Thailand	1.05	1.02	1.18	0.83	1.04	0.86
Vietnam	0.57	0.66	0.82	0.08	NA	NA

Source: Centre for Monitoring Indian Economy (CMIE).

Table 5.7: Percentage Change in Exports and Imports in India with ASEAN

Countries	*Exports*			*Imports*		
	2005-06	*2007-08*	*2008-09*	*2005-06*	*2007-08*	*2008-09*
Indonesia	9.71	−11.79	77.66	6.76	42.82	28.10
Malaysia	−9.74	62.62	60.49	0.72	26.28	37.96
Myanmar	NA	NA	NA	NA	NA	NA
Philippines	22.68	−19.44	55.04	1.24	NA	NA
Singapore	68.35	−16.92	81.08	19.80	29.29	25.74
Thailand	24.11	11.49	53.86	46.69	51.52	17.82
Vietnam	14.22	22.82	66.82	38.39	NA	NA

Source: Centre for Monitoring Indian Economy (CMIE).

4. *Potentials of Exchange in North-East India with ASEAN Countries for Socio-Economic Development of the Region*

The potentials of North-Eastern Region of India arising as an exporter of different goods and services to the neighbouring East Asian countries due to the rapid growth of development in such countries and the process of growing regional cooperation among them. With this development, the North-East India could emerge as a business transit centre for the BCIM, SAARC and ASEAN group of nations and certain strategic places of the region would come out as commercial hub of the regions bustled by business executives, hotels, clubs departmental stores, etc. For this the North-East requires to identify a few well defined thrust areas having comparative advantage and concentrate itself by specialising those areas of production so that it can produce in excess of local demand. On the basis of specialisation based on the thrust areas, the North-Eastern region has the following potentiality of items to export to the East.

(a) *Biodiversity*

North-Eastern region is one of the richest botanical treasury houses of the country. A few valuable items of such rich biological and habitat diversity of the region could be commercially exploited for export purposes such as:

(i) *Orchids*

The region can be a major exporter of orchids as more than 600 varieties can be grown in the region out of 925 varieties of orchids in India. Due to its favourable soil and climatic conditions approximately 200 varieties are unique to the region and 60 per cent of these are ornamental in nature with high demands in international markets.

(ii) *Horticultural Crops*

North-East India is famous for production of apple, orange, pineapple, banana, walnut, kiwi and several spices (cardamom, black pepper, ginger, etc.) including 4,500 species of flowering plants.

(iii) *Major Forest Products*

The commercial use of some valuable timber trees like hillock, pine, chir, tick, firewood, etc. along with its scientific captive plantation can earn substantial revenue for the region. Value added products from such trees can be exported to the neighbouring countries.

The region's forest are the natural habitat of several species of wild animals, birds and flowers and for preserving these species the region has a number of national parks and wildlife sanctuaries which can attract tourists from all over the world.

(iv) *Minor Forest Products*

These above said items mostly include the herbal plants, aromatic plants and some other minor forest products. The North-Eastern region has a rich tradition of herbal health care. The tribes of the region have so far identified over 1,500 species of plants, having medicinal properties. However, some of these medicinal plants are yet to be authenticated by appropriate authority (*State Forest Research Institute Bulletin*, 2003). Herbal medicines produced from these herbal plants could capture the world market and compete out the chemical medicines currently available in the world market because there is an international trade towards herbal medicines shifting the focus from chemical ones.

The increasing international demand for natural perfumes and room fresheners will facilitate the export promotion of aromatic products from the region. The aromatic plants such as citronella, lemon-grass, vanilla, patchouli, agaroo, etc. which can be used in aromatic industry for the manufacture of perfumes, incenses, etc. for export purposes.

In addition to herbal and aromatic plants North-East India is rich in several other minor forest products which include bamboo, cane, reeds, thatching-grass, sun-grass, rubber, honey, tamarind, lac, shellac, tendu leaf, charcoal, pole, boulders, shingle, etc. India's minor forest product exports are presently to the tune of $362 million, comparing 4 per cent of the global trade.

(v) *Bio-Diesel Plantation/Jatropha*

Another emerging potentialities of the North-East is the plantation of Jatropha plants from which bio-diesel can be produced. This plant is grown widely in the entire North-East. If its scientific captive cultivation can be undertaken in a large scale, the region can save lot of foreign exchange in terms of reduced import of crude oil, the price of which is increasing sharply. The plant produces seeds with an oil content of 37 per cent and the oil can be used as fuel without being refined. It burns with clear smoke-free flame and is fit for diesel engine. The by-product is pressed-cake which can be used as fertilizer. The plant grows relatively quickly, producing seed within 4-5 years and survives for about 40-50 years.

The Government of India has emphasised for the plantation of Jatropha plants throughout the country. The Ministry of Petroleum and Natural Gas, Government of India has announced Bio-diesel Purchase Policy, 2005, declaring the procurement price of bio-diesel at ₹ 25 per litre. Due to such technical viability and economic feasibility several NGOs, Government/Private companies, etc. have shown interest for Jatropha plantation in the North-Eastern Region. If large scale cultivation of these plantation crops is undertaken in the region, it will not by immigrants from neighbouring countries which is at present taking place in alarming manner.

(b) *Hydro-Electric Power*

The North-Eastern Region has the rich potentiality of power in the form of hydel which is estimated to be 75,000 MW. The National Hydro-power Corporation (NHPC) has undertaken different survey, investigation and initiated preliminary works on Siang and Subansiri Basins for establishing mega hydro-power project with an installed capacity of 20,700 MW. Thus, the region can be a major exporter of cheap hydel power not only to its neighbouring countries like China and Myanmar.

(c) *Tourism Products*

Different sites of North-Eastern Region can be developed into world class tourist spots for religious tourism, adventure tourism, eco-tourism, wild life tourism, etc. Tawang, Kamakhya, Hajo, Imphal, Parasuramkund and Malini, Than, for religious tourism; Kaziranga, Manas, Pobitora, Namdapha Tiger Project, Mowling National Park as wild life tourism;

Sivasagar, Lake of No Return, Bhismak Nagar, Itafort, War Cemeteries at Kohima, Jairammpore, Bomdila for historical tourisms and Logtak Lake, Brahmaputra river, etc. water sports tourisms are worth mentioning. Also there is world's wettest place Cherrapujee in Meghalaya. The multi-coloured seasonal festivals of the major tribes of north-east can also attract cultural tourists from different parts of the world.

(d) *Plantation*

Plantation sector of the region mainly includes tea, coffee and rubber which have comparative advantage for the region.

Assam alone produces 50 per cent of country's tea and tea industry in India needs new international markets. In India the yield rate has, however, fallen from 1996 kg/hect in 1998-99 to 1614 kg/hect in 2001-02. The yield rate was found to be the highest in Karnataka (2709 kg), followed by Kerala (1789 kg), West Bengal (1735 kg), Tamil Nadu (1697 kg) and Assam (1601 kg). The yield rate of other minor tea producing states of North-East like Tripura, Sikkim, Manipur and Nagaland were found to be below 960 kg/hect during the same period. Thus, among the major tea producing states the yield rate in Assam *vis-à-vis* North-East was found to be the lowest. On the contrary Sri Lanka achieved an impressive jump from 1056 kg/hect in 1991 to 1641 kg/hect in 2002, while Kenya's yield rate also increased form 2031 kg/hect to 2175 kg/hect during the same period leading to comparative advantage over Indian tea at global market.

In India the major coffee producing states are Karnataka (53%), Kerala (28%), and Tamil Nadu (11%). Despite these areas, a small quantity is grown in non-additional belts of Andhra Pradesh, Assam, Nagaland and Arunachal Pradesh.

In the World, Asia is the largest producer of natural rubber accounting 86 per cent of world production. The world natural rubber production was 6.8 million tonnes in 2002 but its demand is projected at 7-9 million tonnes by 2010. At present India is producing about 6,13,000 tonnes and India's production is projected at 7,20,000 tonnes by 2010. During the Tenth Five Year Plan (2002-2007), the North-Eastern Region is selected as a major production centre of natural rubber by the Government of India.

(e) *Economic Mineral Resources*

Among the valuable minerals spotted in the region are petroleum, limestone, marble, coal, dolomite, fuller's earth and natural gas reserves are worth mentioning. Table 5.8 shows some mutual economic cooperation between India and ASEAN countries.

Table 5.8: India and ASEAN: Areas of Mutual Economic Cooperation

Sl.No.	*Countries*	*Important Areas of Mutual Economic Cooperation with India*
1.	Indonesia	Food and energy security, oil exploration, healthcare, infrastructural development, ICT cooperation in IT related services and sourcing of manpower.
2.	Malaysia	Infrastructural development, ICT cooperation in IT related services and sourcing of manpower, healthcare, oil exploration, education services.
3.	Philippines	Healthcare, ICT cooperation in IT related services and sourcing of manpower, education services.
4.	Thailand	ICT cooperation in IT related services and sourcing of manpower, gems and jewellery, food processing, heritage tourism.
5.	Singapore	ICT cooperation in IT related services and sourcing of manpower, financial services, logistics and infrastructure development, tourism, education services.
6.	Myanmar	Food security, technical assistance, development of infrastructural links, agriculture and natural resource monitoring, establish institutional linkages in financial sector.
7.	Vietnam	Food security, technical assistance, development of infrastructural links, ICT cooperation in IT related services and sourcing of manpower, healthcare, oil and mineral exploration, education services.
8.	Cambodia and Laos	Food security, technical assistance, development of infrastructural links, ICT cooperation in IT related services and sourcing of manpower, healthcare, oil exploration, education services.
9.	Brunei	Energy security, oil exploration.

Source: Compiled from Asher, *et. al.*, (2003).

From Table 5.8, it is observed that there are some possible areas of mutual economic cooperation between India and ASEAN countries. These areas span a wide range of areas from food and energy security to infrastructure and human resource development (HRD). Asher *et. al.* (2003) argues that India is seeking to diversify its conventional energy sources and significantly increase exploration of oil and gas in its territory. ASEAN countries, viz. Indonesia, Malaysia and Brunei, possess enough expertise in this area, which can provide considerable scope for energy cooperation. The energy sector companies from ASEAN and India could cooperate with each other in oil and gas exploration and in down-stream processing activities. *As an example, India's national oil company is already involved in a joint venture to explore oil and natural gas in Vietnam. Thus, the two countries are already cooperating in the energy sector, but there is definitely scope for further strengthening it.*

Cooperation in the civilian nuclear power sector for energy is also feasible and desirable. Mineral exploration and processing is another area that could be actively explored by India and some countries in ASEAN. For India as well as most ASEAN countries, food security is an important area of concern. There is scope for cooperation in improving productivity and in reducing wastage through application of knowledge, including biotechnology, to various components of agricultural and agro-processing value chain. More specifically, India faces persistent shortage of cooking oil, while Malaysia and Indonesia are major palm oil producers, creating opportunities for mutual beneficial cooperation. India is a major importer of forest products, while Indonesia and Myanmar are major exporters of these products. This indicates another potential area of expansion of bilateral trade.

Similarly, Thailand's expertise in food-processing industry, particularly in deep-sea fishing and other marine related activities represents another area wherein cooperation is likely to be fruitful. Singapore's largest supermarket operator, NTUC Fair price, could consider using India as a procurement base for variety of food related and other products. This may assist in Singapore's goal of food security and in strengthening the supply-chain for non-food essential household goods. Among the lower income transition ASEAN countries such as Vietnam, there are several other areas — particularly those relating to agricultural research, and biotechnology — where the scientists from India and ASEAN could fruitfully cooperate. They could also seriously consider facilitating trade and investments in agro-chemicals and fertilizers. As an example, less cumbersome registration procedures in these countries for pesticides, and related products, could be considered. *The emerging expertise of India in the ICT services*, ASEAN countries are likely to significantly benefit from cooperating in the areas of Information and Communication Technology, particularly in the development of human resources and on software programmes in the local languages of the respective ASEAN countries. India has expressed its willingness to assist less developed ASEAN countries in enhancing their capacity in the application of information technology (IT). Governmental organisations and companies in Malaysia, Indonesia and Singapore have an opportunity to gain from outsourcing IT works to Indian companies. It has created a dynamic Indian Diaspora with positive externalities for both countries. A related area of cooperation is that of the entertainment and multimedia sector. Firms from ASEAN and India can consider joint production of films, television programmes, and Internet content for both domestic and international audiences, particularly those whose main language is Malay or Bahasa Indonesia. Bollywood movies and some Indian TV channels and serials currently do enjoy some popularity. Restrictive practices in this area among ASEAN countries need to be reviewed.

Thus, these are the most potential areas through which both border and formal trade of North-East India can be strengthened.

5. *Obstacles of India's Economic Integration with the ASEAN Countries*

India has also signed an agreement to establish free trade with Thailand at Bangkok in October 2003. It covers 82 items for exchange of concessions items coverage between the two countries and was implemented in September 2004. The Trade Negotiating Committee is now in the process of working out the free trade agreement (FTA) in goods, services and investment. Apart from this Framework Agreement on Bay of Bengal Initiative for Multi-sectional Technical and Economic Cooperation (BIMSTEC), Free Trade Area (FTA) was signed in February 2004 among India, Bangladesh, Bhutan, Myanmar, Nepal, Sri Lanka and Thailand.

However, what still remains to be a cause of concern is that the Free Trade Area (FTA) agreement with ASEAN countries, that are supposed to be the largest participants in trade under Look East Policy is yet to be formalised. Though the framework agreement on comprehensive economic cooperation was signed between the ASEAN and India at Bali in 2003, the Trade Negotiation Committee is still in the process of arriving at an FTA on goods under negotiation list (Choudhary, 2007).

Sarma (2007) argued that the conventional age-old problems like basic physical infrastructure including road and communications faced by the region, the development initiatives in the NEI lacks a well-articulated policy framework. The paradigm dominated Government of India's policy is related to overstress on security/strategic consideration rather than on development efforts. Again, it is related to the minimum intervention in traditional systems and institutions of the hill economy, which is what has led to their non-compatibility with the functioning of market system.

Yumnam (2005) also argued that the Government of India considered the region as a "Signalling device to monitor the movement of commodities and people" and in insurance against the perceived threat of Chinese dominance of the region. Border trade agreement between India and Myanmar through the Moreh route was not accompanied by domestic economic reforms on the Indian side as expected in a normal Regional Trading Agreements. In the opening of economic trade from NEI (Singh, 2008), the problem of NE is mainly due to the fact that the process of nation formation is not yet complete. The problem of NEI lies in the inability of Indian policy makers to appreciate the region reality in proper perspective. More seriously, NEI is now confronting problems like identity crisis and ethnic violence.

However, India is seen as a good investment destination by Thai enterprises. Thailand ranks the third investor in India among ASEAN countries, after Singapore and Malaysia. Unfortunately, neither the Indian government nor its diplomatic mission in Bangkok seems to be truly interested in projecting the country and its business and cultural interests in Thailand through strong visible programmes and sustained campaigns as done by the other big countries in the Asia-Pacific region.

More interestingly the ongoing authorised bilateral trade (Indo-Myanmar) between the two countries is mostly en-routed through Kolkata port particularly for exporting commodities to Myanmar, Singapore and Thailand. The route is quite long and uneconomical. But this trade agreement between the countries to and from Kolkata port does not serve the interest of NEI. This idea of by-passing the geographical proximity, cultural and other similarities, India's economic integration with ASEAN countries will not materialise the purpose of long cherish (Look East Policy). In fact the attempts and initiatives taken up so far for the region are slightly slipped off from the main track.

Suggestions and Conclusion

So far, the economic integration between India and ASEAN is considered. It is obviously true that with the introduction of Look East Policy, Government of India made an attempt to develop the trade relations with the Asian, specially the South-East Asian nations. After the end of the Cold War, the ASEAN (Association of South-East Asian Nations) emerged as a major actor in the politics of the Asia-Pacific and it offered opportunities to India to come closer. Because both India and South-East Asia were facing similar challenges in the post-cold war period since the United States began transforming the world order and thus emphasis was given on promoting democracy, human rights, environment and free trade, at the global level, to the advantage of Western powers. But even after the sixteen years (almost) of the introduction of "Look East Policy" most of the export and import of India is taking place with the Western countries like European Union and United States of America. Still the policy is not fully materialised and the picture looks gloomy. Of course, there is a possibility to increase the trade with the South-East Asian countries and there are some factors which create problems towards the growth of border trade with India's eastern neighbours. The major impediment is found to be the absence of strong regional economic cooperation, and efficient transport and communication networks between India and these countries in spite of their geographical proximity. Achieve benefits from border trade, the physical linkages among the trading partners in the Trans-National Highways, Railways, Waterways and Airways, wherever possible is of utmost importance. To build such infrastructural facilities a huge amount of capital expenditure is necessary. If it is possible to remove such bottlenecks then a better physical infrastructure can make the region a developed one by way of opening new market opportunities for local producers and service providers and help income and employment generation of the region. It is also possible only through financial cooperation among all the trading partners and the international financial institutions.

The movement of human and non-human goods between India and Myanmar through Manipur is not a recent phenomenon and it is from the pre-historic times. It would not have been a difficult task for linking the country with ASEAN through the same route, if the India Government put their heart and soul. At the same time the region has to adopt proactive measure to boost up India's trade with ASEAN nations. If the NEI market rigidities is removed by the individual states or collectively within each constituent and between them then the mindset of the people needs to be turned in favour of free movement of people, goods and services not only within the country, but also across the border. For the competition of the global economy the substantial investment in the social sector, physical infrastructure, energy and power, health care, hotel and tourism are urgently required. Therefore, the East-West Corridor must be extended up to Imphal in Manipur and the project of four-lame Express Highway in the NEI requires to be completed in the stipulated time.

Thus proper steps should be taken both by the Central and State governments to develop the instruments for cross border trade and to make the people aware of the benefits from such trade. Good governance and people's participation are also the prerequisites for making the success of our Look East Policy.

REFERENCES

Asher, M.G. and S. Srivastava (2003): "India and the Asian Economic Community", *Discussion Paper No. 53*, Research and Information Systems for the Non-Aligned and Developing Countries (RIS), New Delhi, India.

Gogoi, J.K., Borah, K.C. and Goswami, H. (2003): "Regional Cooperation Among Bangladesh, China, India and Myanmar (BCIM) and its Impact on the Economy of the North-East" in proceedings of *The Eighth Annual Conference of North-Eastern Economic Association (NEEA)*, November 16-17, Organised by Department of Economics, Mizoram University, Aizawl, Mizoram.

Gogoi, J.K.; Borah, K.C. and Goswami, H. (2003): "Regional Cooperation between China, Myanmar, Bangladesh and India through Bilateral Trade: Impact on North-East India", *Assam Economic Journal*, Vol. XVI.

Karmakar, Suparna (2005): "India-ASEAN Cooperation in Services — An Overview", Indian Council for Research on International Economic Relations, *Working Paper No. 176*, November.

Patikar, Gautam and Singha, Komal (2009): "Indo-ASEAN Economic Ties — A Study of North-East India" *Southern Economist*, May 1, Vol. 48, p. 79.

Sen Rahul; Asher Mukul, G. and Rajan Ramkishen, S. (2004): "ASEAN-India Economic Relations: Current Status and Future Prospects" RIS (Research and Information System), *Discussion Paper RIS-DP"73*, May.

Saikia, Biren and Kachari Khagen (2009): "Indo-China Economic Cooperation: Prospects and Challenges" presented in Lakhimpur Commerce College, at 6th and 7th November sponsored by UGC.

The Assam Tribune, 27th October, 2004.

Websites

rediff.com/money/.../23of-economices-and-indias-look-east-policy.htm
mar.sagepub.com/cgi/content/refs/1/4/359
www.idsa.in/publications/strategic-analysis/2004/april/Naidu.pdf
www.ipcs.org/article_details.php?articleNo=2474

6

LOOK EAST POLICY AND SECURITY DYNAMICS
A Note

Manoranjan Goswami

Economic integration and political cooperation among the South-East Asia countries became a most viable necessity at the end of 'cold war' and fall of Soviet Union. The Look East Policy (LEP) was launched in 1992 at this juncture when India was also in desperate need for a new and strategic support base. India's vision and place in global economy was also redesigned and redrafted with the policy of 'Look East' since then.

India's link with South-East Asia goes back to history and the historical common objective was end of colonialism. The LEP gave rise to signing of Free Trade Agreement (FTA) between India and South-East Asian nations with about two thousand million dollar Foreign Direct Investment (FDI) with India today from South-East Asia countries only. India looks east for economic exploration today and LEP is a policy that binds the ASEAN countries together for all immediate economic advancement with India in the lead. We must remember that the most important development of twenty-first century will be the rise of Asia. Our ancient relation with SE Asia has a civilizational background and the new economic strategy of the country to open up and encourage more and more economic transaction between India and ASEAN countries in the matter of trade, commerce and industry has brought together and closer these countries politically too with better understanding. It is also a fact that LEP has also helped in creating a perception that India can be or should a counterbalance to the growing influence of China in the region.

Security Angle to the 'Look East Policy'

As briefly stated above Look East Policy, adopted by India was or is a historical necessity for the economic development of the country and to establish a strong tie with the South-East Asian countries with India in the lead position in the region, but there is an angle of 'security' that cannot be brushed aside. The security dimension of the region, which includes North-East of India as well as rather primarily, has to be addressed, taken care of and tackled, diplomatically or otherwise in a prompt and professional way so that the threat that looms around does not take away or destroy all the beneficial effects of LEP. LEP must stay and grow but security dimension must be looked into with equal urgency and professionally. If we do not, it may not only take away the benefits, but may subvert all that LEP aims at.

Security and North-East

India shares boundary with China, Nepal, Bhutan, Bangladesh and Myanmar. In India, North-East, however, is connected to the rest of the country with only a small corridor of just 22 km, which is about 1 per cent of the total international boundary India has in the region. North-East has about 200 ethnic groups, small or big, not on high co-cordiality in relation. There are around fifty active insurgent groups operating in the region, some asking even for separation from India. The North-East, being what state of economic progress it is or is aiming at needs special attention if LEP has to succeed. This is stark truth we cannot ignore if LEP has to achieve what it aims at. Recently, rather only a few days back, in the meet of leading investors of India in Guwahati, Ratan Tata has admitted that North-East still remained a doubtful and risky area for investors in the country in view of security risks involved and he assets that LEP can have no meaning unless North-East gets a boost in matter of infrastructural investment. He and other leading industrial or business giants of the country did opine that for LEP to succeed the security aspect of North-East has to be improved. We must remember that expression of patriotism is one matter and hard investment in millions is another.

Phase II of LEP

The Look East Policy in Phase II rightly includes security issues apart from economic ones including joint efforts by countries concerned to protect the sea lanes and to have effective coordination to counter terrorism. Today terrorism is not just an internal issue of any country. The hand of terrorist groups is spread across the geographical boundaries of any nation. ASEAN countries must work purposefully and trustfully with India to combat terrorism while simultaneously devising ways and means to promote trade and economic cooperation. This is the message of Phase II of LEP.

Among the factors that threaten a nation's internal security are:

— Bad governance, corruption and insensitivity to the actual need of the people.
— A feeling of alienation by a group or by the majority.
— Agitation and militancy approach adopted by the aggrieved parties.
— Grievances of religious and ethnic minorities.
— Exploitations by the external power on the grievance and discontentment that grows within.
— Absence of effective national security management and intelligence machinery.

The above factors are, singularly or together, are prevalent in India and more so North-East and the government and people must try united to bring a congenial environment for rapid economic growth of India through the window opened on the east by LEP. It is not only India, but security threats are there and rather growing in some other South-East Asia countries also and a joint effort is called for to usher in the gift of economy through political cooperation rather than helping the fake dream of insurgents. LEP cannot be left alone and if we do, it will fail. Terrorism and insurgency within and outside India must be tackled as a part of LEP only.

Before we examine the security perception of the region as a whole, we must remember that in today's context, the ultimate objective of Pakistan is not annexation of J&K but to weaken the fabric of India as a whole and to create a clear divide between Muslims and Hindus in India. Osama may go for 'Look East' and spread its virus to the Muslim population staying in Bangladesh, Thailand, Malaysia, Indonesia and even Myanmar. The threats on the religious fanatic is cutting the very unity chord of India and neighbouring countries in the East and South-East and this disturbance will affect and harm the very ideology and aim of LEP. LEP must take care of this threat. A strong and practical strategy to combat terrorism threat in the region is absolutely necessary for LEP to succeed.

Phase II of LEP is an honest effort to combine fight against terrorism and economic progress in the zone of ASEAN countries as a whole.

The Field of Terrorism

The rise of transnational crimes by emergence of criminal syndicates poses asymmetrical threats leading to the very nature and direction to security challenges and radical transformation in combat against the same. There are two issues — (a) Terrorism emanating from religious fundamentalism, and (b) terrorism from transnational crimes through criminal syndicates. Transnational crimes give rise to energy and maritime security aspect also. Energy security involves the need for countries to ensure continued access to energy resources, specially oil and gas, both at home and abroad. Maritime security is a matter that is looked after by respective Naval Force primarily. China, who still dominates the South-East Asia zone, has a very strong base located in Taiwan Straits. About 890 ships of all sorts and capacity are located there and they can be shifted anywhere in the Pacific Ocean region at a short notice. It has few strategic island base in South-East Asia water also. India's naval strategy is primarily designed to counter Pakistan and we have not seriously taken China as an adversary for possible naval conflict so far. It is felt necessary now, that India secure an ally such as Indonesia, Singapore or Australia for convenient deployment of Naval ships, if needs arises with expanding business and commerce interactions with South and South-East Asia. It is to be particularly noted and appreciated that India's Strait of Malacca is an important waterway for India, but is also a security threat. Earlier never East has been any focus of attention so far as India's security deployment is concerned.

Apart from age old malady of piracy, it is maritime terrorism that is of great concern now in the South-East Asia region and that affects trade movements. We have excellent rapport with our neighbours in the ASEAN region. In fact South-East Asia is a role model on collaboration in maritime security. This vigilance and initiative has to be maintained to crackdown on piracy because, if we do not, it would have serious consequence on maritime trades.

The Myanmar Factor

Myanmar shares 1,600 km of borders with four insurgency prone states of North-East — Manipur, Nagaland, Arunachal Pradesh and Mizoram. India stands for democracy and it cannot support the military Junta government of Myanmar, but that has not deterred India in seeking all help from Myanmar in the matter of LEP or in the matter of internal security where terrorist group of the Myanmar is deeply involved. The drug trafficking along these borders are also on increase. Drug and money lures innocents also and terrorist groups are taking full advantage of it for promoting their activities inside and outside India.

There is another very big factor while we discuss security dimension of Look East Policy. That is the China factor. China has built road connecting its Yunnan province to Upper Myanmar and it is learnt that the road will touch the NE border. India needs Myanmar's assistance and cooperation to halt China coming to the border of North-East. Militant groups of Myanmar is already giving arms and providing money to more than one militant group from North-East. Under such situation, India has to play a very delicate diplomatic role with Myanmar. We need Myanmar if we aim at getting more and more FDI from Asian countries and cutting across China's share drastically. In fact, in spite having some irritants within in some other South-East Asia countries like Indonesia or Philippine, their threat level remains well localised and pose no danger to itself or to neighbours. Myanmar's case is little different. As stated already, in spite of all terrorists' activities in the border, Myanmar has emerged as a centre piece for promoting New Delhi's Look East Policy. Myanmar also has geo-political importance to India as it provides China an access to the Bay of Bengal and strategically India will try to stop it always. We have also proposal to rebuild the Stilwell Road and we have proposal to have a new rail link — Silchar-Imphal-Moreh-Tamu. We have improved road Moreh-Tamu. But unfortunate it is that road linkage has not accelerated business between these two countries, as was expected. Rather, unfortunate it is that terrorists groups from North-East are getting better communication sometime through these routes. This is an example how security dimension is getting importance and how we cannot think of LEP without solving the threats towards security that goes with it. I cannot suggest, but it may come to reality one day that for better use of LEP, for the Sake of India's prosperity through the window in the East and for the development and peace of North-East, hard military option may become necessary.

LEP is call of the day and at the same time it cannot be looked upon in isolation of security dimensions, as I have tried to touch very briefly above.

PART II

Look East Policy and North-East Indian Perspective

7

LOOK EAST POLICY AND NORTH-EAST INDIA Political and Economic Implications

Nripen Dhar

Introduction

India's North-East is composed of eight states, i.e. Assam, Meghalaya, Mizoram, Manipur, Nagaland, Arunachal Pradesh, Tripura, and Sikkim. The composition of people in the region has a unique feature which is characterised by multi-ethnic, multi-cultural, multi-linguistic and multi-religious conglomerations. Moreover, the region varies in composition of land having hills and plains and char lands too. The climate in one way is scorching hot during summer and bitter and pinching cold in winter.

With all this natural composition during long British period and post-Independence era, India has been experiencing a threat from immigrant population and India's refugees settlement along with settlement in the vast char lands of the Brahmaputra river bed — out of which long Assam agitation and violences, IMDA, and finally "Assam Agitation", all this become a historical development now facing certain common interest/opportunists for economic development in general and political settlement in particular.

India's "Look East" policy have come into force represent its efforts to cultivate extensive economic and strategic relations with the nation of South-East Asia in order to bolster its standing as a regional power and counterweight to the growing People's Republic of China.

India's "Look East" policy was developed and enacted during the Government of P.V. Narasimha Roa (1991-1996) and later followed by

A.B. Vajpayee (1999-2004) aiming with economic liberalisation and moving way from "Cold War" era politics and activities India's strategy has focused on forging close economic and commercial ties increasing strategic and security cooperation and the emphasis of historical, cultural and ideological links. India sought to create and expand regional markets for trade investment and industrial development till UPA Government of India. It also began strategic and military cooperation with nations concerned by the expansion of China's economic and strategic influence.

Relation shifted steadily need based with Burma (now Myanmar). India's policy change in 1993 making friendly overtures to the military junta and therefore, several encouraging steps have been taken by the Government of India aiming to isolate Pakistan and China from the scenario of economic and political relations from the ASEAN. The following points explained in a brief manner in subsequent paras of this chapter relevance of the purpose and objectivity of the "Look East" policy including special emphasis with North-East India for better life in the field of political and economic relations.

Political Economic Implications

With a view to India's Look East Policy (LEP), India enjoys, indeed, excellent political relations with China, Bangladesh and Myanmar. In his address, Secretary, East, at the 6th Bangladesh-China-India-Myanmar Forum held in New Delhi on March 30, 2006 mentioned that it is not just that we are neighbours sharing common borders, all of us also face similar opportunities and challenges in our respective neighbouring countries for rapid economic growth, national development and prosperity of our people. That the current forum is the sixth of its series is testimony to the utility aiming to initiative in exploring sub-regional cooperation among the four countries. It has attracted much attention in India, as it has the potential to bring our three most important neighbours closer to us in a joint pursuit of common interest and prosperity through the increasing use of mechanisms of regional integration. With this policy formulation, it is necessitated a strategic vision to India's commitment to economic integration and political cooperation in SEA as a logical outcome of its LEP. Due priority is, therefore, given considering the geopolitical map of North-East India's security and economic development. North-East India, on the other hand, derived exactly on geo-political truth that South-East Asia begins. Today, one-third of India's trade volume is with SEA and not yet attractive involvement and participation is reflected in true sense of the term, though the LEP passed more than fifteen years back since its inception of Policy. It is a constraint rather than achievement. It is, therefore, proper priority viewing execution of its policy to review its commitment of achievement at the earliest.

There is increasingly greater focus on economic issues, which will enable us to realise the untapped potential of our economic cooperation and make it commensurate with the level of our political relationship. India is actively engaged in a sustained endeavour to strengthen bilateral engagement with Myanmar, Bangladesh and China. Therefore, cooperation with these three important neighbours is a core component of India's 'Look East' policy, which occupied high priority in India's foreign policy and reflects recognition of the strategic importance of Asia in tomorrow's world and India's place in evolving global economy. It is also belief that developments in our eastern neighbourhood directly affect India's security and development. Thus, the bonds of friendship and cooperation that we are actively creating with our eastern neighbours have a strong economic foundation as well as a positive convergence of security interests.

Bangladesh is a key member of the South Asian fraternity and a most important neighbour and regional partner for India. It is, indeed, special and unique for India, because the Indian state of West Bengal, Bangladesh and the North-East region of India have historically constituted an integrated space. India's multi-dimensional relations and traditional friendship along with wide ranging cooperation with Bangladesh were given a boost. With our respective rich natural and human resources, India and Bangladesh have a significant convergence of interests in taking full advantage of the shared opportunities, complementaries and synergies that flow out of our historical, geographical, political, economic and cultural closeness and in tackling some of the challenges such as, terrorism and drug trafficking.

India's relations with Myanmar rooted in shared historical, ethnic, cultural and religious ties are marked by friendship, mutual trust, economic cooperation provides an important understanding of India-Myanmar ties. Sharing with India a long land and maritime boundary, Myanmar is practically India's gateway to South-East and East Asia. We are involved in a number of infrastructure projects in Myanmar to improve road and rail connectivity demands immediate attention our energy needs and promote development. A step, therefore, taking ongoing cooperation in the field of space. India is assisting Myanmar since early 2006 with remote sensing capabilities. Also sharing with them data from our IRS Satellite. An agreement is already made for setting up a ground station in

Myanmar for receiving directly the IRS data. It is of great importance to its economy. It uses in agriculture, crop forecasting, soil surveying, mineral surveys and watershed management. The whole series of technological involvement for the last several years building up capabilities in Myanmar this data directly receiving and analysing to this data to their great advantage. The other area, working together is an energy side involved in a couple of exploration ventures essentially on the Arakan coast which is just opposite India's own eastern seaboard. India is looking an agreement between the two sides for the exploration of natural gas which would be produced in these exploration blocks. India can do it either by pipeline from Myanmar directly into our North-East. India and is also looking at the possibility of a pipeline from Myanmar through Bangladesh to India. India have also kept an option to look at some other routing for the pipeline. Besides, having the option of converting this into LNS and shipping it to India. In fact, the distance is short and could be quite cost effective. There are various options India is looking at. India have been helping Myanmar in the telecom sector and also in the transportation sector.

Another project, in the process of execution, is the Kaladan multimodal transport project. This is found to be very important because, this is, really a transport again going through the Arakan province of Myanmar from the ancient port of Sitwe which was in the old days used to be known as Akyat. Akyat is very old trade route in the region. Also very important route for rice trade. Since earlier days, rice and other commodities from Myanmar use the sea route going down to Kolkata, to Chennai and back again. The project stated above, is also viewing upgradation of this port and use both river transportation as well as highway which would enter southern Mizoram. So, we could have Kolkata to Sitwe shipping route and then, this would link up with a river and highway route straight into southern Mizoram. It gives a kind of an alternative access to our North-East and also an exit from North-East. It is very important both economic as well as significance in terms of increasing the economic viability of projects for our North-East. It is with this viewpoint initial work has been started. India have from very early days, a strong cultural link with Myanmar. Myanmar is a country where Buddhism enjoys very great reverence among the people. Buddhist link, therefore, between our two countries is a very strong bond. A project is initiated for promoting exchanges in the field of Buddhist studies between the two sides. India have also a special programme for Buddhist pilgrims to visit from Myanmar to India. The groups of pilgrims who come to India, a visa free entry for those groups is extended and thereby people of Myanmar highly appreciated it.

It is also informed that the then (2006) President of India would visit Myanmar and during his stay in Yangon visiting the much revered Shwedagon pagoda, which is a very ancient pagoda. Legend is that there were two traders from Myanmar who were visiting India during the life time of Lord Buddha himself and they were privileged to have two strands of hair of Buddha which they brought to Myanmar and the original Shwedagon pagoda was actually built around these relics which were enshrined.

Another, a very strong historical link between the two countries would be reflected from the then visiting President of India also used to visit the Mazaar of Bahadur Shah Zafar. History would recall us that Bahadur Shah Zafar, the last emperor of India, was exiled to Yangon and the last king of Burma was exiled to Ratnagiri in Maharashtra. It is, therefore, a strong historical link between the two. The visiting President of India will also be visiting Mandalay which is one of the most important cities of Myanmar. The visit of President of India shall follow by Senior officials, which will cover a whole host of bilateral as well as regional issues.

As we know, Myanmar is in a sense our gateway to ASEAN. It is also an important Country, because, we have 1,400 km long boundary with Myanmar. In addition, land boundary really straddles the four most important and sensitive North-Eastern states of India starting from Arunachal Pradesh, Nagaland, Manipur and Mizoram. From this point of view, a very important neighbour for us. We also share the Bay of Bengal another strategic stretch of sea for both our countries. This is, therefore, a very important geo-political position as far as Myanmar is concerned.

As a matter of fact, India's largest neighbour and a key player in the international arena, China remains an important priority of India's foreign policy. It is through joint efforts, India-China relations have progressively developed and diversified. The overall trend of the relationship in recent years has been overwhelmingly positive and marked by regular high-level exchanges. Based predominantly on shared convictions that they have more than just a bilateral dimension, India-China relations have now acquired a long-term global and strategic character. The fact that trade and economic relations have emerged as the trendsetter in the overall India-China relations is not mere coincidence but rather the result of a conscious effort on both sides to bring our relationship in tune with the present realities by building upon mutual complementarities. There is enough space and opportunity in the region and beyond for both India and China to grow together rather. The economic dynamism of India and China offers an unprecedented opportunity for growth and development in the region and in the whole of Asia including four countries in our immediate neighbourhood. India-China partnership is an important determinant for regional and global peace and development.

India has changed significantly in the last decade and a half since, India launched a bold agenda of economic reforms and liberalisation. India has also emerged as one of the largest and fastest growing economies of the world with a leadership role in many cutting edge technologies. India increasingly felt our growth and prosperity as being interlinked with the rest of world, specially with our larger neighbourhood in Asia. Our "Look East Policy" has acquired greater dimension and depth. India have a vision of more robust regional integration in Asia, perhaps in the form of a Pan-Asian Free Trade Area or even an Asian Economic Community. The vision of a prosperious South Asia, the PM of India has emphasised that it is essential that India unlock the potential of this region by dismantling the existing barriers that restrict the movement of people, goods and investment within and across the region. The same logic applies to our extended neighbourhood to the East. Meaningful sub-regional and regional cooperation on India's East, that would create an arc of prosperity from Himalayas to the Pacific, is dependent upon greater connectivity and a dismantling of barriers between us to allow free movement of goods, people and ideas.

Mutually interacting with one another through a wide array of many bodies promoting regional and sub-regional cooperation is in progress. India and Bangladesh, for instance, are close partners in ASSRC where China will also be a observer. Besides, Bangladesh and Myanmar closely cooperate with us within the framework of the Bay of Bengal. Initiative for Multi-Sectoral Technical and Economic Cooperation with Myanmar, India shares another regional organisation the Mekong-Ganga Cooperation (MGC), besides cooperating within the India-ASEAN Summit framework. Both India and China are Summit partners of ASEAN, with China and Myanmar, we have joined hands is an important initiative in the form of the East Asia Summit launched in Kuala Lumpur, which has laid the foundation for a cooperative regional architecture in Asia leading to the long term goal of creating an East Asian Community. Our three countries, on the other hand, are also cooperating within the framework of the Pent Lateral Group on Drug Control. As an observer, in the Shanghai

Cooperation Organisation (or SCO), India shares with China yet another forum for regional cooperation in the case of Central Asia. India's regional engagement with China also includes the trilateral cooperation that the two of us have with Russia.

Talks between India and Bangladesh held in New Delhi on March 21, 2006: (1) on terrorism, both sides agreed that we are victims of terrorism and therefore, to join hands in fighting this scourge. Agreed upon on bilateral cooperation between India and Bangladesh, the areas are noted, (2) on trade, (3) promotion of Indian investments in Bangladesh. There is a proposal, for instance, that the USD 2.5 billion worth of Tata investment in Bangladesh, (4) the other issue like water and security. It was felt that institutional mechanism which are available for the two sides must be strengthened, security issue and Joint River Commission issue should be held more regularly viewing successful implementation, (5) also agreed that SAFTA needs to be implemented as soon as possible, (6) the Sealdah-Jadavpur rail link, (7) Tista river issue. At last, not the least, question on Terrorism since recognised by both sides its very nature is a kind of phenomenon which can be tackled by joint cooperation with desired determination.

During the question hours in Parliament (Lok Sahba, March 8, 2006), another important issue regarding Exchange of Enclaves between India and Bangladesh came up for discussion, where the House informed that (7) There are III Indian enclaves in Bangladesh and 51 Bangladesh enclaves in the Land Boundary Agreement (LBA) signed in 1974. But the exchange of enclaves has not yet taken place. However, the joint Boundary working Groups again envisages that all constitutional or legal barrier to the exchange had been completed in accordance with the Land Boundary Agreement. There was not a pre-condition to the exchange of enclaves.

During the 13th SAARC summit held in Dhaka on 12-13, 2005, the Chinese proposal to join the SAARC, agreed in principle, that the People's Republic of China may be associated as observer and further decided that modalities regarding observer status will be decided at the twenty-seventh meeting of the SAARC Council of Ministers next in July 2006.

In fact, the Government are considering to approve to the proposal of railways for setting up of a rail link with Burma through the North-Eastern States. The feasibility study conducted for on India-Myanmar rail link suggested the following alignments:

1.	In India	Construction of new rail link between Jiribam-Imphal-Moreh at a cost of ₹ 2,941.08 crore.
2.	In Myanmar	Construction of a rail link between Tamu (Moreh)-Kalay-Segyi at a cost of ₹ 1,339.02 crore and rehabilitation of existing line from Segyi-Chaungu-Myohaung at a cost of ₹ 2,839.59 crore.
3.	The Jiribam-Imphal (Tupui)	Sector is scheduled to be completed by March 2010. No decision has been taken as per No. 1 and No. 2 stated above and the security in the border areas is under constant review.

With a view to New Delhi's efforts to strengthen bilateral relations on various defence hardware items and counter China's influence, Myanmar will get from India an unspecified number of BN2 "Defender" maritime surveillance aircraft and deck-based air-defence guns alongside offering a host of training programmes. This is India's first significant defence sale to Myanmar. New Delhi traditionally pursued on adversairal relationship with outgun, most visibly through its support of the pro-democracy movement and anti-Government ethnic insurgent groups. Now, it reversed this policy in the late 1990s and began courting Myanmar. It is to be noted that the policy sifted was partly aimed at counteracting Chinese influence, which New Delhi viewed with concern. India also looked to counter balance inroads by rival Pakistan. The new policy was further intended to better address a range of cross border issues, including drug trafficking and the use of Myanmar's territory as a sanctuary for anti-government militant groups active in India's North-East. Another salient point as observed, Myanmar is still close to Beijing but less dependent on China's support than it was 15 years ago when both countries were internationally isolated. India, its partners in the Association of South-East Asian Nations and several other countries provide Yangon with a range of alternatives. However, cross border cooperation has produced mixed results. Myanmar's ruling junta has declared its willingness to cooperate with the Indian military, but this has so far produced little at field level.

Another area of cooperation and coordination, ASEAN call for coordinated response on natural disasters. The initiative comes as the first anniversary approaches of the devastating tsunami that areas around the Indian ocean at the end of 2004. It gained the formal support of ASEAN defence chiefs who convened separately in Manila. The defence attaches from the ASEAN countries to coordinate disaster response and coventer-terrorism operations initiating an information exchange an military capabilities in place for disaster response operations and establishing a working group to explore intensified military to military cooperation within ASEAN. The disaster response initiative represents a new direction for ASEAN, a political and economic grouping that has traditionally shied away from multi-lateral military activity. Disaster relief operations would provide the organisation with a benign platform for military cooperation.

Summarisation and Conclusion

Following the explanation and probability in achieving the desired goal in the areas of political and economic relations basing the India's Look East Policy and North-East Region, certain achievement likely to be reflected in course of execution of the steps taken by the participants. It is delayed since its inception, yet the beneficiaries are the states of N.E. India with the policy (LEP) paid some dividends resulting successful negotiation of bilateral and multilateral trade agreement with the ASEAN grouping which undoubtedly enabled India to break the artificial political barriers between the subcontinent and South East Asia.

Over and above, sub-regional exchanges among our four core countries (i.e. Myanmar, India, Bangladesh, China) could help realise the latent potential that exists between us for meaningful cooperation based on mutual complementarities and equal partnership. But the impressive web for our regional and sub-regional interaction with one other does bring out that the conceptual framework offered by the BCIM initiative is already subsumed within the existing collaborative architecture in our region. Given that we already have between us a number of overlapping regional and sub-regional groups that provide established platforms for exploring mutually beneficial cooperation, we need to examine deeply, critically and clearly whether a proliferation of sub-regional groups is desirable without establishing their economic utility or viability.

More important than formal structures is the vision of practical cooperation that the scholars of different disciplined and businessmen from the BCIM countries gathered here can bring to our common objectives of getting the four countries to harness their respective advantages for all-round benefit. In that Forum (6th BCIM) Secretary (GoI) East welcome the ideas for project based cooperation in specific sectors, such as, trade, transport and tourism. It is also urged that projects in these areas, must be concrete, economically viable and interlink the major production and commercial centres of all the four countries.

It is also encouraging that civil societies in our respective countries are increasingly coming together to explore the avenues for greater contacts and exchanges between the four countries. Our scholars and trade bodies have done good work in putting forth various ideas to enhance economic integration and people to people contacts in the sub-region. It has also come up with ideas for subregional cooperation in some important areas such as, trade, transport, tourism, energy security, etc. Some of the interesting ideas include test transportation of cargo from Kunming to Kolkata through Myanmar and Bangladesh, Kolkata-Kunming motor car rally *via* Bangladesh, enhancement of civil aviation links, development of tourism circuits and promotion of cultural exchanges between BICM. The same effort will continue in the present Forum and specific proposals would emerge from its deliberations for consideration by the Governments of these four countries. It is, therefore, true that signing the free trade agreement has signalled India's commitment to economic integration and political cooperation in South-East Asia as a logical outcome of its India's Look East Policy.

8

DEVELOPMENT OF NORTH-EAST INDIA AND LOOK EAST POLICY
A Critical Review

Sailajananda Saikia and *Bishmita Medhi*

Introduction

Today when we speak about Look East Policy it seems like something new, a new policy for the development of North-Eastern states of India. In real sense "Look East Policy" has been here from the Vedic past. As we know India is an old civilisation of Sun worshippers and according to Hindu mythology Sun is regarded as the most powerful. In this respect, it may not be correct to trace India's Look East Policy (LEP) to the beginning of the nineties, when the Cold War ended as is usually done. The Look East Policy of India, framed by the Narasimha Rao government in the early nineties, is a substantial manifestation of India's focused foreign policy orientation towards South-East Asia; an immensely resourceful and flourishing region.

The North-East India is commonly referred to the eight states of Assam, Arunachal Pradesh, Manipur, Meghalaya, Mizoram, Nagaland, Sikkim and Tripura. The whole area encompasses 2,62,230 sq.km. with a total population of 3,84,95,089 (2001 Census), which is about 3 per cent of India's total population. These states are only connected to the "mainland" of India through the so-called chicken neck. This small channel constitutes of only about 1 per cent of the region's borders, and the region is surrounded by thousands of kilometres of international border. The partition of the land and the creation of East Pakistan led to the North-East being virtually disconnected from other parts of India with the only remaining link being "chicken neck", the narrow 27 km Siliguri corridor (*North-East Region Vision Document*). This had immense effects on the economic situation of the region and its capability to trade its goods. Further, the variety of different identities and cultures represented in this region, together with the geographical distance to the main part of India and a feeling of 'distinctiveness', led in many parts of the North-East to violent conflicts. Demand of independence in some states led to armed insurgencies since the early 1950s. Thus, "the quest for ethnic and regional identity, nationalism, and ideological motivations have fomented a climate of insurgency in several parts of North Eastern region, which has led to political fragmentation of the region; the climate has been further fuelled by the slow pace of development" (*North-East Region Vision Document*, 2020), that followed the aftermath of independence. There are ample possibilities for North-East India to reap benefits from India's thriving relations with South East Asia as the process of globalisation provides the countries with the opportunities to grapple with cross-market accessibility and enabling them alleviate their poverty and economic backwardness.

North-East India stands as a geostrategic point from geographical point of view and many things need to be looked in while considering this region. It is the deviation from complete economic issues to the broader agenda involving security cooperation, actively constructing transport corridors and erecting pillars of linkages and connectivity. This phase of India's Look-East Policy renders ample relevance to the development of its North-Eastern Region because of its geographical proximity to South-East Asia. The incessant conflict scenario in this part seems to be far away from the "mainland" of India, not only from the geographical perspective, but also from the notion of how it is perceived. To engage in the region is a great challenge for the Government of India, as well as a necessity. Therefore, this chapter aims at reviewing the involvement of Government of India in its North-East. However, due to the limited scope here the focus only on particular aspects of those broad and complex issues surrounding the North-Eastern Region (NER).

Before coming to the present context on the importance of LEP we have to look at the matter from the historical perspective in order to understand the importance of the very policy that has generated so much debate for the last two decades.

Historical Evolution of LEP

Evidence is there about India's dynamic and extensive relations with its eastern neighbours since the first century. This phase lasted until the 12th century and can be described as the first wave of "Look East" in cultural and commercial engagement. During this period, the first Hindu Empire (in what later became the Indo-China region) flourished based entirely on cultural and philosophical contacts. No military mission was launched and no war took place in the East despite the South Indian emperor Rajendra Chola's periodic encroachments into the Srivijiya Empire in Malaya and Indonesia in the 10th and 11th Century.

Colonial Period

The advent of Islam in the 12th century and the colonial expansion that followed Muslim rule in India disrupted these cultural and commercial links. During the British colonial period, the Second World War engulfed East Asia rather extensively. The war added a strategic dimension to British links with South-East Asia and the importance of North-Eastern Region increased geopolitically. The British grasped the strategic centrality of India in Asia and sustained their colonial presence in the "East of the Suez" including in South-East Asia, on the basis of their Indian empire. They built India as the bastion of their power and influence in Asia that protected their colonial holdings as far in the east as possible, up to Hong Kong. This period may be considered as the second wave of India's LEP under colonial rule when strategic interests were brought upfront along with the commercial interests, at the cost of cultural and civilizational links. The legacy of India's colonial sway persists in many subtle and diverse ways. It alerts East Asian countries and interested major powers to project and even exaggerate India's possible, expansionist and adventurist intents even when there is no evidence to support such intents.

Post-Independence Period

The third wave of India's LEP was set in motion with the advent of independence. The eastern neighbours constituted one of the priority areas in India's commitment to work for Asian resurgence. Nehru called the Asian Relations Conference in March 1947 even before the formal beginning of "India's tryst with destiny". He, as the philosopher and architect of independent India's foreign policy, in general and its Asia policy, in particular, articulated this commitment while underlining the rationale and significance of Asian resurgence in India's worldview.

The emphasis on geography and culture in Nehru's early eastward policy was aimed at building Asian solidarity. He took into account the aspirations of a new, independent and resurgent Asia. The first Afro-Asian

Conference held in Bandung, Indonesia, in 1955, was the culmination of these early Indian initiatives and efforts to promote Asian resurgence. India strongly pleaded for China's integration into the international community in the interest of Asian solidarity and pleaded that China should be treated more as a nationalist country than a communist revolutionary force. The characteristic feature of the third wave of India's LEP was decolonisation and Asian resurgence. Both of these aspects were primarily emotional and ideological in content. The Nehruvian vision had a strong political content to back them, but was bereft of much tangible substance of commerce, culture and economy, as was evident during the first wave period. Nor was much attention paid, save rhetorical recognition, to the security imperatives of the developments in Indian Ocean, except during the late sixties and early seventies when India encouraged and backed the proposals for reducing the great powers' arms race in the Indian Ocean by getting it recognised as a "Zone of Peace". Therefore, India's efforts and initiatives with regard to Asian resurgence and Asian solidarity, though appreciated, could not be sustained as desired.

The present Look East Policy is viewed as post cold war development in the realm of India's foreign policy. Although, many policies have been initiated by the Central Government for the development of North Eastern Region, most of the policy had been on chapters only and never reached the ground. In the post independent era, the policy had shifted many a times. While discussing LEP we need to look into the main paradigm and in recent years the paradigm has shifted from Cultural to development.

The first of these paradigms is the '*Culture Paradigm*': that the North-East is a phenomenally diverse mosaic of cultures which have to be preserved and enriched; this paradigm was perhaps preponderant largely in the 1950s and the 1960s.

Somewhere in the mid-1960s, the '*Security Paradigm*' came into greater prominence. Probably after the Chinese invasion of 1962, the North-East began to be seen as a strategically significant region not only in a geographical sense but in a larger geopolitical sense of India's role in East Asia and South-East Asia.

In the early 1970s, a transition to the '*Politics Paradigm*' the region required political representation; the diverse tribal cultures and diverse sub-nationalities required participation in 'mainstream' democratic process. This was when new states began to be formed on the idea that people here required a voice — representation in the democratic process —and that once they have voice and representation through the instrument of representative, pluralistic parliamentary democracy, many of the problems associated with this region would tend to get nullified or minimised.

As we moved from a culture paradigm to representative politics, in the 1980s, we hit upon the new *mantra*, the fourth for the North-East — the '*Development Paradigm*'. We have to look back on the factors responsible for this paradigm shift from the Central Government for North-Eastern region. The main points are:

1. The end of cold war and the eventual rise of the US as the only superpower making the policy of non-alignment virtually redundant.
2. The worldwide trend towards regionalism since, the nineteen eighties posing new challenges before India and considerably weakening India's faith in multilateralism.
3. East Asia's exemplary growth performance under an outward looking strategy of development contrasting with India's sluggish growth under protectionist and all pervasive government control policy regime.
4. The "China factor" — China was seen as the principal source of insecurity and the greatest potential threat to India's long-term interests. Closer links with the East and the South-East Asia were thus considered to be possible ways to "set limits on China's influence" or perhaps to "balance" China's expanding power in the region.
5. The emergence of the Look East Policy as a role model of development for the North-East is often dubbed as the new development mantra or a new paradigm of development in the North-East development perspective.

It is here to understand the main reasons that had led the Central Government to divert its policy for the development of North-Eastern region. The main points for this new emphasis can be summed up as under:

Security Concerns: Security is one of the main factors for the economic development of any region and it is the most important issue for the North-Eastern states both external and internal. As for the external concerns, the China factor again emerges as the crucial one. China even today does not openly accept Arunachal Pradesh as part of India.

The *Internal Security Problems* relate to the North-East India having serious international dimensions as follows:

(i) The extremist/insurgent outfits are internationally well connected;
(ii) The porous borders are frequently used by the extremists/outfits to escape from the Indian army;
(iii) These outfits have their hideouts in the neighbouring countries; and
(iv) Pakistan through their ISI is also involved in fomenting trouble in this region using Bangladesh as a base.

New Paradigms of Development

The admission of Myanmar to the ASEAN Club in 1997 could be another reason since the Myanmar is strategically situated between India and Indo-China. It is here to be mentioned that Geopolitics plays an important role in the change of government's attitude or policy on North-Eastern region, as both India and China are two of the fast emerging economic powers in the world. And in order to grow their economy both needs new areas for their trading purposes. And for India the geostrategic situation of Myanmar is important as it gives an alternative way to reach out to the East and South-East Asian markets.

The North-East being a "top priority" for the Government of India today, this seems to be a justifiable reason for the inclusion of North-East in the Look East Policy (LEP). Clearly, this demonstrates a development concern for the North-East. This new development paradigm in a way was the result of the failure of the "Old development paradigm" where the major thrust of development policy as articulated by various packages of development under the aegis of successive Prime Ministers since, Deve Gowda was to pump inasmuch money as possible for the development of this region.

But this new paradigm of development will have if at all only a very limited on the development of the region. The region was exposed to a massive scale of international trade during the 19th century, but its impact, if any, on the economy was very negligible. This is a sad lesson from the past history of the region.

The Real Issue with LEP and North-East Region

Though India's trade with countries bordering the North-East has seen the most dramatic expansion, this expansion has had little or no impact on North-East economy as most of this trade expansion is through seaports. In spite of huge potential, the Indo-Myanmar trade remained insignificant, amounting to few crores per year. The traded items between India and Myanmar are mostly third country products and there is no concerted effort on the part of the government to develop the border regions and expand the tradable items.

Following their research on India, Goldman Sachs, Co. economists Jim O'Neill and Tushar Poddar have come up with a report on "Ten Things for India to achieve its 2050 Potential". Some of the findings like improve governance, increase trade with neighbours, increase agricultural productivity and improve infrastructure are very much needed in this region. In order to reap the benefits of this policy and from FTAs with the economies of the East, the key variables are transit arrangements, proliferation of trade routes and customs check post, easy visa regime making it possible for traders, businesspersons and transport operators to move in and out of the region.

It thus requires massive investments in infrastructure: construction of roads, railways, air transport and communication facilities, which are largely absent. Hotels, restaurants and resorts needs to be built for tourists. The Shukla Commission on "Transforming the North-East", estimated that such investment would exceed ₹ 25,000 crore. As envisaged in *North-Eastern India Vision 2020*, a substantial increase in investments as well as improvement in productivity is required for the North-Eastern region to catch up with the rest of the country by 2020. This huge investment cannot come from the government alone. As a result, private investment and loans from Asian Development Bank and World Bank is needed. However, the present political and security environment cannot attract private investors. The government needs to create a secure environment by initiating dialogue with radical elements to bring peace and stability in this conflict-ridden region.

Industries in the region need to produce goods that can be exported to the neighbouring countries. Processing industries would be set up to manufacture quality goods that can be offered in international markets at acceptable prices. Agriculture has to be improved to match the requirement of the industries. The new North-East Industrial Policy 2007 practically made the whole region a special economic zone. The industry departments of various states of the region have only benefited the "subsidy eaters" till now. Otherwise, the region would just be a corridor between mainland India and South-East Asia. India's policy of strengthening its ties with eastern neighbours has so far been limited to counter insurgency efforts as seen in Bhutan and Myanmar. Here Look East Policy is used as a means to convince the neighbouring countries to drive out insurgents taking shelter in these countries. Sincere and political negotiations and not military approach to insurgency would bring lasting solution. Such negotiations should involve, as Das (2001) stated, "civil society and all the contending parties as one negotiation may antagonise the other group/groups."

The role of North-Eastern states in the Look East Policy is negligible till date. So far, it seems to be a dictated policy of the Central Government. This is in sharp contrast to the role played by Yunnan province of China in search of closer relationship with its South-East Asian neighbours. The Yunnan province plays a role in the institutions of the Greater Mekong sub-region. However, there is little room for India's North-eastern states in the Mekong Ganga Cooperation or in BIMSTEC. It is through concentrated efforts in various thrust areas that North-East India will be able to stand not only the challenges of the Look East Policy, but also to fully participate in the new milieu. Only then, North-East can hope to be a part of the bridge connecting India and South-East Asia. Giving the North-Eastern states a direct role in this policy by taking advantage of the region's history and shared cultural ties with East and South-East Asia can ensure a successful Look East Policy.

Problems of Development

The crux of the problem of development is, therefore, not the lack of integration with the booming East and the South-East Asian markets. The crucial problems of development faced by the region are:

(i) The lack of intra-regional as well as intra-state connectivity,
(ii) Infrastructure, and
(iii) The issues of security and governance.

The new paradigm of development seems to ignore these issues by diverting attention to an issue (like connectivity with the outside world) which may have if at all marginal impact upon the economy. The correct strategy of development should, therefore, be to address the latter issues more seriously instead of focusing upon connectivity with the outside world.

The region should have both short-term and long-term visions of development where the ultimate objective should be to increase the size of the market by allowing scope for trade and specialisation within the

North-East through the improvement of intra-regional connectivity, creation of infrastructure and maintenance of proper security and governance and by initiating a participatory development process with the grassroots levels of participation in order to increase agricultural productivity.

The failure of the old paradigm of development set the tone of the new *mantra* or the new paradigm of development — integrate the North-Eastern region with the booming markets of the East and the South-East Asia through the so called "The Gateway of India" — a possible land route from the North-East to the China and the other East Asian markets — an attempt to rediscover the old Silk Route.

The basis of this argument is that integration will increase opportunities of trade for the North-Eastern region with the promising markets of the East and the South-East Asia. International trade is expected to play the role of an "engine of growth" so as to transform the North-East into a highly modernised industrial region and also as an alternative route to reach out the outside markets as entrecote trade facilities for the hinterland.

The real issue is not the lack of integration which caused slow growth in the North-Eastern region, but insurmountable developmental constrains resulting in the failure of the region to integrate with the rest of India. The region has relatively very high levels of cross border trade with the neighbouring countries, which will continue to exist irrespective of any policy. But such border trade was mainly determined by scarcity and surplus situation in the geographical proximity of subsistence village economies, and not market economies where production is mainly for marketed surplus.

The distance to be covered from the "gateway to the East and the South-East Asia" is very long covered by uneven topography causing high transportation cost, uncertainties and perhaps too many borders to cross.

The Real Facts on Development Policy

Constraints

Connectivity within the region and absence of internal security and governance are the primary constraints. Many believe that the opening of Stilwell Road will open new avenues for trade and commerce. But in reality it may act in a different way, firstly in India we have only about 60 km of road length, in Myanmar more than 1000 km, which is not under control of government and most of the insurgence groups had their hideouts in this region, and the rest about 600 km with China.

Moreover, it is here to be mentioned that with the opening of Stilwell Road, China will be the beneficiary as Yunnan province will be developed, which is the most underdeveloped province of China and landlocked. China will have an easy passage through North-East India to Bangladesh port that will help their trade to boom in a massive way.

If we observe carefully, we can see that there is no market as such in this region and the interstate connectivity is also not up to the mark. Moreover, majority of the traders in this region is always from outside. From the recent document published by the Planning Commission clearly reveals the North-Eastern states in terms of transport cost and law and order situation is at very bad shape.

What Can be Traded?

To put it in other words given the present pattern of India's trade with the East and the South-East Asian countries, do we find any array of goods that are being produced in the North-East and in the production of which the region can possibly realise comparative advantage? The answer is an absolutely no. The region does not have any product that we can bank upon to sell once the policy is implemented. The region will only consume other's products instead of exporting any product.

It is here to be mentioned that India experienced a spectacular 10 per cent cumulative annual rate of growth in tea exports over the period 1858 to 1901 and Assam's contribution to India's exports of tea was nearly 90 per cent. Why then such a massive trade could not play the role of an engine of growth for the region? The region failed to boost up any other sector that can induce growth or development.

Conclusion

The Look East Policy is expected to usher in a new era of development for the North-Eastern part of India through network of pipelines, road, rail and air connectivity, communication and trade. However, several hurdles need to be overcome of which the region is embroiled for the past several decades before any meaningful activity can take place. Starting from various forms of insurgent activities to the problem of illegal migration and drug trafficking, which are all transnational in character; the Government of India need to forge cooperation from the neighbouring countries.

The trans-border communities can be restored through border trade and inter-country trade which the border region should not act merely as a transit corridor but as a source of local manufacture and enhancing people-to-people contact. The emphasis should be on industrialisation and growth. The Indian government and the North-Eastern states must adopt proactive role and provide not only infrastructures but also political stability and good governance. Greater participation of the local people in production and distribution activities and raising agricultural productivity should be given prime importance. Trade alone will not be sufficient to transform the region into a sustained development path. In addition, growth in trading activities will only benefit those people who possibly are from outside the region and who are economically more powerful to exploit the resources of the region. India's Look East Policy should include goals such as encouraging public debate and participation as well as opening doors and windows in the political and economic arena.

In order to develop the region the interstate communication should be developed. As the Shukla Commission report (Shukla, 1997) states, the regions' infrastructure should be developed in order to develop North-Eastern region. The Central Government should look into this matter more seriously before any other activity taken in the region.

The policy envisages the region not as the periphery of India, but as the centre of a thriving and integrated economic space. Thus, many people see it as an excellent opportunity to integrate not only with Indian mainland economy but also with India's neighbouring countries and even beyond. In contrast, others view this policy as an extension of India's new imperialism in a new form in that the region will only provide a bridge between the rest of India and South-East Asia. The main argument of the critiques is that India is more concerned with the East, but not to India's North-East.

Increased regional and international trade can shape the future destiny of the North-Eastern region by providing the scope for industrialisation and growth. But mere facilitation of trade through the region with the neighbouring countries will have only marginal impact on the economy unless the region can be converted into a production hub. For this the Central Government and the various State Governments of the region must adopt proactive role. Instead of providing tax holidays for investment in the region, the Governments should provide infrastructures, political stability and good governance. They should adopt more outward rather than inward looking policies for development.

Greater participation of the local people in production and distribution activities, the education sector should be given the prime importance. However, the vast rural masses have to be brought into the process of industrialisation for political viability of the trade as a strategy of industrialising the region. For this the utmost importance should be given to raise the agricultural productivity in the region with proper flood control measures and other steps. As it had happened in the past, without a parallel agricultural revolution in the region, trade alone will not be sufficient to transform the region into a sustained development path. The growth in trading activities will only benefit those people who possibly are from outside the region and who are also economically more powerful to exploit the resources of the region.

In conclusion, it seems that there is an urgent need for the policies and approaches for North-Eastern Region to be specifically applicable to the needs and specificities of the region. The policies for the development of the region must not only be framed keeping local needs in mind, but also, be implemented efficiently in order to achieve desired results.

REFERENCES

Mukherjee, P., External Affairs Minister, Government of India (2007): "India's Look East Policy", address at the Institute of Foreign Affairs and National Security, Republic of Korea on 17/09/2007.

Ahmed, R. and P. Biswas (2004): *Political Economy of Underdevelopment of North-East India*, Akanksha Publishing House, New Delhi.

Baruah, Sanjib (2004): "Between South and South-East Asia: North-East India and the Look East Policy" *CENISEAS Paper No. 4*, OKDISCD, Guwahati,

Kumar, B.B. (2007): "India Looking East", *Dialogue*, July-September, Vol. 9, No. 1.

Das, G. (1995): *The Tribes of Arunachal Pradesh in Transition*, Vikas Publishing House, New Delhi.

Das, S.K. (2001): "Tribal politics in Contemporary India", in Rakhahari Chatterji (ed.), *Politics India: The State Society Interface*, New Delhi, South Asian Publishers.

Das, S.K. (2007): "Conflict and Peace in India's North-East: The Role of Civil Society", *Policy Studies 43*, East-West Center, Washington.

Dong Zhang (2006): "India Looks East: Strategies and Impact", *AUSAID Working Paper*, September 2006, p. 19.

Das, H.N. (2007): "Preparing North-East for Look East Policy", *Dialogue*, July-September, Vol. 9, No. 1.

Hussain, W. (2004): *Interaction on the North East*, Observer Research Foundation, New Delhi, November 18.

Miri, M. (2001): "North-East: A Point of View", *Dialogue*, October-December, Vol. 3, No. 2.

Mukherjee, P. (2007): "Geography as Opportunity", Speech at Seminar on "Look East" Policy, June 16, Shillong.

Press Statement by Pranab Mukherjee, Minister of External Affairs after the Meeting on Look East Policy, 31-10-2007.

Raha, M.K. (1998): "North-East India and Nehru", in M.K. Raha and A.K. Ghosh (eds.), *North-East India: The Human Interface*, Gyan Publishing House, New Delhi.

Sikri, R. (2009): *Challenge and Strategy: Rethinking India's Foreign Policy*, Sage Publication, New Delhi.

Ramesh, J. (2004): *Northeast India in a New Asia*, Inaugural Lecture in CENISEAS Forum, "Towards a New Asia: Transnationalism and North-East India", held in Guwahati, 10th and 11th September, 2004.

Ramesh, J. (2005): "*Northeast India in a New Asia*" Gateway to the East: a symposium on North-East India and the Look East Policy, Seminar, 550, June 2005. http://www.india-seminar.com/2005/550.htm

Khanna, S. (2005): "Economic Opportunities or Continuing Stagnation" Gateway to the East: a symposium on North-East India and the Look East Policy, Seminar, 550, June 2005. http://www.india-seminar.com/2005/550.htm

Gordon, S. (1995): *India's Rise to Power in the Twentieth Century and Beyond*, New York, St. Martin's Press, p. 299.

Sachdeva, G. (2000): *Economy of the North-East: Policy, Present Conditions and Future Possibilities*, Konark Publishers, New Delhi.

Shukla Commission Report on Transforming the Northeast-High Level Commission Report to the Prime Minister, March 7, 1997.

Singh, B.P. (1987): *The Problem of Change: A Study of North-East India*, Oxford University Press, New Delhi.

Datta, S. (2000): "Security of India's North-East: External Linkage", *Strategic Analysis*, Vol. XXIV, No. 8, November.

Verghese, B.G. (2004): *India's North-East Resurgent: Ethnicity, Insurgency, Governance, Development*, Konark Publishers, New Delhi, 1996 (2nd revised).

9

ANALYSING 'SPACE' AND 'REGION FORMATION' IN INDIA'S NORTH-EAST
Interpreting the Look East Policy

Gorky Chakraborty and *Asok Kumar Ray*

Introduction

'Capital' aspires to 'create' and 'annihilate', 'space' simultaneously in order to augment its attempt for dominance and accumulation. While some argue that in order to satisfy capitalism's insatiable urge for cheaper raw materials, newer sources of labour and markets, it *annihilate space by time*,[1] others argue that it is only through the production of fixed and immobile territorial organisations in the form of *space-time compression*[2] that capitals circulation process is accelerated. Without entrapping oneself to anyone of the particular viewpoints, it can certainly be argued that capitals surge for accumulation is multi-scalar in nature whereby there is a dialectic interplay of annihilation and compression of both space and time accordingly.

In this vein, it is observed that the recent phase of globalisation has moved towards *annihilating* the production process from the state-centric territorial traps but in the process has also given rise to regional formations facilitating *compression*. So, space instead of being self-enclosed cartographic unit becomes a liberated despatialised entity, whereby annihilation and compression occur simultaneously. Thus, instead of the complete withering of the nation-states we observe the emergence of region-states for initiating the ways for capitals insatiable urge for dominance and accumulation.

In this regard, scholars may argue about the complimentary and contradictory nature of these formations *vis-à-vis* capitals insatiable urge or may analyse whether the *status quo* of the existing cartographic space of nation-states will be maintained or will it bring about a new phase of deterritorialisation and subsequent reterritorialisation or may even question as to whether despatialisation for enhancing profits remain limited to the economic sphere or will it reactivate the socio-cultural and ethnic fault lines which hitherto remained self-enclosed within the existing territorial limits of the nation-states?

Without attempting to settle these issues, we will try to carry it forward by restricting ourselves to understanding the process of region formation in India's North-East and then attempt to interpret the much hyped Look East Policy and the imperatives associated with it.

Pre-Colonial Frame

The pre-capitalist form of region in North-East was rather a bio-region with clan boundaries, which, thought occupied varying geo-spatial areas, was essentially non-territorial in nature. In the North-East, such clans had multitudinous political formations ranging from republican, authoritarian and convivial systems that in turn corresponded to the state of economic formations. We can find two distinct economic formations in the region — the subsistence economy in the hills and the surplus-yielding economy in the valley areas. The nature of these two economic formations — (i) subsistence and (ii) surplus virtually divided the region in two spatial entities — hills and plains. This followed the simple logic that *smaller the surplus, less elaborate is its public authority and less extensive is its territorial space* and *vice versa*.

There emerged three distinct yet interactive modes of production in the North-East, namely: the Domestic, the Intermediary and the Capitalist. The Domestic mode of production was accompanied by shifting cultivation and forest gathering, with a communitarian ethos and the wet field agricultural economy generating limited surplus. The Intermediary mode of production was based on petty trade and small mercantile base created by surplus agriculture. The foothill areas were the sub-peripheral entry points for trade. The capitalist mode of production superseded such spaces and converted these into the colonial sites of accumulation.

History bears testimony to the fact that early trade in the North-East helped to mediate between the differentiated spaces created by domestic and capitalist modes of production but could not bring about structural changes in the economy. In the pre-capitalist phase trade and mercantile economy did not scale-up; it was based on barter system, limited goods;

lacked monetisation and an aggressive mercantile class. The stagnancy and immutability of the economy, warfare and luxuriant practices of the kings, nobles and their associates did also hinder the larger space creation for capital accumulation.

Colonial Frame

The Treaty of Yandaboo (1826) for the first time initiated the process of re-creation and de-creation of spaces. Later the colonials made series of regulations to re-define colonial space. They also made a distinction between the natural space of the hills of Assam and civilizational space of the British territory through the promulgation of the Inner Line Regulation of 1873. The similar distinction was made through the Scheduled District Act and Assam Frontier Tract Regulation. Things culminated in the visit of Simon Commission and eventual Government of India Act, 1935 under which the tribal areas of the North-East were re-constructed as 'Excluded Areas and Partially Excluded Areas'. Colonial trade and strategic interest led to re-structuring of the tribal constellations in North-East India. As a result of which, the Mizo chiefs were given 'Boundary Paper' (*Ramri Lekha*) that gave the chiefs the British-defined rights over certain territorial spaces and not beyond; the Kuki chiefs were given Settlement Rights and the Assam Chieftainship Act made and unmade the bio-spaces governed by the numerous chiefdoms. These were acts of structured subordination by the British.

The second mode of spatial re-definition was conversion of common property resources through the twin instrument of *res nullius* and *lex loci*. Draining out the incredible resource endowments of the region and accessing to south China's natural wealth were the major targets of the colonials. This converted bio-spaces into British-defined territorial spaces.

The third mode was artificial demarcation of forest areas through the 'Reserved' forest which denied natural right of the forest dependent communities over the commons. The Assam Forest Regulation, 1891 created certain type of 'spatial enclave' with administratively defined forest boundaries that prohibited entry of tribal and forest dependent people. Such 'spatial enclave' was created in different hill areas of the region at different points of times depending upon the exigencies of colonial expansion. The Assam Forest Regulation, 1891 denied acquiring of right of people except by succession or under a grant of contract in written and made or entered into, or on behalf of, the Government of some persons in whom such rights or power to create such right was vested when the proclamation was published, and on such land no new house shall be built or plantation formed, no fresh cleaning for cultivation or for any other purpose of trade or manufacture except as hereinafter provided. Both the *Land Acquisition Act* and the *Forest Regulation Act* defined space to fit in with colonial region formation and thereby changed the hitherto use and ownership patterns.

The fourth mode was Land Revenue administration. The Assam Land Revenue Regulation was promulgated in 1896. In the hills, Hill House Tax was imposed through the Chin Hills Regulation. Whereas most part of Assam came under the Ryotwari system, some areas were brought under the Permanent and Temporary Settlements. The Regulation was brought into force in Cachar, Goalpara, Kamrup, Darrang, Nowgong, Sibsagar and Lakhimpur and with certain exceptions in North Cachar Hills, Garo Hills District, Khasi and Jaintia Hills, Naga Hills and Lushai Hills districts. The Regulation was brought into force in the tract transferred from the Mokokchung sub-division of the Naga Hills district to the Sibsagar district. There were, however, subsequent modifications in the Regulation. Rights over land were converted from natural right to acquired right. In Tripura the Chakla Rosanabad areas were brought under the Zamindari system and the King of Tripura, the tributary of the East India Company, was accorded Zamindari rights in Chakla Rosanabad. The state of Manipur followed the Assam Land Revenue Regulation and Ryotwari system was thereby followed there.

The fifth mode was road and infrastructure building that also de-constructed and re-constructed space and in the process of which many a people and villages went into oblivion only to be recreated in historical research.

Revenue interest of the colonials squeezed the community space through individualisation of rights that prolonged in the post-colonial era too. There were great roles of administration, institutional power, warfare and forcible annexation in re-definition of space. However, it is to be understood that the colonial de-construction and re-construction of space was not a one stroke affair rather it was a process that depended on colonial requirements and the associated incremental market opportunities.

Similarly, in 1913-14, the British administrator, Sir Henry McMahon, drew up the 550 mile long McMahon Line as the border between British India and Tibet as Britain sought to advance its line of control and establish a buffer zone around its colony in South Asia. In the same light, in 1914 British India brought some tribes of Assam under North-East Frontier Tracts comprising two sections: the Central and Eastern Section (comprising the erstwhile Dibrugarh Frontier Tract, created in 1882, and some more areas in south) and the Western Section. The Central and Eastern Section was subsequently renamed as Sadiya Frontier Tract, while the Western Section was renamed as Balipara Frontier Tract. By the North-Eastern Frontier Tracts (Internal Administration) Regulation, 1943, Tirap Frontier Tract was created by amalgamating certain areas of Sadiya and Lakhimpur Frontier Tracts. In 1946, Balipara Frontier Tract was further divided into two administrative units: Sela Sub-Agency and Subansiri Area. A combined outcome of these was de-creation of the bio-spaces and incorporation of these spaces into the colonial space.

Liberal Frame

The post-colonial Indian state viewed North-East through security and threat prism due to its long international border. The mega project of spatial re-structuring was confronted by countervailing ethnic spaces some of which symbolised 'rebel consciousnesses'. This created (i) hiatus between the two spatial realities — nation and ethnic; and (ii) a dyadic face-off between the dominant integrationist view of the Indian state and the ethno-spatial view of the emerging regional elites. The region was viewed as a cartographic space of the grand polity of India whereas the contesting bio-regional and ethno-cultural spaces countervailed such view. Partition of the country in 1947 and eventual overnight refugee formation gave a sudden shock to the people whose bio-spaces were divided by international boundaries. Whereas as kinship units their affinities died hard across the borders, partition divided them spatially. Things took more serious turn when the Post-1971 Bangladeshi refugees sought for space and cognition in certain parts of the North-East.

Post-1947, North-East Frontier Tract became a part of Assam state. In 1948, Sadiya Frontier Tract was bifurcated into two districts: Abor Hills district and Mishmi Hills district. In 1950, the plain areas of these Tracts (Balipara Frontier Tract, Tirap Frontier Tract, Abor Hills district and Mishmi Hills District) were transferred to the Assam state government and the rest became one of the Tribal Areas within Assam (under Part-B of the table appended to paragraph 20 of the sixth schedule of the Constitution of India). In 1951, Balipara Frontier Tract, Tirap Frontier Tract, Abor Hills district, Mishmi Hills district and the Naga tribal areas were together renamed as the North-East Frontier Agency (NEFA) in 1954. It was divided into six frontier divisions: Kameng (formerly Sela Sub-Agency), Subansiri (formerly Subansiri area), Tirap (formerly Tirap Frontier Tract), Siang (formerly Abor Hills district), Lohit (formerly

Mishmi Hills district), and Tuensang. On 1st December, 1957, Tuensang was separated and attached to the newly formed Naga Hills District to form Naga Hills — Tuensang Area. The administration of NEFA was placed under the Ministry of External Affairs with the Governor of Assam acting as agent to the President of India. In 1965 the administration of the agency was transferred to the Ministry of Home Affairs. Consequently, in 1965, the five frontier divisions (Kameng, Subansiri, Siang, Lohit, and Tirap) became five Districts. A Deputy Commissioner became the administrative head of these districts in place of a Political Officer. In 1967, an Agency Council was constituted for better administration. Till 1972, it was constitutionally a part of Assam and was directly administered by the President of India through the Governor of Assam acted as its Agent. In 1972, the North-East Frontier Agency was promoted as Union Territory and was placed under the charge of a Chief Commissioner. It got statehood in 1987. The other Constitutional spaces that were created through grants of statehood; Autonomous District Councils; Autonomous State; Autonomous Territory and so on.

In the economic front, different programmes and schemes for development extended the space associated with Intermediary mode of production as more and more community space (which may be referred as 'lived space') got entangled in this exercise of nation building. These came under the purview of market forces and exchange relationship. But this transformation of space from a 'lived' to 'used' entity generated tension and conflict, as those associated with this transformation did not belong to the *in situ* community. This could be exemplified by the presence of Bangladeshi/Nepali farmers in different parts of the North-East region.

On the other, the emerging elites of North-East India had plethora of imaginations about the spatial status of their own. The ethno-spatial movements of the Naga, Khasi, Mizo, Bodo and the Kuki groups are classical examples. These can be broadly classified under the integrationist, isolationists, pan-ethnic, and the trans-territorial categories. Now, that there was a great transformation from the pre-capitalist bio-space, territorial politics became volatised in the region. The accidental proximity of the two regional spaces — India and North-East India exposed the paradox of discordance.

Post-Liberal Frame

The 'Look East' policy viewed North-East as a strategic point through which India could really look East farther towards South-East Asia and sought closer economic and security ties with maritime South-East Asia. This policy as initiated in the context of liberalisation. Re-creation of region was necessary for pioneering trade and market niches through the north-eastern region towards the South-East Asia. Globalisation thus 'unbounded' the region and simultaneously 'narrowed' down its vision to market expansion.

On the other hand, there emerged continuous struggle of various ethnic groups for re-drawing the territorial boundaries according to the imagined spatial blueprints. This created a deadlock. While the Indian state liberated its economic space it was not adequately responsive to the latter. Market economy demanded a highly centralised state as a support institution that discarded any imagined blue-prints. The question of region-formation thus got entrapped in a paradox: de-territorialisation and a centralised state. The dissenting views of subaltern region formations added on to this paradox and added further criticality to the spatial spread of capital.

At the meso level, region formation was driven by the logic of economic rationality whereby region was conceived as natural economic zones engulfing the 'space' of more than one nation state. Thus, we found emergence of different regional groupings, apart from SAARC and ASEAN (India became full dialogue partner of SAARC in 1997), in the market economy frame. These include BISTEC (later re-constituted as BIMSTEC). Nepal and Bhutan also joined this block and it was re-named as 'Bay of Bengal Initiative' for a multi-sectoral, technical and economic cooperation in 2004. The Ganga-Mekong Cooperation (GMC) included India, Myanmar, Thailand, Laos and Vietnam.

The other sub-regional groupings included the South Asian Growth Quadrangle (SAGQ) comprising Bangladesh, seven north-eastern states, West Bengal, Nepal and Bhutan; South Asian Business Forum under South Asia Sub-regional Economic Cooperation; and the Kunming Initiative for integrating the resource rich areas of Yunnan province of China, northern Myanmar, North-East India, Bangladesh, Nepal and Bhutan into Asian communication network. Space reconfiguration under market economy in reality thus went well beyond the South to the South-East Asia and North-East India came to implicate in both these regional spaces.

Concluding Remarks

Space, instead of being self-enclosed cartographic unit becomes a liberated despatialised entity under globalisation that *annihilates space by time* or deterritorialisation, but simultaneously there is also *space-time compression* which is leading to newer region formation or reterritorialisation. In case of trade, this phenomenon is amply reflected, where there has been certainly more openings in terms of global trade under WTO regime yet it is also simultaneously evident that reconfiguration of regions for trade are happening within the WTO regime itself. The regional dominos, therefore, becomes the tool through which the big global players facilitate their dominance and accumulation in the global market. It is in this context that the emergence of region-states without the withering of the nation states becomes important. If we consider the Look East Policy from the above view point, certain criticalities emerge, whose resolution seems pertinent for the Policy to attain its desired objectives.

The Look East Policy primarily aimed at prioritising market interest through trade whereby the state policies were geared towards global financial players for attracting Foreign Direct Investments, so that the resource endowed North-East India spearheads economic growth and leads to the forward market integration with the immediate South-East Asian region, an opportunity that was suddenly lost during the post-colonial era. To attain this desired objective, the cultural affinities of the people in the North-East and its immediate neighbours were sought to be highlighted, which it was believed would augment the economic imperative of trade promotion. But in reality since the cultural affinity of the people in the region and their proximate neighbours became trade policy assets, it remained entrapped within the precincts of state rather than embedded within the society and therefore, failed to deliver the expected dividends.

The desired forward market integration of the region with South-East Asia as envisaged in the Policy was sought to be implemented through connectivity and infrastructure development but existential reality suggests that this is inseparably linked with security environment of the region at large. So rather than trade, trade-related securitisation is often found to occupy the centre stage at all the regional forums associated with the region.

The complementarity assumption between regional trade and global trade needs to be demystified and analysed properly. It is observed that both in the Indo-China and Indo-Myanmar borders brisk business is done not with *in situ* produced industrial goods from the North-Eastern region, but from those produced either in mainland India and/or outside India. Thus although, it is a truism that the region is richly endowed with natural resources and has huge potential yet North-East has yet to make a mark in the regional trade other than acting as a conduit in the entire process.

Lack of common market denies the producers in the region with the benefits of minimising the cost of production and shifting resources to more efficient products. Similarly, inter-state movement of natural person is highly problematic considering the problem of influx associated with the region. Moreover, the uneven levels of development, limited taxation power of the states and lack of connectivity in the region pose threats towards proper economic development and participation in regional trade.

Domestic reforms in laws, regulations and institutions got limited to liberalisation of quantitative restrictions and high subsidisation policies of the states. This resulted in restriction of North-East and its products to international competition, on one hand and on the other did not expand regional integration which hampered the growth of common market at both the inter-state and intra-state levels. So, trade creation as thought about in the Look East Policy did not materialise.

On the contrary, this brought about opportunities for the global market players to take full advantage of liberalisation in quantitative restrictions and policy subsidies given by the states in the region. While the regional trade initiatives could not go beyond the mechanisms of Preferential Trade Agreements and/or Free Trade Agreements under the present arrangements, there also due to the lack of *in situ* produced industrial goods from the region, North-East remains a mere *pathway* for trade with the South-East Asian region. Under such a scenario, securing this *pathway* thereby would be the sole priority of the Indian state, which obviously would lead to further resecuritisation of the region of course, associated with the countervailing backlash from the region.

NOTES

1. 'Annihilation of space by time' is an expression used by Marx to illustrate capitals globalising dynamics whereby the world market is referred essentially as a historical product and a geographical expression.
2. 'Space-time compression' is an expression used by Harvey for arguing that it is only through fixed and immobile configurations of territorial organisations that capital's circulation process is accelerated temporally and expanded spatially.

REFERENCES

Brenner, Neil (1999): "Beyond State-Centrism? Space, Territoriality and Geographical Scale in Globalization Studies", *Theory and Society*, Vol. 28.

Chakraborty, Gorky and Ray, Asok (2009): "Contextualizing India's North-East *vis-à-vis* South Asia: The Realities and Imaginaries", Paper presented at International Conference, *Region Formation in Contemporary South Asia*, 25-27, November, University of Delhi.

Harvey, David (1980): "The Condition of Post-Modernity" as cited in Soja Edward, "The Socio-Spatial Dialectic", in *Annals of the Association of American Geographers*, Vol. 70.

Marx, Karl (1973): *Grundrisse: Foundations of the Critique of the Political Economy,* New York: Penguin.

Roy, Kumar Asok (2010): *Whither North East?* (New Delhi: Om Publications).

10

INDIA'S LOOK EAST POLICY AND STILWELL ROAD
An Economic Analysis in Context of North-Eastern Region of India

Tarun Dutta

Introduction

North-East India is strategically located and being projected as India's gateway of commerce to the East and South-East Asia. Even historically, it was always a part of large, dynamic Brahmaputra-Yangtze-Mekong economic region. In today's liberalised Global Era, the geographical location of North-East, particularly Assam, offers a position at strength that can help the region to regain its past glory by integrating more closely with the national economy and opening up to the dynamic economies of the Eastern and Southern Asia and beyond. South-East Asia is a continuously growing formidable region having the best potential of emerging markets with 220 million households. Due to the high rate of growth, the ASEAN country markets are expanding and there is a massive rise in consumer demand. North-East thus has the potential to charge as the strategic base for foreign and domestic investors to tap the vast potential of contiguous market of Myanmar, China including Hong Kong, Malaysia, Thailand, Philippines, Laos, Cambodia, Indonesia and other East and South-East Asian countries, which constitute nearly half of the world population. Such changes certainly would transform Assam as well as the entire North-East into one of the fastest growing economic regions of the world. In such an environment the forces behind insurgency in the North-East bound to be inoperative. "In growing economies especially, a wide range of solutions may be available for constructive bargainers."[1] There are many vistas open for the economic prospects of North-East. If the Stilwell Road would open, it would definitely bring trade, travel and tourism benefits to both sides.

Trade

Economically prospects of North-East India are very vast. Its natural resources show the possibility of the future prospects. This region is very resourceful and proper utilisation of these resources could develop the whole region along with China and Myanmar. These three nations indicate economically underdeveloped or developing through it has rich natural and human resource. According to HDI of 2002, prepared by UNDP, China with 0.726 HDI ranks 96 out of the total 173 countries in 2000; India with 0.577 HDI ranks 125 and Myanmar with 0.552 HDI ranks 127 in the same year.[2] The per capital income of these three countries is extremely low in comparison to USA. Export share slowly increasing in China — 4.72 per cent, India — 0.70 per cent and Myanmar export share was slightly insignificant in the year 2001.

Among this export share India exported its commodities to China in the year 2001-02 as shown in Table 10.1.

Table 10.1: India Exported Commodities to China in the Year 2001-02

Sl.No.	*Item*	*Value (millions)*	*Value (in % of total)*
1.	Iron ore	197.58	21.34
2.	Plastic and Linoleum products	141.55	15.28
3.	Other ores and minerals	107.91	11.65
4.	Marine Product	84.88	9.16
5.	Drug, pharmaceuticals and fine chemicals	78.83	8.52
6.	Cotton yarn fabric	74.20	8.07
7.	Inorganic/Organic/Agro chemical	47.95	5.17
8.	Processed minerals	17.90	1.93
9.	Residence chemical and allies products	16.38	1.77
10.	Electronic goods	15.91	1.71
11.	Others	142.63	15.40
	All commodities	925.74	100.00

Source: CMIE, Foreign Trade and Balance of Payment, October 2002.

Except China, India exported its commodities to other major destinations also which are shown in Table 10.2.

Table 10.2: India Export Commodities to Other Major Destinations Except China

Sl.No.	Country	Percentage
1.	Japan	3
2.	UAE	6
3.	Italy	4
4.	USA	19
5.	Hong Kong	5
6.	Germany	4
7.	Belgium	3
8.	UK	5
9.	Others	51

Source: CMIE, Foreign Trade and Balance of Payment, October 2002.

India is not a self-sufficient country. She also imports commodities from various nations which as follows:

Table 10.3: India's Import Commodities from Various Nations

Sl.No.	Country	Percentage
1.	Japan	4
2.	Germany	4
3.	China	4
4.	Belgium	5
5.	USA	6
6.	UK	5
7.	Switzerland	6
8.	South Africa	3
9.	Others	63

Sources: CMIE, Foreign Trade and Balance of Payment, October 2002.

Table 10.4 shows that India imported some commodities from China and it covers 4 per cent of total import. The commodities of India's import from China are as follows in the year of 2001-02.

Table 10.4: India's Import from China

Sl.No.	Items	Value	Percentage of Total Value
1.	Electronic Goods	380.74	18.68
2.	Coal, coke and Briquettes	262.84	12.89
3.	Organic chemicals	236.87	11.62
4.	Raw silk	122.07	5.99
5.	Medicinal and pharmaceutics	103.33	5.07
6.	Silver	94.41	4.73
7.	Non-Electrical Machinery	70.66	3.46
8.	Electrical Machinery	59.73	2.93
9.	Inorganic chemicals	38.53	2.87
10.	Non-Ferrous metals	54.47	2.67
11.	Professional/optical goods	54.33	2.66
12.	Others	540.67	26.53
	All commodities	2,038.65	100.00

Source: CMIE, Foreign Trade and Balance of Payment, October 2002.

From above tables, we see that India's import from China increased as compared to its export. If we make a comparison with imports-exports of them we will able to get the difference of both nations (Fig. 10.1).

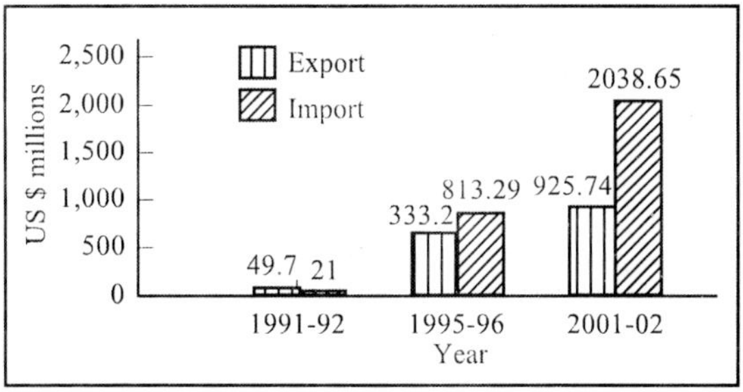

Figure 10.1: Growth of India's Trade with China (1991-92 to 2001-02).

The Stilwell Road, if it transformed as a Trans-Asian Express Highway and along with it if a Trans-Asian Railway line, then in near future the entire nation, could have direct access by both road and railway not only to Myanmar and South Chinas trading centres, but also to entire East and South-East Asia.

From the border point of Arunachal Pradesh exports of India could reach by the Stilwell Road to Kunming in South China 1,079 miles, within two days, Yangon in Myanmar within two and half days, Bangkok in four days and Singapore in five/six days. This land route of trade would be shorter and cheaper in comparison to existing maritime routes. India's trade may take a diametrically opposite direction from the West to the East and that too with much more gains, since the buyers and sellers of these markets of the East are culturally more akin to the buyers and sellers of North-East India.

With these developments, the North-East with its locational advantage could emerge as a business transit hub for both the SAARC and ASEAN groups of nations. In that case in certain strategic places of the North-East, large warehouses with business offices to exporters and importers from both sides would be built up. Such places would emerge a commercial hub of the region busted by business executives, hostels, clubs departmental stores, etc.

In North-East, there are some thrust areas which can emerge as producers of export items to the East.

Flora and Fauna

North-East India is famous for its flora and fauna. Out of the 925 varieties of orchids available in India, as many as over 600 can be grown in the region due to the favourable climatic conditions. In fact, approximately 200 verities are unique to this region and 60 per cent of these are ornamental in nature with high demand in the international market. It also ideally situated to produce spices, fruit and vegetables, flowers and herbs. Therefore, the North-East India can emerge as an exporter of orchids, flowers, apple, orange, pineapples, spices, herbs, etc. Moreover, the forests of North-East after a vast array of aromatic plants which can be used in the aromatic industry for the manufacturing of perfumes, incenses, etc. In fact, there is an increasing international trend towards natural perfumes and room freshner, shifting the focus from chemical ones. With proper planning, there exists scope for establishing aromatic industry in the region.

Minerals

The trijunction of India, Myanmar and China, Arunachal Pradesh and Assam lies over the Eastern Himalaya, Mismi Hills and Naga-Patkai belt of Mountains comprising geological formations of different ages and it bears potentiality for occurrence of economic mineral deposits. Huge reserves of coal are present in Dilli-Jaipore and Margherita coal belt of Assam. Most remarkable fact is that the Stilwell Road originates from this place and along with Arunachal's mineral belt the road has a great potentiality to become an international corridor. The Road expected to play a key role for export and import of economic minerals among East Asian countries.

The region is a deposit house of mineral resources. After exploration in 1960, Arunachal focuses out its resources. According to GSI investigation the minerals of the region are as follows:

Table 10.5: Minerals Production in Arunachal Pradesh

(*in thousand tonnes*)

Item	*1992-93*	*1993-94*	*1994-95*	*1995-96*
Petroleum (encode)	59	49	30	25
Limestone	1	2	1	3

The eastern part of Arunachal is also rich in mineral resources. So far investigated minerals are as follows which bear the potentially of a great industry. Abrasive minerals garnet and quartz are two minerals that occur as grains in sufficient quantities in river sand. Garnet is found in Khetabari formation while quartz occur in abundance in sedimentary rocks, granite geris can be separated easily and used for making sand paper in cottage industry. Brass-metals, copper, nickel, cobalt and zinc are found in different parts of Arunachal Pradesh. Poly-metallic Sulphide is also available in this region.

Sulphide minerals in Lohit, Limestone in confluence of Tidding and Tellu rivers, Marbals in Tezu river, Dona river, Lohit valley, Dibong valley, Mica in Dibong valley, Pyrite and Pyrrhotite in west Orsam village of Lohit valley, platinum in the sand of the Noa-Dihing river, Graphite in Lalpani, Malybdenite in near Apruni village in Dibong valley, coal, petroleum, etc. some important deposit of minerals in this region. Among these minerals coal and petroleum are two most important with respect to the Stilwell Road. In the time of Second World War, along the Road a pipe line also followed up to Kunming for fuel supply.

The economic mineral resources of this region have not been properly assessed. Out of the minerals discovered so far, the limestone and marble can be used for manufacturing of cement and decorative slabs, respectively. Huge deposits of graphite will find its importance in different industries. Extensive intrusive of Mishmi massif may prove to be store house of many metallic minerals in future. The ophiolite, serpentinites and other ultra-basic convergent boundary rocks bear prospect for occurrence of many sermonic minerals in the Lohit complex of Mishmi Hills, which is believed to be northern continuation of the Precambrian rocks of Mogok belt of Myanmar which is very rich in precious gemstones. One may hope for finding the same in Arunachal Pradesh also (Tables 10.6 and 10.7). The huge reserves of coal in Assam and Arunachal Pradesh, very close to the Stilwell Road are to be given due importance. There is a great possibility of export of the coal from India to adjacent countries through this important Road in future.

Table 10.6: Mineral Deposits for Quick Exploration

Sl.No.	*Deposit*	*District/State*	*Industry Proposed*	*Capacity*
(1)	*(2)*	*(3)*	*(4)*	*(5)*
1.	Granite Bura Mayangh	Morigaon (Assam)	Dimensional Stone	4,000 sq.m. polished slab
2.	China clay Upper Deopani	Karbi-Anglong (Assam)	Ceramic industry at Bokajan Insulators and white wares at Deopani	300 TPD for insulators and white wares

(Contd.)

Table 10.6 (*Contd.*)

(1)	*(2)*	*(3)*	*(4)*	*(5)*
3.	Coal Margherita/Bora Golai	Dibrugarh (Assam)	Thermal Power Station	1 m.t. annually
4.	Limestone New Umrangshu	NC Hills (Assam)	Cement plant at Lanka	1 m.t. annually
5.	Glass Sand Jiyajuri/Borhola	Nagaon (Assam)	Glass Industry	
6.	Cement plant based on Phungvor limestone	Ukhrul (Manipur)	Cement	200 TPD
7.	Limestone Maumluh-Maswsmai Ichamati/Shella	East Khasi Hills (Meghalaya)	Export oriented cement plant	3 lakh TPY
8.	Limestone Litang valley	Jaintia Hills (Meghalaya)	Cement plant Sutnga	3 lakh TPY
9.	Limestone Lumshong	Jaintia Hills (Meghalaya)	Paper grade lime plant	200 TPD
10.	Kaoline Muleih	Jaintia Hills (Meghalaya)	Ceramic plant	
11.	Limestone Ichamati/Shella	East Khasi Hills (Meghalaya)	Calcium/Carbide plant	45 TPD

Table 10.7: Known Mineral Resources of North-Eastern Region (Exploration Status)

State	*Name of Mineral*	*Locality*	*District*	*Reserves*	*Remarks*
(1)	*(2)*	*(3)*	*(4)*	*(5)*	*(6)*
Arunachal Pradesh	Coal	Chanhlang-Namchik Namphuk	Changlang	93.0 mt	for cooking blend, synthetic petroleum, power generation
	Limestone	Tidding	Lohit	91.00 mt	Suitable for cement and lime burning
		Dali	Siang	225.0 mt	Suitable for cement and lime burning
		Hunli	Lohit	—	Suitable for cement and lime burning
	Dolomite	Rupa	Kameng	185.00 mt	SMS and Refractory
		Menga	Kameng	3.75 mt	SMS and Refractory
		Dedza	Kameng	58.00 mt	SMS and Refractory
	Graphite	Taliha Lalpani-La-Ramdak	Lohit-Sibansiri-Siang	84.673 mt	
	Quartzite	Kalaktang	Kameng	3.13 mt	Ferrosilicon grade

(*Contd.*)

Table 10.7 (*Contd.*)

(1)	(2)	(3)	(4)	(5)	(6)
Assam	Coal	Makum	Dibrugarh	235.00 mt	High sulphur, low ash, high caking index and calorific value
		Koliajan	Karbi-Anglong		High moisture, high ash and high sulphur
		Dilli-Jeypore	Dibrugarh	55.36 mt	Low ash, high sulphur coal
	Limestone	Garampani	NC Hills	104.00 mt	Cement grade blendable, high R_2O_3 limestone
		Koilajan	Karbi-Anglong	124.00 mt	Cement/Lime burning
		Sylvetta-Meyongdisa	Karbi-Anglong	2.00 mt	Ferro-Portland cement
		Umrangshu	NC Hills	35.00 mt	Cement grade, High R_2O_3 limestone
	Fireclay	Koilajan and Sylvetta	Karbi-Anglong	0.71 mt	For pottery and fire bricks
		Namdang-Lido	Dibrugarh	0.05 mt	Fire bricks
	Kaolin	Sylvetta	Karbi-Anglong	0.06 mt	Ceremic and refractory purposes
	Clays	Upper Deopani	Karbi-Anglong	0.61 mt	Gr. I Type
	Fuller's Earth	Subankhata	Nalbari	0.24 mt	Petroleum refining and fertilizer mfg.
	Iron Ore (BMQ)	Chandardinga	Goalpara	30.00 mt	Suitable for sponge iron
	Dimension stone		Karbi-Anglong, Goalpara, Kamrup, Nagaon	2700 m cubic metre (540 mcm)	Polished blocks and Dimension stone industries
	Sillimanite	Chipilangso	Karbi-Anglong	50.00 mt	Mostly of more than 10% sillimanite concentration-Refractory
Manipur	Limestone	Ukhrul	Ukhrul	4.60 mt	Cement grade mostly being utilised by mini cement plants 50 TPD of Department of Industries, Manipur
		Phungyer	Ukhrul	3.20 mt	
		Hundung	Ukhrul	1.80 mt	
	Clays	Kongvan	Churachandpur	2.52 mt	

Sources: The Report of the Task Force for the North-Eastern States, 1996, Government of India.

Tourism

The North-East India is well known for its bio-diversities and heritage sites too. In Arunachal Pradesh, Tawang, Namdapha, Tezu, Parshuramkunda, etc. are very attractive places for tourist. In Assam Majuli, Kaziranga, Manas, Pabitara, etc. can be developed further as tourist spots. If modern transport and communication systems along with the requisite infrastructural facilities between the ASEAN countries and India are developed, then tourists visiting the ASEAN countries are likely to extend their tour programmes to the North-East India, for visiting its exotic bio-diversity and heritage sites. In 1996, an internationally reputed consultancy firm, Coopers and Lyband submitted a report to the Government of Assam, which states that if the vast tourism potentials of the North-East India are fully tapped and developed, within 20 years the region will receive more tourists than Singapore or Bangkok. Because almost all the Western and Japanese tourists visiting South-East Asian region would fly or drive a few hundred kilometres more to enjoy the scenic and cultural beauties of the North-Eastern region.

The adjacent areas of the Stilwell Road provide great scope for development of tourism. The Pangsau pass located at an altitude of 1,242 metres and short drive about 3 km from this point, a panoramic view of Hukoong valley can be observed where mystic 'Lake of no Return' is located. In this lake large number of airplanes of Allied forces had crashed during the Second World War and many soldiers also vanished from the lake when they gone for bath or swimming. That is why the American called it the 'Lake of No Return'. Another tourist place of the area is the Cemetery of War, where thousands of unknown soldiers rest for ever. The Dibru-Saikhowa National Park is also an attractive tourist spot in Assam and Arunachal Pradesh.

The areas, through which passes the historic Stilwell Road is a virgin area and here lies a great potentialities of growth of tourist industries. The unpopulated ever green forest and natural beauty as well as valuable resources are available in this area. These have the potentialities of multi-dimensional tourism prospect like sight-seeing tourism, wildlife tourism, advantage tourism, eco-tourism, river-cruise tourism, heritage tourism, cultural tourism, business tourism, tea tourism, sports tourism, festival tourism, educational tourism, etc. (Table 10.8).

Though the area has potentialities to develop the tourism industry, most of the areas yet to be explored. If materialised properly, each and

Table 10.8: Tourist Spots and Functions of North-East India

Sl.No.	*Tourism*	*Places*	*Functions*
1.	Site-seeing tourism	All over North-East	Site visiting by road/ waterway/air
2.	Wildlife tourism	Namdapha, Kaziranga, Manash, Pabitara, Dibru-Saikhowa	Visiting and observing the sites
3.	Adventure tourism	Patkai hill, River Brahmaputra, Dihing, Dibru, Lake of no Return	Tracking, racing, rafting, gliding, rock climbing, para-sailing
4.	Eco-tourism	Stilwell Road and its adjoining areas	—
5.	River-cruise tourism	Brahmaputra and other Rivers	Fishing, rafting, boating, para-sailing, river cruising, etc.
6.	Heritage tourism	Historical place of Assam like Sibsagar, Majuli, Arunachal Pradesh, etc.	By visiting the places
7.	Cultural tourism	Culturally rich zone of NE at India	By attending of ethnic groups' cultural ceremonies
8.	Business tourism	NE and its adjoining areas	—
9.	Tea tourism	Tea gardens of NE	Ceremonies of Tea-tribes, visiting bangalows, tea garden, etc.
10.	Sports tourism	Rivers and land of NE	Swimming, golf, racing, etc.
11.	Festival tourism	North-Eastern zone	Celebration of different festivals organised by various ethnic groups
12.	Educational tourism	Whole NE	According to their interests
13.	Pilgrimage	Holy and religious places of NE	By visiting the places

every area will be able to attract both the domestic and foreign tourists from all corners of the world. it is not that tourist will go back to their homes after visiting these places near Stilwell Road, rather, Stilwell Road will act, if reopened, as an arrow-mark for the tourists to visit other tourist spots of India. Again Stilwell Road would not link India with Myanmar and China only, but will be a road link to other South-East Asian nations like Thailand, Malaysia, Philippines, etc. Realisation on these potentialities and prospects will be possible only when there exists a suitable and planned tourism policy. The policy should certainly will have the strategies to overcome the infrastructural problems, and administrative barriers like the 'Restricted Area Permit' system, etc. Again, the reopening of Stilwell Road is alone not enough for tourism development without developing the other aspects, especially the border trade. So, both will be complementary and the tourism policy should be supplemented by another pragmatic cross-border trade policy. But for this road and airways between the South-East Asian region and India have to be developed.

Tea Industry

No more explanation is required about tea industry of Assam. Assam alone produces about 50 per cent of country's tea and this needs some new international markets. Assam tea exported to Thailand, Canada, Germany and for this some special treaty already been signed. Thus, tea industry of Assam can find new outlet for exploring its products to the South-East Asian countries, if Stilwell Road is developed.

Conclusion

In conclusion it can be said that the making of Stilwell Road is an important aspect of the economic, cartographic and strategic history of frontier. The Road had an importance in military history itself, for which the road was built. Besides, the road has a prosperous past and potential future. If the potentialities are properly utilised the region must be a developed one in the history of mankind. Cooper and Lyband, one internationally recognised firm said that North-East will become a developed region than Singapore within twenty years if its tourism prospects are fully utilised. For the development of the region, the local entrepreneurs must hold the key instead of outsiders. Otherwise the road will be a transit path and the areas will be a transit point without any benefits. If the key goes to the foreigners and the local people will not be aware then the area will be dumping by outsider communities and the region suffers most. To establish some beneficial projects local youth should come forward and start to set their dreams to reality by establishing firms like food processing, horticulture, floriculture, tourism, craft industry, etc. which are continuing in the neighbouring countries like China. Otherwise the making of Stilwell Road will be a history, instead of reopening of the road and implementing of Look East Policy. So to honour the great work of Joseph Warren Stilwell, which was considered as strategic and military importance, should be converted to economic interest, which will boost the region to a developed one. According to J.L. Nehru, "*Assam has the look of great reserve of strength and potential power. . . . I have no doubt that great highways by road, air and rail will go across her connecting China with India, and ultimately connecting East Asia with Europe, Assam will then no longer be an isolated far away province by an important link between the East and West.*"

Recently Government of India has attracted top priority in opening all traditional trade routes between the North-Eastern states of India and the neighbouring countries to encourage trade and commerce leading to economic development of the region. Recent diplomatic developments hinted at the major policy shift and expressed that "The North-Eastern states have to have an access eastward. Opening up of the natural outlet for the north-east is a challenge and have to be achieved. The natural movement of goods, people and services from North-East is not through Kolkata.

NOTES

1. B.G. Powell, *Contemporary Democracies: Participant, Stability and Violence*, p. 43.
2. H. Goswami and J.K. Gogoi, "Economic Prospects of Stilwell Road: An Analysis", in *Reopening of Stilwell Road: Prospects and Problems*, (ed.) D. Nath, p. 110.

REFERENCES

Antrobus, T.R. (1929): *The History of Assam Tea Company*, DHAS, Guwahati.

Aung, Maung Htin (1967): *A History of Burma*, New Delhi.

Bagchi, P.C. (1950): *India and China: A Thousand Years of Cultural Relations*, Bombay.

Barbara, W. Truchman (1971): *Stilwell and the American Experience in China, 1911-45*, Macmillan, New York.

Bhagawati, A.K.; Bora, A.K. and Kar, B.K. (2001): *Geography of Assam*, New Delhi.

Caddy, J.F. (1976): *South-East Asia—Its Historical Development*, McGraw-Hill Publisher, New Delhi.

Das, G. and Purakayastha, R.K. (2000): *Border Trade: North-East India and Neighbouring Countries*, Akanksha Publishing House, New Delhi.

Deka, P. (2007): *The Great Indian Corridor in the East*, Mittal Publication, New Delhi.

Dutta, S. (ed.) (2002): *Cross-Border Trade of North-East India*, Hope India Publication, New Delhi.

Elwin, Verrier, (ed.) (1962): *India's North-East Frontier in the Nineteenth Century*, London.

Gogoi, P. and D. Gogoi (2006): *Patkai, Stilwell Aru Lack of No Return*, Banalata, Dibrugarh.

Gogoi, J. Nath (2002): *Agrarian System of Medieval Assam*, Delhi.

Hunter, W.W. (1998). *A Statistical Account of Assam*, Vol. I, Spectrum Publishing, Guwahati: Delhi.

Mukharjee, B.N. (1992). *External Trade of Early North-East India*, Har-Ananda Publication, New Delhi.

Mukharjee, B.N. (1992). *Trade and Trade Route in North-Eastern India*, H.P. Publication, New Delhi.

M'cosh, John (1861). *Various Lines of Overland Communication between India and China*, Proceeding of Royal Geographic Society, London.

Nath, D. (ed.) (2004). *Reopening of the Stilwell Road: Prospects and Problems*, Delhi, MAKAIAS.

Ray, H.P. (2003). *Trade and Trade Routes between India and China*, Kolkata.

Reid, R. (1997). *History of the Frontier Areas Bordering on Assam from 1883 to 1941*, Spectrum, Guwahati.

Periodicals

Frontline, October 21-November 3, 2006.

National Geographic Magazine, November 2003.

Prantik (Ass), December 16, 1997, August 1, 2006.

Gariyasi (Ass), January, 2006-November, 2007.

Proceedings, NEIHA, Souvenir.

Dehing Patkai Festival, 2002, 2003.

Souvenir, *17th Shapawng Yawng Manau Poi Festival*, 2001.

Primary Sources

Assam State Archive Resources, Guwahati.

11

LOOK EAST POLICY AND NORTH-EAST INDIA
The Growing Prospects

Ajay Kumar Mishra

Introduction

The North-Eastern part of India possesses a distinct regional character because of its distinct geopolitical location, diverse physiographic framework with more ethnic diversity, economic backwardness with disparity in levels of development. Moreover, the region is flanked by four foreign countries — China, Myanmar, Bangladesh and Bhutan. The terrain conditions of North-East India also make it an isolated region. The Himalayas on the North and the Patkai-Barail range on the North-East, the Meghalayas and Karbi Plateau in the West and Central region, the Nagaland, Manipur, Mizoram and Tripura Hills, with dense monsoon forests, have great bearing in the development of separatist tendency amongst the people.

Through the treaty of Yandaboo in 1826, the British administration took up the reins of development of this region and started exploiting the national resources and accordingly formulated strategies to achieve its ends. The strategies which were adopted by the British here were different from that of the plains. As a result, it gave rise to distinct political formations in the two regions. On the other hand, modernisation processes led to the emergence of an elite group first in the plains, which realised the exploitative nature of the colonial administration and raised its voice against it. Moreover, the disparity that the region gained due to the development process widened the gulf between the developing plains and underdeveloped hills.

Against this background of inherited socio-economic inequities, in the post-independence scenario, the Indian nation-state building processes have been facing serious problems of conflict, such as: the sub-national movements, boundary disputes, demands for regional autonomy, etc. But most of these conflicts have their roots in the historic past, i.e. from the pre-colonial to the colonial period.

Strategic Importance of North-East

India's North-East comprises seven states: Assam, Arunachal Pradesh, Manipur, Meghalaya, Mizoram, Nagaland, Tripura. Later on Sikkim is also included in the North-Eastern Council. The region is characterised by a pronounced ethnic, culture and linguistic diversity. In addition to the non-tribal populations, the region has more than 160 Scheduled Tribes.

North-Eastern India is blessed with many natural resources (e.g. oil, coal, limestones, forest and hydropower potential). Many of these resources are being exploited as national resources for the benefit of the entire country, but local sentiment has often referred to these activities as internal colonialism. It is also the case that many recent immigrants, or "non-tribal" Indians have been employed to run these industries and have been given good positions in the formal economy (for example in state-run factories and institutions). However, it would be incorrect to state that the region is an exploited corner of the country. May of such resources are also exploited by the local inhabitants to export and earn their own revenue (e.g. coal and limestone in Meghalaya) and hence not contributing much to the local development. The aggregate data also suggest that with the exception of Tripura and Assam, all the states have a per capita income around or substantially above the national average. Literacy levels, with the exception of the remote state of Arunachal, also substantially higher than the rest of India.

The region is connected with the rest of India through a narrow corridor, the "chicken's neck". At its narrowest, around Siliguri in North Bengal, separating Nepal and Bangladesh, it has an approximate width of 21 kilometres on the western side. Practically, the entire boundary of the region is an international border: China on the north, Bangladesh on the south-west, Bhutan on the north-west, and Myanmar on the east.

The cultural diversity in North-East India, with its various ethnic and linguistic groups, was made more complex due to the British policy of "importing" large numbers of administrators, tea plantation workers, and cultivators from other parts of India during colonial rule, which started with the submission of Assam in 1826. The prospect of integration with the local community was systematically undermined by the British policy of segregating the tribal populations into so-called non-regulated or excluded areas that were administered differently. Laws that prevailed in the rest of British India were thought to be unsuitable to the stage of development of the populations of the hill areas of the North-East. Also from the point of view of political expediency, given the emergence of the nationalist movement in the rest of British India, spatial integration with the rest of the subcontinent was deferred.

The "Inner Line" system prohibited access to these areas to all "outsiders" except those who obtained special permission from the government. It created a frontier within a frontier, accentuating the political and cultural division between the tribal areas and the plains. The conversion to various forms of Christianity is a good illustration of the simultaneous working of segregation (from the rest of India) and subordination within the system of colonialism. Many tribal clans, while rejection the "alien cultural invasion" of mainstream Indians, thus, more readily came to cleavage in the modernising influence from the West. This has contributed to the cultural cleavage in the region.

After independence, such isolationist policies persisted, partly because of the chicken's neck connectivity, which made the area marginal to the rest of India. The cumulative impact of these policies was a deepening of fissures between tribal and non-tribal populations. Many areas were also excluded from the process of modernisation that affected the rest of the country. Such exclusion was by and large unsustainable in a modernising world to which the tribal elites were also attracted.

North-East India faces daunting developmental challenges because of its landlocked condition. The Partition of 1947, as B.G. Varghese puts it, "caused the extreme isolation of the North-East". He describes the region as South Asia's third landlocked "state" along with Bhutan and Nepal. The loss of connectivity and market access as a result of the partition, he said, "set its economy back by at least a quarter century" (Varghese, 2001). Historian David Ludden puts the same point even more forcefully. Partition, he said, referring to its impact of North-East India; cut old routes of communications and mobility across new national borders more dramatically than almost anywhere in the world. The Bengal Assam railway tracks from Guwahati to Dhaka were torn up at the Cachar-Sylhet border, in 1965. Now it is much easier to communicate by phone or mail between Dhaka and London than between Dhaka and Guwahati (Ludden, 2003).

However, on the east and the north, North-East India's isolation from its neighbourhood has much older roots: that which came about as a result of the advent of Western dominance over sea routes and over global trade and more particularly the British conquest of the region and the decisions to draw lines between the hills and plains, to put barriers on trade between Bhutan and Assam and to treat Myanmar as a strategic frontier — British India's buffer against built French Indochina and China. While the British colonial rulers built a major new transportation infrastructure, aimed primarily at taking tea and other resources out of Assam, the disruption of old trade routes remained colonialism's most enduring negative legacy.

North-East India was on the southern trails of the Silk Road. A review of the historical literature on a related theme by Francoise Pommaret, a French historian of North-East India's neighbouring country Bhutan, gives a useful picture of North-East India's place in these trade routes. Pommaret summarises the state of scholarly consensus as follows: "Kamrupa was on the trading route between south-west China and India. Even though, the existence of this route seems well established and its importance as a trading route and its age are controversial" (Pommaret, 1999).

In 1947, Assam became India's most proximate borderland with revolutionary China. In this strategic location, the US Army built the so-called Stilwell Road, in 1943, running from Ledo in Assam to the China-Burma Road, to form a link with the Bengal-Assam Railway and carry support for US and UK warfare against Japan (and later, against Chinese Communists). The Burma Road ran from Lasio railhead in Burma to Kunming in Yunnan, about 700 miles, across rugged mountains. The Burma Road became initiated by China in 1934 during the Sino-Japanese war, and completed in 1938 and more important to China when Japan took control of coastal China and Indochina. After Japan conquered lower Burma, the British began building the road from Ledo to the Burma Road, in December 1942, when the only way for Allies to send supplies to China was by air "over the hump". General Stilwell assigned 15,000 American troops to construct the Ledo Road, later named after the General, which ran 271 miles to a junction on the old Burma Road. Construction work trudged across Patkai Mountains, as high as 4,500 feet, required moving 100,000 cubic feet of earth every mile, and reached its goal at Shingbwiyang on 27 December, 1943.

Table 11.1: Stilwell Road

Length of Roads Lies Within	*Kilometres*	*Miles*
India	61	38
Myanmar (Burma)	1,033	646
China	632	395

India's Look East Policy

The end of cold war has made the international atmosphere conducive to and compelling for greater cooperation and understanding at the regional level. Most of the cold war rivalries and tensions that had intensified for the past forty-five years and vitiated regional divergence and conflicts have declined. Rather, throughout the world, regional economic cooperation has become a trend. This trend, especially in Third World Countries, has assumed great importance and keeping pace with the changed international scenario, India, one of the most important country of the Third World can play an important role in strengthening regional cooperation measures. The economic reforms embarked upon since 1991 have provided India with a new outward orientation that seeks greater integration of India into the global market place.

Initiated in the early days of the post cold war era, in 1992 the Indian Prime Minister P.V. Narasimha Rao followed "Look East" Policy that continued to peruse India's interests in the security of South-East Asia while instituting two significant changes: it reduced resistance to regional cooperation and committed itself to a new, more open economic policy. India has begun to explore new regional groupings, most of them linking parts of its own region to South-East Asia. As far as states like India and China are concerned, no epoch in history is complete by itself; it is both a continuation and a beginning. Former Prime Minister Narasimha Rao underlined this basic reality in his famous speech "India and the Asia-Pacific: forging a new relationship" in October 1994 at the institute of South-East Asian Studies in Singapore. The closer relationship, which India seeks today with South-East Asian countries, has to be fashioned on twin foundations. The benign interaction of the past and the mutuality of interests that exist at present.

In its relations with South-East Asian countries, India has several plus points. Historically, Burma, Thailand, Malaysia, Indonesia, Laos and Cambodia have been deeply influenced by Indian political ideas, religion, art and culture and language. The spread of Indian influences, leading to the cultural enrichment of South-East Asian countries, constitute a glorious chapter in Indian and South-East Asian history alike. Historians and political leaders have acknowledged South-East Asia's cultural indebtedness to India.

Not much work has been done by Indian scholars on the impact of culture on foreign policy. As far as South-East Asia is concerned the general tendency to look at the region as an extension of India —

"Greater India" — is resented by South-East Asia scholars. On the other hand, we should consider South-East Asia as an area of confluence. This does not mean that we have to reject the unquestionable evidence of tremendous Indian influence. It is only an acknowledgement of virile indigenous and non-Indian external influences in the cultural evolution. This balanced approach alone an provide the basis for benign cultural interaction. Secondly, the example of India-Sri Lanka cultural relations could be meaningfully applied in South-East Asia. The Governments of India and Sri Lanka have come together and have started the India and Sri Lanka Cultural Centre which has given a fillip to cultural interaction between the two countries. Thirdly, Indian and South-East Asian Universities should undertake collaborative research programmes relating to the fascinating area of cultural evolution.

India has land and maritime boundaries with Myanmar and maritime boundaries with Thailand and Indonesia. These countries are not only our next-door neighbours; they have been, as stated earlier, profoundly influenced by India in the cultural sphere. It is interesting to note that historians like K.M. Panikkar, Nilakanta Shastri and R.C. Majumdar used the term South-East Asia to cover both South Asia and South-East Asia. By accepting the American concept that South-East Asia countries stretching from Myanmar to the Philippines is a different area, we intellectually distance ourselves from our immediate neighbours.

Historically, all members of the Bay of Bengal Community — India, Bangladesh, Myanmar, Thailand, Malaysia, Singapore, Indonesia and Sri Lanka — have witnessed dynamic interaction between maritime trade and cultural evolution. The Bay of Bengal is a composite geographical and ecological unit. It is about the same size as the Mediterranean Sea. The littoral state contains almost one-fourth of the world's population. Bay of Bengal is a gift of "Mother Nature" and the littoral states can cooperate with one another for common well-being. If the littoral states could cooperate with one another in the crucial area of weather forecasting, preventive measures can be adopted and population could be removed from coastal areas well in advance of nature's fury. Similarly, Bay of Bengal is being used by the North-East insurgents in India and the Liberation Tigers of Tamil Eelam (LTTE) in Sri Lanka earlier for the smuggling of weapons. This maritime terrorism could be contained if the littoral states share intelligence and take joint action. The list can be multiplied. In short, exploitation of living and non-living maritime resources; development of maritime communications; ship building and ship repair; weather forecasting; prevention of maritime pollution and combating of maritime terrorism — these tasks which are the exclusive responsibilities of individual countries at present can best be accomplished through regional cooperation.

Neo-liberal Paradigm and Look East Policy

The Western trajectory of LPG development based on liberalisation, privatisation and globalisation was contemplated to be a panacea for the crises-ridden nations. The state was to retreat from the economic sector to propel the market forces for domestic growth and flourishing global trade. De-territorialisation became the common idiom in economic integration. In the backdrop of this, India circumspectly treated on neoliberal path mooting structural reforms in the nineties. It formulated Look East Policy in 1991 for developing economic cooperation with the East Asian neighbours. Interdependence replaced state centralism. India was cognizant that all the regions have tremendous potentialities in geographical sense and its dividends should be reaped by the people through direct and participative way. It viewed the geo-economic importance of North-East India as the link between East and South-East Asia in an era of regional and global cooperation. In this context, north-eastern states through cross border market corridor could bring India's economic integration with the East. "Justifying India's Look East Policy", former External Affairs Minister, Shri Pranab Mukherjee once said "Geography is an opportunity and the very geographical location of the north-east makes the doorway to South Asia and East Asia and *vice versa*, a doorway to India." Trans Asian Highway — Multinational Project South Asia — Thailand, Manipur and North-East India (Myanmar, Thailand and other countries of South East Asia), Bengal, Bihar, UP and go through Pakistan and Afghanistan.

Look East Policy and North-East India

After declaration of the Look East policy, some positive steps have already been taken to promote trade in other parts of North-Eastern region. Nathu La Pass was opened in 2006 after 44 years for trade with Tibet/China. There is proposal to re-construct Stilwell Road to connect Brahmaputra valley with Myanmar and China. The Moreh in Manipur and Tamu in Myanmar have been opened up for trade between the two countries. The Champhai (Mizoram)-Hri (Myanmar) Road and a third opening in Lungwa (Nagaland) aims at promotion of Indo-Myanmar border trade. The road-network and Asian Railway network will connect

India with the countries of South-East Asia and China. With the aim of creating big trading block, India is moving towards Comprehensive Economic Cooperation Agreement (CECA) covering free trade agreement (FTA) in goods, services, investments and identification of the areas of economy cooperation.

The "Look East Policy" and opening of the trade has started paying dividends. The share of the trade with our eastern neighbours has started increasing. The share of our trade with China has increased from 2.5 per cent of total trade in 2001-01 to 7.0 per cent in 2005-06 and 7.7 per cent during April-October 2006. During this time the share of our trade with Singapore and Malaysia has increased to 4.0 and 2.2 per cent respectively. The quantum jump in our trade with these three countries has been to \$21.8 billion from \$7.0 billion during 2000-01 to 2005-06.

The trade share with other countries has also increased considerably. It needs mention that the Look East Policy provides enormous possibility of the development of the whole country, especially the North-Eastern region of India. Most of the trade through land route will pass through the North-East region, benefiting it the most. The border trade will benefit the region also because of its being land-locked. The sea trade will benefit other parts of the country equally.

To take maximum benefit from the policy, the North-Eastern region should be develop industrially. The NE Industrial Policy has particularly made the whole region a special economic zone (SEZ). This, however, is not going to bring benefits if the lethargy and the corruption are not controlled. After all, the industry departments of various states of the region have only benefited the subsidy eaters up till now. For the flow of fund from South-East Asia, the roads, power and security is a must. We must bid farewell to the culture of *bundhs*. This is needed also for developing tourism. For this, the North-Eastern states must administer properly. Insurgency and extortion enterprises must give way to production oriented industry. Undue complacence towards the illegal migration from Bangladesh and huge illegal trade with that country must not continue.

Responding to the India's Look East Policy, apart from the other state of North-East, even the Government of Arunachal Pradesh also introduced reforms in various sectors to steer the course of development. It created a new Trade Department called Trade and Commerce in 1998 to facilitate the border trade. The government located Bleating (Namtsering), Bongkhar and Dongshengmang of Tawang district on Indo-Bhutan border, Pangsau pass (Manpong) in Changlang district of

Indo-Myanmar border, Kibithoo of Anjaw district, Bumla and Kenzamane (Zeminthang) of Tawang district, Gelling (Kepangla Pass) of upper Siang district, Mechuka (Lolla Pass) and Monigong (Dumla Pass) of West Siang district in Indo-China border as possible trading points. It is also considering for infrastructure development in Indo-Bhutan and Indo-Myanmar border for beginning formal trade. The World Trade Centre (Mumbai) is also in touch with the State government to open up one centre at Itanagar contemplating the potentiality of border trade inconsonance with the Look East Policy of the Centre. The Mumbai Centre is keen to promote trade by organising business Centre for meeting, conference, workshop, and video conferencing, facilitating research studies, training on foreign language and dealing with the trade missions. Materialisation of this would renew urban centres, open up vistas of business opportunities, empower the trading community and bring all-round development of the state. Experts on border trade also suggest for rebuilding of old Stilwell Road to connect Ledo with Kunming in Yunnan province of China through Pangsau Pass and Wauling at Mongya. They expect that the reopening of this strategic route would enhance the prospect of cross border trade with China as well as Myanmar. The connection of Stilwell Road to the Asian Highway was project through Hukwang valley of Myanmar may expand economic cooperation and pave the way for formation of growth triangles or growth zones in future. However, its success depends upon the pragmatic considerations and the multilateral approach of India, Myanmar and China.

Look East Policy and New Vision

India realised the importance of its relationship with East and South-East Asia, formulated 'Look East Policy'. The country is trying to strengthen its ties, including the Trade ties with the countries of the region. None can deny that strategically and economically strong Eastern neighbourhood of India shall provide strategic safety and economic strength to this country. India needs to develop all-round bilateral and multilateral relationship with the its eastern neighbours.

The end of cold war and the onset of economic globalisation are generating new atmospherics for inter-regional economic cooperation around India some of which can be harnessed for speeding up growth in the states of the North-East. In a nutshell, if the air, road communication links of the North-East with the rest of India are strengthened this region can benefit from India's Look East Policy.

India's relations with South-East Asia and ASEAN countries have grown considerably over the last decade. ASEAN countries have recently been negotiating and concluding multi-faceted and multi-layered economic cooperation partnerships in the region. We need to show innovative response to the realities of the new age and the new economy. In the first few decades after our independence India did not attain the full promise of relationships with the neighbouring countries partly because of the divergence in economic ideology, political outlook and security assumptions privileging in the cold war era. Now, that India is jointly developing the India-ASEAN vision 2020, we look forward to more India-ASEAN summits. In pursuit of specific socio-economic goals in the region, India is strongly supporting Mekong-Ganga Cooperation (MGC) bringing together Cambodia, Laos, Myanmar, Thailand, Vietnam and India. Sub-regional cooperation is also accelerated by the BIMSTEC (Bangladesh, India, Myanmar, Sri Land, Thailand Economic Cooperation). Currently, India is closely collaborating with ASEAN countries in various fields, such as trade and investment, science and technology, tourism, human resource development and transport and infrastructure. Some of the joint projects and joint studies can be routed in the North-East in order to develop employment opportunities here.

There has been much discussion about the potential of the Look East Policy transforming India's North-Eastern region that borders ASEAN. In this foreign policy vision North-East India is often described as the gateway to South-East Asia. The ASEAN-India car rally in 2004 was flagged off in Guwahati. According to Rajiv Sikri, Secretary of the Ministry of External Affair, the Look East Policy "envisages the North-East region not as the periphery of India, but as the centre of thriving and integrated economic space linking to dynamic regions with a network of highways, railways, pipelines, transmission lines, crisscrossing the region." The opportunities that economic integration with its transnational neighbours could open up for North-East India are enormous. The region's difficulties as result of the loss of connectivity and market excess are well known.

Now, that India has become a summit partner of ASEAN, it provides an opportunity for the top leadership to visit South-East Asia every year for political interaction. Unlike in the past, it appears the current phase of the Look East Policy is much more substantial. While developing links with ASEAN and other ASEAN-led multilateral institutions, India is also pursuing to qualitatively improve bilateral links with member states. The three distinct features of the Look East Policy are: one, India has managed to develop a multi-faceted relationship; two, successful defence diplomacy has been put in place; and three, unlike in the past, India is not averse to participate in regional multilateralism security or economic cooperation.

There is now a vision for the North-Eastern region. The Eleventh Plan has included most of the proposals and provided ample resources to implement them. For exclusive growth of the region, there are various departments like DoNER and NEC, who are effectively working and getting financial support from the Government of India. However, it is important that both the centre and states need to engage themselves on the various issues. If the desired results are to be obtained, serious efforts need to be made sooner rather than later. Since, North-East India as region is surrounded by a number of foreign countries many of its policy, challenges are inherently transnational in nature. Therefore, the place of North-East India in India's Look East Policy might be benefited from India's growing integration with other major Asian countries.

Conclusion

Undoubtedly, the Look East Policy has once again emerged as a major thrust area of India's foreign policy after some hiccups in the mid-1990s. Although, it is claimed that this policy encompasses the whole of Asia Pacific region, it is apparent that much of the emphasis so far has been on South-East Asia. Despite enormous progress made since, its enunciation in the early 1990s, India lags behind other great powers in terms of geopolitical or economic importance, but New Delhi has carved an important place. And the Look East Policy is responsible in making India an inalienable part of Asia Pacific's strategic discourse. The current phase marks the beginning of a vibrant relationship on economic, political and strategic fronts. A number of institutional mechanisms have been put in place so that there is a regular interaction at all levels and simultaneously bilateral linkages with individual member states have also been strengthened.

A close scrutiny of India's Look East Policy reveals that it was not simply meant to improve relations with South-East Asia, but there were a number of other dimensions too. What started an attempt to assuage negative reaction to the navy, the post-Cold War political atmosphere offered an opportunity to convert that into a policy initiative by expanding the scope considerably to include aspects political as well as economic. Devoid of any policy statement or document explaining the details or objectives, gradually it took shape to be known as the Look East Policy. It was a multi-faceted and multi-pronged approach to establish strategic links with many countries as possible, evolve closer political links with ASEAN, and develop strong economic bonds with the region. Second, it was an attempt to carve a place for India in the larger Asia Pacific. Third, the Look East Policy wa also ment to show India's economic potential for investments and trade. In a way this policy also started influencing India's foreign policy in a significant way, India, which has all along been wary of participating regional multilateralism, was willing to partake actively for the first time.

By way of conclusion, it can be suggested that for inclusive development of the North-Eastern region an interface between academicians, policy maker, and industrialists is to be stimulated for removing the pitfalls in the process of development in terms of India's Look East Policy.

REFERENCES

Acharya, Amitav (2003): "South-East Asia: Imagining the Region", *Himal South Asian* (Kathmandu) 16(1), January 24-29.

Baruah, Sanjib (2003): "Look East, but *via* the North-East", *Indian Express*, December 12.

Hindu (2001): "India, Myanmar Road Opened", *The Hindu* (Chennai), February 21.

H.N. Das (2003): "Economic Consequences of Insurgency in Assam", *The Indian Police Journal*, Vol. L, No. 1, January-March, New Delhi.

Indian Institute of Entrepreneurship, Guwahati, "Prospects of Border Trade with Myanmar and Bangladesh", Pre-investment Feasibility Study done for NEDFI. Similar studies are required for the other countries of South and South-East Asia.

"India: Looking East", Editorial in *Sapra India Bulletin*, November, 2006 Issue, New Delhi.

J.N. Dixit (1997): *My South Block Years: Memories of a Foreign Secretary*, UBS Publishers, New Delhi.

Liebenthal, W. (1956): "The Ancient Myanmar Road — A Legend?" *Journal of the Greater India Society*, XVI (1): 1-17.

Ludden, David (2003): *Where is Assam? Using Geographical History to Locate Current Social Realities* (CENISEAS Papers 1) Guwahati: Centre for North-East India, South and South-East Asia Studies, OKD Institute of Social Change and Development.

Misra, Udayan (2000): *The Periphery Strikes Back: Challenges to the Nation-State in Assam and Nagaland*, Indian Institute of Advanced Study, Shimla.

North-Eastern Development Finance Corporation Limited (NEDFI), *Resources and Investment Potential in North-Eastern Region*, Guwahati.

Pommaret, Francoise (1999): "Ancient Trade Partners: Bhutan, Cooch Bihar and Assam (18th-19th centuries)", *Journal Asiatique*, 287: 285-303.

Sanjib Baruah (2004): *Between, South and South-East Asia: North-East India and the Look East Policy*, Omeo Kumar Das Institute of Social Change and Development, Guwahati.

Taylor, Charles (1994). "The Politics of Recognition", in Charies Taylor *et al.*, *Multiculturalism: Examining the Politics of Recognition* (Amy Gutman ed.), Princeton: Princeton University Press.

The Economic Times, issue dated February 12, 2007.

Verghese, B.G. (2001): *Unfinished Business in the North-East: Pointers Towards Restructuring, Reform, Reconciliation and Resurgence*, Seventh Kamal Kumari Memorial Lecture.

12

LOOK EAST POLICY AND PROMOTION OF ENTREPRENEURS
Opportunities and Challenges

D.D. Mali

Introduction

The North-Eastern region of India accounts for about 8 per cent of the total geographical area and 3.8 per cent of total population of the country. The region shares 98 per cent of its border with Bhutan, China, Myanmar and Bangladesh and only 2 per cent with the mainland. The region has been lagging behind the rest of the country despite the fact that it is endowed with rich resources capable of utilising for economic and industrial development. This is partly because of geographical isolation, difficult terrain, coupled with its narrow corridor connecting with the mainland India and poor infrastructural facilities within the region. Besides, the Central Government policy towards this region was also partly responsible for this situation. For a long period of time, it did not open its border with the neighbouring countries of South-East Asia which may be because of security concern or greater emphasis on following a Look East Policy. This policy had hindered the development of the region.

Look East Policy

India's link with South-East Asia can be traced back to history and legend, though this link was not used earlier for the benefit of the region. Gradually, the government began to realise the importance of looking more to the East. Hence, when the country started the process of economic liberalisation, one of the important steps taken in 1991 was the adoption of the Look East Policy (LEP). Though this policy was announced in the early 1990s, it becomes a talking point in the region towards the end of the last century only.

The LEP is basically, an adjustment of India's foreign policy priorities based on the changing global scenario. The essential philosophy of this policy is that India finds it advantageous by linking itself more with its Asian partners. Besides, India's future and economic interests are best served by greater integration with East and South-East Asia. India's relationship with ASEAN (Association of South Asian Nations) forms the key element of the LEP (Charles, 2006; Bhattacharjee, 2010; Agarwal, 2010). In this policy framework, North-East India and Myanmar, with their geographical continuity, provides the fast growing relationship between India and ASEAN (Charles, 2006). The primary objective of LEP in the context of North-East India is to take advantage of the emerging new opportunities in trade and investment by improving socio-economic and political relationship with the neighbouring countries (Bhattacharjee, 2010).

The BIMSTEC (Bay of Bengal Initiative for Multi-Sectoral Technical Cooperation) forms the second key element of the LEP. Along with BIMSTEC, the Mekong-Ganga Cooperation (MGC), consisting of 6 countries, namely India, Myanmar, Thailand, Cambodia, Laos and Vietnam has been formed to supplement and complement the growing India-ASEAN relationship. Thus, we have in the India's LEP the growing India-ASEAN relationship at the top with BIMSTEC and MGC acting as two supporting pillars. In all these, from India's perspective, the North-East is seen "as the centre of a thriving and integrated economic space linking two dynamic regions" (Charles, 2006).

India became a sectoral partner of ASEAN in 1991, a full dialogue partner in 1995, and a member of the ASEAN Regional Forum in 1996 (Adhikary, Bora and Sikidar, 2007) and finally, a summit level partner in 2002 (Agarwal, 2010). Trade between India and ASEAN countries has been expanding fast. Pranab Mukherjee, the then former External Affairs Minister once stated that by gradually integrating this region through cross-border market access, North-East India can become the bridge between the Indian economy and the fastest growing and dynamic region in the world (Vishwanathan, 2008). However, North-East India should not just be a bridge, but a bridgehead for its benefit.

Look East Policy and Development Initiatives

The initiatives taken by the government after the announcement of LEP can be grouped under few heads, namely signing of bilateral and multilateral trade agreements, organising seminars and conferences, holding of trade fairs and exhibitions, developing infrastructure, creating export development fund, etc.

Trade and Economic Cooperation Agreements

- The first important development was the signing of first Indo-Myanmar Trade Agreement on 31 January, 1994.
- Signing of first framework for bilateral free trade agreement with Thailand in October 2003.
- Again, signing of comprehensive economic cooperation agreement (CECA) with Malaysia in December 2003 and with Singapore in June 2005. Further CECA signed with Malaysia on 18 February, 2011.
- In October 2004, Myanmar's Head of State, General Than Shwe visited India and signed three bilateral agreements. This has signaled a new approach of government to security and trade (Kuntala, 2005).

Indo-ASEAN Car Rally

- Organisation of Indo-ASEAN car rally in November 2004 was the first concrete step in this direction. The rally organised from Guwahati passed through North-East India and eight other countries covering about 8,000 km. This rally aimed at establishing people to people contact among the nations, exhibited road connectivity between India and ASEAN countries. It could create awareness among the states of North-East India and bring them closer to South-East Asia (Saikia, 2004; Sarma, 2008).

Trade Fairs and Exhibitions

- International Trade Fairs are being held at Guwahati and other places of North-East India and several South-East (SE) Asian countries started to participate in the trade fairs. In 2005, most of the South-East Asian countries who had participated in the Trade Fair expressed their willingness to promote trade with North-East India especially Thailand, China and Bangladesh.

Seminars and Conferences

- In 2003 an Export Promotion seminar was held at Shillong to identify areas of trade and joint ventures between North-East India and neighbouring countries. Later on, a number of seminars on LEP were held at different places to create awareness of the Look East Policy and investment opportunities in the region.

Infrastructure and Connectivity

- BSNL started working on an optical fibre project to set-up telecommunication network between North-East India and South-East Asia. Several other projects to improve connectivity between North-East India and Myanmar including road, rail links, telecommunication, IT, science and power have been started (Vishwanathan, 2008).
- Government of India has created some facilities for facilitating border trade such as construction of warehouse, cold storages, weigh bridges, trade centres, etc. in border towns of the region.

Export Development Fund

- The Central Government has created Export Development Fund for North-East India. Under this, trade-*cum*-exhibition centre at Guwahati, laboratory for testing agriculture and food products at Balipara (Tezpur), Integrated Trade Information and Stay Facility Centre at Moreh (Manipur), Integrated Marketing Cell, Inland Transport Assistance Scheme for the exporters from the region. Agro Processing Zones for pineapple (Tripura), Floriculture and cherry (Sikkim), ginger (Assam and Sikkim), Bamboo Industrial Complex (Mizoram), Integrated Pack House Facility (Guwahati), 32 Land Customs Stations at different places have been set-up.

Opportunities

These are important developments noticed after initiation of the Look East Policy. This policy has been gradually creating opportunities for entrepreneurs including the entrepreneurs of this region. Opportunities are emerging both in trade and industry, and also in agriculture and horticulture sectors. Besides, there are enormous possibilities for people to people contract, once the LEP is implemented in the true sense of the term. At the same time there are also many challenges. It is for the entrepreneurs how to take advantage of the opportunities and overcome the possible challenges of the LEP.

Opportunities in Trade

There can be opportunities for border trade with the countries having common border. A number of organisations have already identified opportunities for border trade. Among the organisations, Indian Institute of Foreign Trade (IIFT), New Delhi, Indian Institute of Entrepreneurship (IIE), Federation of Indian Chamber of Commerce and Industry (FICCI), Tata Consultancy Services (TCS), North-Eastern Chamber of Commerce and Industry (NECCI), Federation of Industries and Commerce in North-Eastern Region (FINER), etc. are a few to name. Some of the items having potential for border trade are identified as processed fruits and vegetables (orange, lemon, jack fruits, ginger, papaya, potato, chilli, pine apple, guava, brinjal and turmeric), tea, rubber, medicinal plants and herbs, drugs and pharmaceutical products, paints and varnishes, handloom products and silk (Khanka, 2007). Apart from these products, potentiality also exists for border trade in gems and jewellery.

The relationship with Bangladesh has improved over the years. Because of improved relationship there are good prospects of trade relations between India and Bangladesh, particularly with Assam, Meghalaya and Tripura states bordering Bangladesh. The prospect of Indo-Bangla trade has brightened with Dhaka-based entrepreneurs setting up joint ventures and opening up a new market for exporting garments to North-East India. MoU is also signed for a tyre manufacturing unit at Agartala with 100 crore Bangladeshi Taka and a readymade garments unit.

Opportunities for Industry

Export-based Industries: The tradable products consist of processed agro products and manufactured goods, except medicinal plants and herbs. Assuming that these products have potentiality for export to the neighbouring countries, it is necessary to examine their production base and capability of meeting the export demand. Existing entrepreneurs can consider expansion of their units and new entrepreneurs may also emerge. New potential areas can also be identified based on the resource endowment of the region. This may require the support of governments and promotional organisations.

Investment from Mainland Entrepreneurs: The proximity of North-East India (NEI) to the commercial hubs of SE Asian nations like Singapore and Bangkok may influence many entrepreneurs from the mainland engaged in consumer goods industries to relocate their units in

NE to take advantage of tax incentives announced by the government. This can happen once the trade route is opened. These units may be mainly export-oriented units. Besides, mainland entrepreneurs can set-up joint ventures with NEI entrepreneurs. Foreign investments from the ASEAN countries are likely to flow to the region precisely for the same reasons with the collaboration of Indian counterpart (Saikia, 2004).

Agro-based Industries: Pineapple production in NE India, medicinal and aromatic plants (more than 50 varieties) can command market worldwide. Cultivation of non-conventional crops such as vanilla, jathropa, alovera, can be foreign exchange earners, sugarcane cultivation, sericulture and fishery, handloom, rich and exotic cane and bamboo furniture (Seshan, 2007) have also good prospects in international markets.

Horticultural Products like strawberry, ginger, turmeric, cashew nut are inherently organic. Investors can invest in these fields also. Morever, bamboo-based industrial products have demand worldwide. The scope for developing this sector exists. This sector can get boost because of LEP.

The Tourism Sector of the region is expected to get a tremendous boost with the implementation of LEP. North-East India has the potential of becoming a major destination of eco-tourism, cultural tourism, and tea tourism. The region has the potential of performing as a key player in the global market in view of its rich reservoir of natural resources. Besides, there is the provision for several attractive sops offered to investors under North-East Industrial Investment and Promotion Policy 2007 and its very location. But due to lack of upgraded infrastructure, it has failed to develop economically. Thailand is keen in tourism and hospitality sector. Nearly 30 million tourists visit Thailand every year. Thailand and North-East India could be packaged together. Even if 1 per cent of Thai tourists visiting NE India will change its profile tremendously (*Yojana*, February 2008). Countries across SE Asia can invest in tourism sector. Thai Ambassador to India Krit Kraichitti stated that NE India can attract substantial investment from Thai companies in tourism, infrastructure and aviation sector with the help of North-East Indian State governments (AT 1 February, 2010). Buddhists sites scattered in upper Assam would be very attractive for Thai tourists. Thus, tourism industry can be a major industry if it is harnessed properly.

There is also possibility of setting up *Joint ventures* and give a new direction to the development of energy, transport and communication, bamboo products and Science and Technology sector. India and Myanmar share more than 1,600 km long border and people residing both sides will certainly find their life much easier with cross-border trade and commerce since marketability will be least costly as compared to the respective mainland alternatives in their own countries.

Revival of Plywood Industry: This industry was one of the important forest-based industries in NE India, which has been closed for several years. There is also possibility of reviving this important industry with raw materials from Myanmar.

Cultural and Social Sector development would also result eventually due to easy accessibility and free mingling of the people of the region (Saikia, 2004).

Challenges

There are also lots of challenges for NE Indian entrepreneurs. The biggest challenge that they face is the *lack of reliable and dependable infrastructure facilities* within the region. The region has high potential for hydro power generation. But there is inadequate power (generation and supply), lack of all weather dependable road and transit facilities.

There is fear that opening of trade route may lead to rise in *smuggling activities* including that of *drug related items* in the region, the route is being proximate to the Golden Triangle. These are security related issues and that should be left to the security agencies to deal with. These should not be a stumbling block for trade and commerce.

There is also the competition from outside with quality products. This is natural in a free market economy. The entrepreneurs of NE India need to think in terms of improving quality of product or services, increasing efficiency to compete, instead of complaining.

At present the focus is more on outward orientation of our trades and dreaming of Guwahati as the business hub of international trade. But this may not help. *International trade is a two way traffic*, both the countries are its beneficiaries as per their comparative advantage. This has to be accepted (Saikia, 2005).

ASEAN is a key pillar of India's LEP and accounts for 10 per cent of the nation's export. But trade is carried mostly through the sea route. Hence, *benefit mostly goes to the mainland* and the very purpose of LEP is defeated. The only *transportation link* is, through a road in Moreh, in Manipur and Tamu in Myanmar. The value of trade through the land route is very small and is limited to local goods. India's rail link with the ASEAN region would also have to pass through the Manipur. India has no significant development in freight transportation by waterways. The

Kaladan Multi-Model Transit Transport Facility envisages connectivity between Indian ports on the eastern seaboard and Sittwe port in Myanmar.

There is also a need for *road connectivity* between North-East India and Thailand *via* Myanmar. Proper connectivity is a must to boost bilateral trade. But unless there is measured improvement in the ground situation, there is little likelihood of NE India initiating trade with SE Asian countries (Dwaipayan, 2005).

Now, the NE is envisaged as a thriving and integrated economic space, linking the mainland India with SE Asia in India's LEP. But mainland India's tie with SE Asian countries have traditionally been maritime. Even today, India finds it cheaper and easier to trade with South Asian countries through sea rather than land. In that case, there is a possible *danger that the policy may get de-linked from the vision of NE India as a gateway*. Whether the LEP envisages the North-East India as a periphery or not, it cannot ignore a robust continental thrust with a thriving North-East region linking the country's economic role to a dynamic SE Asian economy.

The most urgent need is to *build-up the entire infrastructure* of the region that has been waiting for years. What is essential at this moment for the Centre is to develop special economic zones at appropriate places of the region to start with trade venture.

Concluding Remarks

Opportunities are emerging for North-East India's entrepreneurs, so also the challenges. Simple opportunities can attract some entrepreneurs to take advantage of the opportunities and get benefit from them. It is repeated that the entrepreneurs of this region would focus on opportunities and try to overcome those challenges using the available incentives, finance, infrastructural facilities and support from various agencies engaged in promoting entrepreneurship. In North-East India, more entrepreneurs emerge because of compulsion and not by choice. In such cases, incentives, easy availability of finance and infrastructure facilities would encourage them to take advantage of the opportunities. Most important, however, is the improved infrastructure, particularly transport and communication, and power for which the initiatives have already been taken. Much is yet to happen in this direction even after bout two decades of the adoption of the Look East Policy.

Industry and trade between neighbouring countries prepares when there is mutual trust. Political compulsion may demand different strategy.

In a liberalised environment trusting the neighbours is important for mutual benefit. There may be necessity to change the orientation of NE India entrepreneurs towards export trade for their benefit and also for the benefit of the region.

REFERENCES

Adhikary, A.; Bora, B. and Sikidar, S. (2007): "India's Look East Policy" in J.U. Ahmed (ed.) *Industrialisation in North Eastern Region*, Mittal Publication, New Delhi.

Agarwal, R.C. (2010): "North-East Needs Proper Connectivity with ASEAN", *The Assam Tribune*, 17 January.

Borthakur, R. (2004): "Sustainable Investment in North-East", *The Assam Tribune*, 16 October.

Bhattacharjee, S. (2010): "India's Look East Policy on Right Path", *The Assam Tribune*, 29 January.

Charles Chasie (2006): "Look East Policy: Pertinent Issues", *The Assam Tribune*, 20 March.

Dwaipayan (2005): "North-East ASEAN Trade Ties", *The Assam Tribune*, 22 March.

Editorial: *The Assam Tribune*, 22 November, 2004.

Jacob, M.M. (2004): "North-East: The Best Foot Forward", *The Assam Tribune*, 31 January.

Khanka, S.S. (2007): "Look East Policy through North-East — Its Impact on Industrial Economy of North-East", in J.U. Ahmed (ed.), *Industrialisation in North Eastern Region*, Mittal Publication, New Delhi.

Saikia, R.C. (2005): "Chasing India's Look East Dream", *The Assam Tribune*, 19 May.

Sikia, M. (2004): "Indo-ASEAN Car Rally to Boost Economy", *The Assam Tribune*, 22 November.

Sarma, S.B. (2008): "The North-East *vis-à-vis* South-East Asia", *The Assam Tribune*, 18 February.

Sharma, Kuntala (2005): "India Myanmar Ties: Key to North-East", *The Assam Tribune*, 2 February.

Seshan, K.S.S. (2007): "Economic Potentialities of North-East", *The Assam Tribune*, 5 January.

Sumati, Vishwanathan (2008): "Look East Policy", *Yojana*, February.

13

ASIAN ECONOMIC COMMUNITY AND NORTH-EAST INDIA

Amalesh Banerjee

Introduction

Asian countries are heterogeneous with wide dissolution between the rich capitalist country to poor populous country. The economy and culture reflect really a dramatic variety as reflected in Gunnar Myrdal's *Asian Drama*. Over last fifty years, Asian countries experienced many ups and down in economic and political scene. While in Europe a homogenous, community of nations, European Economic Community (EEC) has emerged over the years, in Asia regional groups have emerged as a result of interaction of conflicting forces and pulls. So, there is formation and reformation of Asian groups of countries and there is hardly any trend of dominant groupings of countries like European Economic Community. Instead of being a partner of creative formation like EEC, smaller Asian countries are being treated as prawn of dominant global players in the neo-literal agenda of economic development. As a result, while EEC countries are moving towards a conveyance, Asian countries, having failed to form a community are now moving against each other. In this chapter we tried to see the possibility of formation of an Asian Economic Community and its impact (beneficial or otherwise) on the North-Eastern states of India. In the next part of the chapter, we examined the existing complexion of groups of major Asian countries and then, we tried to see the possibilities of formation of the Asian Economic Community (AEC). After that we attempted to explore the impact of such AEC, if formed, on the North-Eastern states of India. Some concluding remarks are made in the last section.

Asian Formations

A number of groupings of countries with hardly mutual interactions have emerged in Asia over time. (I) Gulf Countries (GC), basically, an oil producing group, have western link. This is because most of the oil producing companies are based in Europe and America. Gulf nations' funds are parked in USA and Europe. (II) Central Asian Countries, primarily oil producing, had thereto been under Russian dominance. Even though they have moved away from the earlier combination, their interaction with other Asian countries are few and far between. India's attempt to build oil transaction with Tazakisthan in recent years in a new move. (III) South-east Asian countries, now combined in ASEAN, is a combination that is almost thirty years old. (IV) SAARC — South Asian Association for Regional Cooperation is also twenty five years old. But instead of showing any interaction, South Asian nations are disturbed by political disputes and terrorism. Recently the SAARC nations resolved to have free trade agreement among them (SAFTA). (V) China is moving along. Chinese economy has a strong influence on South-East Asian countries. (VI) Although not in a combination, South-East and East Asian countries, once considered as Asian tigers, are strong economies — Singapore, Hong Kong, South Korea, Thailand, Malaysia and Vietnam are heterogeneous group. (VII) Japan, Asia's strongest country is almost out of any combination. With a strong economy, Japan is a strong player in the Western economic power grid. (VIII) Besides this inter-Asian combines, some Asian biggies have come together to form inter-continental combine for trade and capital flow, Brazil, Russia, India and China have formed BRIC for coordinated measures to increase trade and capital flow.

Condition for Asian Union

These combinations of countries of Asia hardly indicate any close economic integrated approach with any coordinated objective in view. If we look at the various steps that preceded the formation of European Economic Union, then these Asian dispersed groups hardly give any indication of formation of a union. These different groups themselves are not yet strongly integrated. Strong members of SAARC and ASEAN are making independent approach for inter-continental alignments. Occasional assault spun some member countries to come together for mutual cooperation but no broad umbrella of agreements are in sight. We can count on some necessary conditions to be fulfilled for formation of Asian Economic Community: (a) Agreement of trade on a broad scale among he member nations. (b) Agreement on capital flow among member countries. Most of the Asian small countries are capital-scared. Hence private capital as well as inter-governmental assistance have to be on a large scale to obtain higher level of growth. (c) Rapid industrialisation of under-developed countries for attaining stronger homogeneity among the countries of the group. (d) Formation of Asian Reserve Fund. Table 13.1 indicates that some Asian countries have huge international reserve. At least a fraction of that reserve can be separately pooled for development of the poor nations. This is different from Asian Development Bank (ADB). (e) At least some countries must have a target for a higher level of trade. Inspite of existence of more than a quarter century, SAARC and ASEAN, there is no strong economic, convergence among the nations of each group. Hence, big nations of the region must fix a target for increasing mutual trade, at least on certain areas. (f) On domestic economic front, countries must aim at a higher level of growth. On different sectors, member nations must help each other to overcome scarcity and unemployment. For example, agreement on agricultural improvement. (g) Infrastructure, industry, and services

Table 13.1: Impact of Financial Crisis of Selected Macro-economic Variables

Nature of Crisis	*Period*	*PFCE Gap*	*Investment Gap*	*Savings Gap*	*GD Gap*
East Asian Crisis	1997-	–32.4	14.4	50.1	–27.7
	1998	28.8	–59.8	–52.5	20.7
Datcom B	2000	–34.7	–92.7	–80.5	–30.8
Global Financial Crisis	2008				–18.0
	2008				–22.9

Source: RBI, *Annual Report*, 2008-09.

Table 13.2: Global Recession and the Service Factor
Performance of the Service Sector in Emerging Market

Country	*Service for Share in GDP*			*Service Sector Growth*			*GDP Growth*		
	2001-05	*2006*	*2007*	*2001-05*	*2006*	*2007*	*2001-05*	*2006*	*2007*
India	52	52	52	8.4	11.0	11.0	6.8	10.0	9.0
Brazil	65	65	66	2.8	4.0	6.0	2.8	4.0	5.0
Chile	56	49	49	4.2	6.0	6.0	4.2	4.0	5.0
China	40	40	40	10.0	12.0	13.0	9.4	12.0	13.0
Korea	56	57	58	4.0	4.0	5.0	4.0	5.0	5.0
Russia	59	57	57	6.4	10.0	10.0	6.0	7.0	8.0

Source: World Development Indicator, World Bank, RBI, *Annual Report*, 2008-09.

are the different areas of cooperation and growth. For an economic union to be launched, member nations should agree to have certain areas of targeted coordinated action. (h) Some member countries must agree to maintain some standard level of fiscal discipline.

Table 13.3: International Comparison of Balance on Current Account as Percentage of GDP

Country Group	*2001*	*2005*	*2006*	*2007*	*2008*
Russia	11.1	11.0	9.5	5.9	6.1
China	1.3	7.2	9.5	11.0	10.0
India	0.3	–1.3	–1.1	–1.0	–2.8
Korea	1.6	1.8	0.6	0.6	–0.7
Mexico	–2.6	–0.5	–0.5	–0.8	–1.4
South Africa	0.3	–4.0	–6.3	–7.3	–7.4

Table 13.4: International Comparison of Balance on Current Account as Trading Blocks

(*mn US $*)

Country Group	*2001*	*2005*	*2006*	*2007*	*2008*
Advance Countries	–0.8	–1.1	–1.3	–1.0	–1.1
Central and Eastern Europe	–1.9	–4.8	–6.5	–7.7	–7.6
Developing Asia	1.5	4.0	6.0	6.9	5.8
Middle East	6.4	19.7	21.0	18.2	18.8

Table 13.5: Growth Rate of Major Trading Partners of India, 2008-09 (%)

Country	*Export*		*Import*	
	April-August 2008	*January-March 2009*	*April-August 2008*	*January-March 2009*
World	16.5	—	18.1	—
USA	19.8	–22.3	14.9	–29.9
Hong Kong	7.9	–18.3	9.5	–21.2
Singapore	16.9	–6.2	23.5	–35.8
Japan	16.4	–5.1	–40.6	–29.0
China	29.5	–24.1	40.9	–25.3

Source: IMF, *World Economic Outlook Data*, April 2009, *Economic Survey*, 2008-09, Government of India.

Table 13.6: Export Growth and Share in World Export

Country	*Growth Rate, Annual (%)*			*Share in World Exports (%)*		
	2006	*2007*	*2008*	*2006*	*2007*	*2008*
(1)	*(2)*	*(3)*	*(4)*	*(5)*	*(6)*	*(7)*
China	27.2	25.6	17.3	8.0	8.8	9.1
Hong Kong	9.5	8.7	5.3	2.6	2.5	2.3

(*Contd.*)

Table 13.6 (*Contd.*)

(1)	(2)	(3)	(4)	(5)	(6)	(7)
Malaysia	14.0	9.6	19.1	1.3	1.3	1.3
Indonesia	19.0	14.7	24.4	1.0	0.9	0.9
Thailand	18.7	17.0	12.9	1.1	1.1	1.1
Singapore	1.84	10.1	13.0	2.2	2.2	2.1
India	16.3	16.6	23.2	1.1	1.2	1.3
Mexico	17.1	8.6	7.3	2.1	2.0	1.8
Russia	24.1	16.9	44.3	2.5	2.6	3.2
Korea	14.4	14.1	13.6	36.0	36.2	38.4
World	16.0	13.9	14.3	100.0	100.0	100.0

Source: *Economic Survey*, 2008-09, Government of India, p. 142.

Table 13.7: International Comparison of Foreign Exchange Reserve

(*US $ billion*)

Country/Group	*2001*	*2007*	*2008*
Russia	33.1 (44.6)	466.7 (165.1)	421.3 (114.4)
China	216.3 (9.7)	1531.3 (148.0)	2134.5 (163.6)
India	46.4 (65.0)	267.6 (95.1)	271.7 (79.3)
Asian Excluding China and India	116.9 (37.9)	329.2 (49.9)	339.4 (42.9)
Middle East	157.9 (8.7)	670.4 (114.7)	823.1 (106.7)

Note: Values in brackets represent ratio of reserve to imports.
Source: *World Economic Outlook*, April 2008 and *Economic Survey*, 2008-09.

Table 13.8: Gross External Debt to GNI in 2008

Country	*Percentage*
Turkey	38.8
China	11.6
India	18.9
Indonesia	33.9
Kazakhastan	103.7
Ukraine	52.9
Malaysia	29.4
Thailand	26.5
Russian Federation	29.4

Source: *Economic Survey*, 2008-09, Government of India.

Budgetary deficit, taxation, public expenditure are some major areas, where leading member, nations must agree to maintain certain mutually agreed standard.

(i) Employment and un-employment is another area of concern. Member countries of a group must also agree to maintain a certain level of employment.
(ii) Price level is another area of cooperation. Member nations must agree to maintain stability of price level.
(iii) On monetary front, member countries must agree to maintain a certain degree of monetary stability, money supply so that instability generating in one country does not have a congestions effect on neighbouring country.

Three Majors and Leadership

Asia has three major economies. Japan, the capitalist country is geographically located in Asia, but in many aspects its economic relations are mainly with Western countries, primarily with USA. Japan, time and again, is quickly affected by global economic crisis. Every economic crisis generated in USA has affected Japanese economy seriously.

China is the fourth biggest economy in the world. China has a large diasporas, which provides a large flow of capital in China's mainland. The country has made some successful reforms of its economy, which has yielded good results. In terms of human resources development China is much ahead of many Asian countries. China is now affected by economic crisis but was not affected by South-East Asian crisis of 1997.

India has started economic reform in 1991 and since then made some progress. India's present rate of growth is comparable with that of China.

Leadership of Asian Economic Union rests with India for a number of reasons: Firstly, India is the democratic country. Trade data indicate that India's participation in world trade has substantially increased in recent decade (Table 13.6). Secondly, India has the leadership of modern information technology which has revolutionised the contemporary industrial world. Thirdly, India has the vast reservoirs of technical manpower and virtually supporting the US economy with outsourcing work. Fourthly, India can revolutionise the transport system in Asia by exploiting Trans Asian Railway. Geographically, India can extend its railway network to the eastern as well as to the Western Asia. This will hasten the process of integration of Asia and the convergence process.

India can push up to Russian Federation on the one side and to Indonesia on the other side strengthening the Trans-Asian Railway.

Look East and Asian Economic Community

India's Look East Policy not only means for the development of North-Eastern states, it also means that India will come closer to the Central East Asian countries. If India takes this bold leadership of Asian Economic Community, India's north-eastern states will be most beneficiaries. Not only India's trade with Asian countries particularly the neighbouring countries of Bangladesh, Myanmar would increase but also with East Asian combine of ASEAN countries would be stronger.

Trade and tourism are the most important service activities that would serve as a booster to North-Eastern states. With little industralisation, North-Eastern states use languishing. With the opening of Trans-Asian trade and transport North-Eastern states will have the benefit of stronger trade and employment opportunity. India's trade with Asian countries will definitely increase. As stated in the 11th Five Year Plan, development of the region is linked to the Look East Railway of the Government and development of relationship with neighbouring countries of the entire region. There is wide scope of generating economic activity through interaction with these countries. Look East Policy is, therefore, important to bring these areas out of isolation and gradually developing an economic identity and moving on a higher growth path. Higher income will reduce the incidence of poverty of the region and will set the stage of convergence of the states with the advanced states.

Conclusion

Asian countries are divided in to several regional groups like SAARC, ASEAN. But it is possible to develop an Asian Economic Union. On trade and transport there is wide possibilities of generating economic development of the region. India can strengthen the Trans-Asian Railway. It has a vast possibility in respect of integrating the big and small countries of the region and boosting regional handle and tourism. Asian Economic Union is possible with larger capital flow, with transfer of technology and energy. Thus, process will track isolation of the North-Eastern region and would generate rapid development. Look East Policy not only emphasises on the development of the region but also on improving the regional cooperation with neighbouring countries.

REFERENCES

Asian Development Bank (2009): *Asian Development Outlook*, Oxford University Press.
Banerjee, Amalesh (2009): "SAARC Symphony Voice", *BMR*, Kolkata.
Bank of Japan (2009): *Monthly Report of Recession, Economic and Financial Developments*, March.
International Monetary Fund (2009): *World Economic Outlook*, April.
MEL Cousins (2005): *European Welfare States*, Sage Publications, London.
Stiglitz, Joseph (2006): *Making Globalization Work*, Penguin Books.
Stiglitz, Joseph (2002): *Globalization and Its Discontents*, Penguin Books.
World Bank (2009): *World Development Report*, (World Bank).

14

PREREQUISITES FOR INTEGRATING INDIA'S NORTH-EAST WITH SOUTH-EAST ASIAN COUNTRIES

Pranay Jyoti Goswami

Introduction

India's Look East Policy was formulated in order to strengthen her relationship with the South-East Asian countries. Since 1990s, the partnership between India and the Association of South-East Asian Nations (ASEAN) comprising Brunei, Cambodia, Indonesia, Laos, Malaysia, Myanmar, the Philippines, Singapore, Thailand and Vietnam has been developing at quite a fast pace. India became a sectoral dialogue partner of ASEAN in 1992. Mutual interest-led ASEAN to invite India to become its full dialogue partner during the fifth ASEAN summit in Bangkok in 1995. India also became a member of the ASEAN Regional Forum (ARF) in 1996. India and ASEAN have been holding summit level meetings on an annual basis since 2002. India signed a Free Trade Agreement (FTA) with the ASEAN members in October 2009 in Thailand. Under the ASEAN-India FTA, the ASEAN member countries and India will lift import tariffs on more than 80 per cent of traded products between 2013 and 2016. Also, tariffs on sensitive goods will be reduced to 5 per cent in 2016, while tariffs will be maintained on up to 489 items of very sensitive products. India and ASEAN are currently negotiating Agreements on Trade in Services and Investment. India has made requests in a number of areas including teaching, nursing, architecture, chartered accountancy and medicine; as it has a large number of English speaking professionals in these areas who can gain from job opportunities in the ASEAN region. India is also keen on expanding its telecom, IT, tourism and banking network in the ASEAN countries.

ASEAN is India's fourth-largest trading partner after the EU, US and China. Indo-ASEAN trade, which has been growing at a compounded annual growth rate (CAGR) of 27 per cent since 2000, stood at US $38.37 billion in 2007-08. The bilateral trade between India and the ten-member ASEAN now stands at US $48 billion annually.

North-Eastern Region has a situational advantage to expand trade with the ASEAN countries. The region has a link with thee countries culturally and religiously. But how far this region has been able to reap the benefit of the comparative advantages is a matter of research.

Objectives

In this context the objectives of the present chapter are as follows:

(1) To analyse the background and the current status of India's Look East Policy.
(2) To review the locational advantage of North-Eastern region in the emerging East Asian Regional Architecture. It also covers the prospects of trade with the Asian countries.
(3) To put forward suggestions in order to reap the benefit of regional integration. In other words this chapter will discuss the prerequisites of integration of North-East India with the South-East Asian countries.

For the sake of convenience this chapter is divided into three sections, viz. Section I, II and III respectively which highlight the above mentioned three objectives.

Analysis of India's Look East Policy

India's Look East Policy began in the early 1990s during the Government led by P.V. Narasimha Rao. All subsequent governments have supported the policy and have built in it. Economics has been a prime mover of India's Look East Policy. India has ignored the Asian economic miracle in its early phases since, the lessons of the export oriented economies of a few small countries indulged by West seemed inapplicable to an economy of India's size and ambition. That view, however, was badly shaken by the emergence of China — its spectacular growth since the 1980s that is based on trade and a liberalised economy. Moreover, collapse of Soviet economy, US led Gulf War on Iraq in 1991 and destabilisations in Middle East are the other reasons for India's Look East Policy.

In the days of cold war India's attitude towards ASEAN was ambivalent, but not hostile. India considered ASEAN as the surrogate of the American imperialists and ASEAN considered India as the surrogate of Soviet Union. But that attitude has already changed in both the camps. "If we want to truly get into the globalisation bus" an Indian business professional is quoted as saying, "We must first try and get into the shuttle of ASEAN" (cited in *Manila Times*, 2002). Culturally, India has more commonalties with South-East Asian counterpart. The Look East Policy has aimed at developing closer relation with the so called economic tigers of South-East Asia. In 1997, India became a full dialogue partner of the region's main groups ASEAN. India's efforts to develop closer ties with South-East Asia began paying off in 2002 when the ASEAN heads of Government and India's Prime Minister met in a summit meeting in the Cambodian capital Phnom Penh. ASEAN and India had agreed to work towards negotiating a free trade agreement in ten years. In ASEAN summit at Bali (Capital of Indonesia) in October 2003, India's the then former Prime Minister Mr. Atal Bihari Vajpayee spelled out new initiative for economic cooperation including air and road links. In addition India signed an Indo-ASEAN framework agreement for the establishment of FTA by 2011. By this time, all trade with ASEAN would fully liberalise. ASEAN is a big market of 537 million people with vast trade links and potential for the expansion of India's external sector. This has given rise to talk of establishing an Asian Economic Community by 2020.

In India ASEAN car rally on 22nd November, 2004 former Prime Minister Man Mohan Singh has given stress for the cooperation of India and Asian countries in the areas like trade and investment, technology transportation, energy and tourism.

There are number of bilateral and multilateral agreements that provide the foundation for India's growing relations with South-East Asia. The first major breakthrough was the signing of BISTEC (Bangladesh, India, Sri Lanka and Thailand Economic Cooperation) agreement, with later addition to Myanmar and its conversion into BIMSTEC in 1997. On 28th December, 1998, India signed an FTA with Sri Lanka (ILFTA). There is also BCIM (Bangladesh, China, India and Myanmar) Regional Economic Forum that has its roots in the Kunming initiative in 1999. Official statement by ASEAN and Indian leaders call for deeper integration of the economics of ASEAN and India in coming years.

In November 2000, India floated the Mekong-Ganga Cooperation Scheme with 5 of its neighbours — Myanmar, Thailand, Laos, Cambodia and Vietnam. The stress is given for the trade in services like tourism, culture and education.

In October 2003, India also signed a FTA agreement with Thailand in both goods and services. There was a proposal for implementation of free trade in services with effect from 2006 and goods from 2010. In addition to this, it proposed a land bridge project for linking the Andaman Sea and Gulf of Thailand for oil and gas transportation. India has also signed a comprehensive economic cooperation with Malaysia in 2004 and Singapore on 29th June, 2005.

It is evident from Table 14.1 that India's trade with the Asian countries has increased rapidly during the period 1987-88 and 2004-05. India's export to the Asian countries has increased from 11.9 per cent of her total export in 1987-88 to 29.3 per cent in 2004-05. In the same period the imports has risen from 12.1 per cent of her total imports to 20.1 per cent. India's export to China, Hong Kong, South Korea, Malaysia and Singapore was 0.1, 2.8, 0.9, 0.6 and 1.7 per cent respectively. Again India's export to ASEAN countries in 2005-06 was 9097.28 million dollar (share 10.07 of total export) which has increased to 11,326.50 million dollars. SImilarly, imports in 2005-06 was 9,550.22 million dollar (share 9.97 of total imports) to 16,178.23 million dollar. The export to China was only 1 per cent of total export in 1987-88 which has increased to 6.8 per cent in 2007-08. Similarly, import from China has increased to 11.3 per cent from 0.7 per cent during the same period. The data related to import and export of other countries are shown in Table 14.2.

Table 14.1: India's Foreign Trade with Some Asian Countries

(Percentage of Total Export and Import)

Country	*Export*		*Import*	
	1997-98	*2003-04*	*1997-98*	*2003-04*
China	2.1	4.7	2.7	6.4
Korea	1.3	1.2	2.4	3.9
Japan	5.4	2.7	5.2	4.2
ASEAN-6*	6.9	9.0	8.1	9.0

* ASEAN-6 — includes Indonesia, Malaysia, Philippines, Thailand and Vietnam.

Source: Datt, Ruddar and Sundharam, K.P.M., *Indian Economy*, S. Chand & Company Ltd., New Delhi, 2006.

India's export to SAARC countries has increased to 5.4 per cent in 2004-05 from 2.6 per cent in 1987-88. It may be mentioned here that India's export and import trade with Japan has declined during the same period, e.g. in 1997-98 India's export to Japan was 5.4 per cent which has declined to 2.7 per cent in 2004-05. It may be noted that China

Table 14.2: India's Export and Import to Selected Countries

(million US dollar)

Country	*1987-88*				*2007-08*			
	Imports	*Share*	*Export*	*Share*	*Import*	*Share*	*Export*	*Share*
China	119	0.7	1.5	0.1	27079.8	11.3	10781.6	6.8
Hong Kong	93	0.5	344	2.8	2696.0	1.1	6304.6	4.0
South Korea	257	1.5	112	0.9	6030.9	2.5	2850.0	1.8
Malaysia	648	3.8	70	0.6	NA	NA	NA	NA
Singapur	323	1.9	210	1.7	889.0	NA	660.0	NA
SAARC	75	0.4	313	0.26	2125.4	0.9	8986.1	5.7

Source: Dutt, R. and Sundharam, K.P.M., *Indian Economy*, S. Chand & Co. Ltd., New Delhi.

including Hong Kong has emerged in 2004-05 as India's second highest trading partner after USA, overtaking countries like UK and Belgium. A joint study group have been constituted to examine bilateral agreements with China and Korea. An India Japan study group is examining the feasibility of bilateral trade agreements between India and Japan.

India-ASEAN trade in 2003-04 was about US $13.25 billion, over 5 times the 1993-94 trade figure of US $2.5 billion. India's exports to ASEAN were US $5.8 billion while imports about US $7.4 billion in this period; balance of trade was in favour of ASEAN. Compared to other regional groupings, ASEAN is the fifth most important market in the world in terms of Indian exports and fourth in terms of imports.

ASEAN as a region has displayed great economic dynamic. Growth in India's exports to ASEAN in recent years has been much higher in comparison with other important destinations. Although in case of imports, those from other regions have achieved faster growth than ASEAN's imports into India.

Major commodity groups of India's exports to ASEAN include oil meals, gems and jewellery, meat and meat preparations, cotton yarn, fabrics, made-ups, engineering goods, transport equipment, machinery and instruments, electronic goods, marine products, fruits and vegetables, rice, drugs and pharmaceuticals, chemicals, etc.

India's imports mainly consist of artificial resins, plastic material, natural rubber, wood and wood products, electronic goods, non-ferrous metals, metaliferous ores and metal scrap, organic chemicals, edible oils, coal, fertilizers, etc.

The top ten commodity groups that are of maximum importance in ASEAN's import basket considering the figures of Brunei Darussalam, Cambodia, Indonesia, Malaysia, Myanmar, Philippines, Singapore and

Thailand (2000-2001) are: 1. Machinery and electrical appliances, 2. Mineral product, 3. Chemicals, 4. Base metal and metal articles, 5. Vehicles, 6. Textiles and apparel, 7. Plastics, 8. Optical, precision and musical instruments, 9. Prepared foodstuffs, and 10. Vegetable products.

It is observed from the statistical figures that:

1. Among ASEAN members, Singapore and Malaysia have been India's most prominent trading partners. The growing bilateral economic relationship is reflected in the rapidly rising bilateral trade between Singapore and India. The cumulative FDI inflow to India from Singapore during April 2000-April 2009 was around US $7.9 billion. Singapore continues to be the single largest investor in India amongst all countries, rising to US $3.45 billion in 2008-09. FDI inflows from Singapore between April-July, 2009 stood at US $759 million, taking the cumulative inflows from April 2000-July 2009 to US $8.57 billion.
2. There has not been any significant change in the product composition of India's major exports to ASEAN since 1991-92 with the exception of electronic goods that emerged as one of the leading export items by 2000-01.
3. With the BCLMV countries (Brunei, Cambodia, Laos, Myanmar and Vietnam) India's current trade is rather low both in terms of absolute value and relative share, with Myanmar being an exception. Constraints in bilateral trade are several times more including high shipping cost, lack of contact between the business communities, relatively lower volume of demand and so on.

Locational Advantage of the North-East Region

The North-East with its locational advantage could emerge as an major business transit centre for both SAARC and the Association of South-East Asian Nations (ASEAN).

The trade between North-East and its bordering countries is mostly non-formal. For example, large quantities of gem stone, raw materials, i.e. precious and semi-precious stones are informally traded between Myanmar and India *via* North-Eastern part of India. Moreh (Manipur), India's gateway to the South-East Asian countries has been turning into one of the busiest international bazaar for trading in precious and rare stones. These gem items finally reach Middle East and other European countries after polishing at Guwahati.

It formal trade is developed, it can be said that on the basics of speculation on the thrust area North-East India can emerge as an exporter to the Myanmar, China and other South-East Asian countries of certain items. For example, North-East India is famous for its exotic flora and fauna. Out of the 1925 varieties of orchids available in India over 600 can be grown in the region due to the climatic condition. In fact approximately 200 varieties are unique to the region and ornamental in nature with high demand in international market. It is ideally situated to produce spices, herbs, etc. Moreover, the forest of North-East offers a vast varieties of aromatic plants, which can be used in the aromatic industry for manufacture of perfumes, incenses, etc. In fact there is an increasing international trend towards natural perfumes and room fresheners. With proper planning there exists scope for establishing aromatic industry in the region.

Secondly, Assam produces about 50 per cent of country's tea. Tea industry can find new and newer outlets for exporting its product to Myanmar and other South-East Asian countries if border trade can be developed.

Thirdly, North-East is well known for its bio-diversity and heritage sites. Twang in Arunachal Pradesh, Mazuli, Kaziranga of Assam, etc. can be developed further as tourist spots. In 1996, Consultancy firm, Coopers and Lybrand submitted a report to the Government of Assam mentioning vast tourism potential of North-East. If these potentials are fully tapped and developed, the report remarks, "within 20 years the region will receive more tourist than Singapore or Bangkok", because almost Western and Japanese tourists visiting South-East Asian region could fly or drive a few hundred kilometre more to enjoy the scenic and cultural beauties of North-Eastern region.

What to Be Done?

1. **Development of Rail, Road and Airways.** This is the prerequisite for regional integration. There is a proposal of construction of New Delhi-Hanoi railway line which will go *via* Manipur of North-East India and Myanmar. Again a railway line may be constructed connecting Ledu (Assam) and Dali of Yunnan State of China *via* Tengchog-Myitkyina (Myanmar). Development of Stilwell Road which was constructed during 1942-45 is another agenda. This road runs from Ledo in North-East India and passes through Lekhapani-Panshu pass in India, Myitkyina and Lacio in

Myanmar to Kunming in Yunnan Province in China and *via* express road up to Hong Kong. From Lashio by well developed rail and road one can reach Laos, Thailand, Malaysia and Singapore. If 100-120 miles road from Arunachal Pradesh to Myitkyina is rebuilt, North-East will be well connected with the other East or South-East Asian countries. Triangular Road Project is also taken by Government of India which will link the Mizoram state with East and North Myanmar Border and Falam and Tiddim.

The government has taken up some measures in order to develop water transport also. In line with Look East Policy, the Centre has agreed to take up Kaldon Multimodel Transport Project which will link Mizoram of North-East India with Sittwe port in Myanmar by waterways.

Rail connection with Bangladesh can be developed by connecting Mohisasan station of Assam with Sialdah *via* some of the stations of Bangladesh like Dhaka and Kulaura.

2. **Development of Communication Facilities.** Tele-density and internet facilities in the region are still poor as compared to other parts of country. This need to be developed.
3. **Development of Financial Infrastructure including E-banking.** For international trade development of financial infrastructure including e-banking is most essential.
4. **Development of Law and Order Facilities.** For development of the region a peaceful atmosphere is essential. But insurgency problems of the North-East retard its economic development.
5. **Removal of Quantitative and Qualitative Restrictions.** For free trade this is one of the preconditions.
6. **Skill Formulation for Unskilled Worker.** Though the literacy rate in some North-Eastern states is better, yet many of them are unskilled, so training facilities in the relevant thrust areas should be given.
7. **Introduction of National Identity Card.** In Euro nations, free movement of labourers is possible because every citizen has his/her National Identity Card. In North-Eastern region in order to check infiltration from Bangladesh, Myanmar and Nepal, efforts should be made for the introduction of National Identity Card immediately. In all the countries, the issue of National Identity Card to their citizen will ensure free movement of labourers in the region in future.

8. **Development of Cold Storage and Hotels.** Development of cold storage near airport and important cities is essential for the trade of perishable commodities. Some hotels with star ranking should be constructed.
9. **Transparency, Good Governance.** It is learnt that a truck driver has to pay bribe to the police and other tax officials around ₹ 2000 when he carries goods from Guwahati to Aizawl. This has an adverse effect on cost. So, fast to faster decision making in the areas like sanction of loans, environmental permissions, etc. is the *sine qua non* for increasing our strength in the international competition.

Conclusion

The Union Ministry of External Affairs has made a comprehensive exercise to work for the North-Eastern states and has given thrust to convert diplomatic initiatives to commercial opportunities. For this purpose the MEA in close cooperation with the Union Ministry of Doner, Planning Commission, all economic ministries and the state governments has adopted strategic common actionable plan. The major objectives of the Look East Policy is to develop economic relationship with the ASEAN countries. As a part of this, it is endeavour to renew and strengthen the economic contact with the region and to reinforce its Look East Policy a sub-regional grouping called BISTEC (Bangladesh, India, Sri Lanka and Thailand). In addition BIMSTEC is also formed by including Myanmar, Bhutan and Nepal. India sees an opportunity to address the lack of opportunities for the people in the North-East and convert the region from being a security problem into a land of economic opportunity. To revive and reopen the ancient trade connectivity road between Myanmar, Bangladesh and China besides encouraging investment opportunity in the North-Eastern region, one North-East India investment opportunities week was held at Bangkok in October 2007. The Government of India has approved setting up of two border trade centres — one at Sutarkandi and another at Mancachar to facilitate border trade with neighbouring countries.

In fine, it can be said that along with international trade there is chance for Drug and women trafficking in North-Eastern states. But this problem is universal. South Asian countries must work jointly in order to check the problems of terrorism, informal trade of arms and ammunition, drug and women trafficking for their own survival.

REFERENCES

Ashar Mukul J. and Sen Rahul (2005): "India East Asia Integration", *Economic and Political Weekly*, Vol. XL, No. 36, September 3-9, p. 3932.

Baruah, Sanjiv: *Between South and South East Africa: North-East India and the Look East Policy.*

Boillot, J.J. and Labbouz, M. (2006): "India-China Trade: Lessons Learned and Projections for 2015", *Economic and Political Weekly*, Vol. XLI, No. 26, June 30.

Datt, Ruddar and Sundharam, K.P.M. (2006): *Indian Economy*, S. Chand & Company Ltd., New Delhi.

Economic Survey, Assam, 2008-09.

Ghosh, D.N. (2004): "India and China: Partnership or Rivalry in a Globalising World", *Economic and Political Weekly*, Vol. XXXIX, No. 52, December 25-31, p. 5630.

Gogoi, Jyanta Kr. (2004): "Border Trade and North-East", *Yojana*, September, p. 29.

Islam, Nurul (2004): "Indo-Bangladesh Economic Relations", *Economic and Political Weekly*, Vol. XXXIX, No. 36, September 4-10, p. 4069.

Kumar, Nagesh (2005): "A Border Asian Community and a Possible Roadmap", *Economic and Political Weekly*, Vol. XL, No. 36, September 3-9, p. 3926.

15

TRADE AND ECONOMIC DEVELOPMENT OF NORTH-EAST INDIA
A Note

H.N. Das

Theoretical economics has all along pleaded for removal of all restrictions on trade. The belief is that "in every country it always is and must be the interest of the great body of the people to buy whatever they want to those who sell it cheapest". Stating this in his '*Wealth of Nations*' Adam Smith also clarified that "the proposition is so very manifest that it seems ridiculous to take any pains to prove it; nor could it ever have been called in question, had not the interested sophistry of merchants and manufacturers confounded the commonsense of mankind".

In the practical field it has been noticed that international trade has fostered the wealth of nations. Tremendous economic development has taken place in the six decades since the end of the Second World War and trade has played the most important role in it. During my visit to Taiwan an enquiry was made into the genesis of its transformation from a poor fishing island without any natural resources into one of the most prosperous countries in the world. In 1950 General Issimo Chiang Kai Shnek and his wife Sung Li fled to Taiwan (then called Formosa) after Mao Zedong's Red Army swept into power in mainland China. They started the process of Taiwan's economic development through trade. First, they started to harvest and export fish. Then agricultural and agro-industrial goods. Thereafter, the products of village and small scale industries which included very large consignments of cheap ready-made clothes. This continued for some time when they started manufacturing and exporting computer hardware. This became possible through its technically skilled and rich human resource.

A number of countries including Korea, Thailand, Singapore, Hong Kong, Malaysia, Philippines and others followed a more or less similar growth path and became prosperous. To quote the Nobel prize winning economist Joseph E. Stiglitz "the most successful developing countries in the world have achieved their success through trade — through exports." But he has warned that "opening up markets in the developing countries to goods from the advanced industrial countries without full reciprocation" might not work. He quoted the case of Europe when in 2001 it "unilaterally opened up its markets to the poorest countries of the world" and "almost no trade followed." Stiglitz referred to the various trade agreements and opined that "even if trade agreements have been truly free and fair, not all countries would have benefited — or at least benefited much — and not all people, even in the countries that did benefit, would share in the gains. Even if trade barriers are brought down systematically, not everyone is equally in a position to take advantage of the new opportunities."

These are prophetic words indeed. Their potency can be examined with reference to Government of India's (GoI) Look East Policy adopted in 1990-91 after the liberalisation of the Indian economy. By this policy a new orientation is sought to be given to India's foreign policy and trade by a thrust on south Asian and South-East Asian countries. Former Prime Minister Manmohan Singh described India's Look East Policy as "a strategic shift in our perspective" and further clarified that "the age-old India-ASEAN linkages have been given a renewed thrust with the impressive growth of connectivity and the ever increasing flows of tourism between India and ASEAN." In fact ASEAN (Association of South-East Asian Nations) has reached 40 years of its existence in 2007. Recalling the recent events Singh further said that "in the present phase of our Look East Policy, we in India seek to deepen our economic integration by entering into free trade or comprehensive economic partnership agreements, both with ASEAN as a whole and with individual countries of the region."

The very first agreement in this field was the Indo-Myanmar Trade Agreement signed on January 31, 1994. The agreement provided for "establishment of trade on the basis of equality and mutual benefit." The idea was to put in place a "signalling device to monitor the movement of commodities and people." Probably another objective was to provide "an insurance against the perceived threat of Chinese dominance of the region." A memorandum of understanding (MoU) was also signed between Government of India (GoI) and Myanmar on the same day.

These two agreements were followed up by a delegation level talk on June 10, 1994.

Media comments on these events at that time were favourable to Government of India. For example, *Sapra*, which is a serious magazine on insurgency, national security, etc. under the overall guidance of Gen. (Retd.) Shankar Roy Choudhury said that "improvement in relations with ASEAN as well as other key East Asian countries like China and Japan would only heighten regional economic bonds. India's increasing integration with this region will only help ensure that these bonds do not snap at any time in the foreseeable future." The MoU is concerned with cooperation between civilian border authorities of the two countries. The minutes of the talk related to banking and trading arrangements, immigration and customs inspection and timing of border trade. Indo-Myanmar trade was formally launched on April 12, 1995 by the former Union Commerce Minister P. Chidambaram and his Myanmarese counterpart Lt. Gen. Tun Kyi.

It is appropriate that the Look East Policy first touched Myanmar. Myanmar has a common border of 1643 kms with four of India's states, namely, Arunachal Pradesh, Nagaland, Manipur and Mizoram. For trade with China and the South-East Asian countries by the land route all movement has to be through Myanmar. It is true that Myanmar itself is poor. It does not have as much to offer as the other South-East Asian countries except for smuggled precious stones, gold bars, teak wood, arms and drugs. But its strategic geographical location cannot be ignored. That is why India is proposing to build a trans-Asian railway network through Myanmar to Singapore. The Asian road highway is already under construction through Myanmar. The ultimate idea is to link up the Indian ocean with the South China sea.

Writing about India's foreign policy in the Asian context the former Indian Foreign Secretary J.N. Dixit in his "My South Block Years: Memories of a Foreign Secretary" had suggested that our trade relations with Myanmar should be normalised irrespective of the government that may be in power there because that country is geo-strategically important for India. India is now following a pragmatic policy towards the autocratic junta which controls Myanmar, while at the same time supporting the world community's effort towards freeing the Nobel Laureate fighter for democracy, Aung San Su Ki, who is under house arrest in Yangon.

Sixty five years ago, the then Supreme Commander of the Allied Forces, Earl Mountbatten of Burma, also recognised the importance of North-East India in the Asian context when he penned his Report to the

Combined Chiefs of Staff. Much later, I had travelled on the Stilwell Road as far as the Myanmarese army camp on the hill overlooking the Lake of No Return and spent a night in the camp. It was Mountbatten's South-East Asia Command, which built the famous Ledo Road to Kunming in China for supervising the two oil pipelines, respectively, from Kolkata and Chittagong *via* Tinsukia. This road was also used for movement of troops and military supplies. Its construction was overseen by Mountbatten's quarrelsome Deputy Stilwell. But a magnanimous Mountbatten named the road after Stilwell.

According to media report the Stilwell Road has been rebuilt by China up to their border with Myanmar. On the Indian side the road is quite good up to a reasonable distance of the India-Myanmar border. The damaged stretch is now being repaired. It is the portion within Myanmar which will need very extensive rebuilding. Myanmar does not seem to have the resources to do this. Whether India and China will carry out the repairs is a question which has no answer as yet. India has already undertaken several road projects through Myanmar at its cost besides initiating discussion for a rail connection between Jiribam in Assam and Hanoi in Vietnam. All these measures should lead to the success of the Look East Policy and economic development of North-East India through trade.

PART III

Look East Policy and Manipur

16

LOOK EAST POLICY AND MANIPUR

Ksh. Bimola Devi

Introduction

Manipur, one of the North-Eastern states, is in the eastern most part of India, bordering Myanmar (Burma). The early history of Manipur has been characterised by close association with Myanmar in the form of inter-marriage between the two sides on the one hand and conflict or war on the other. Manipuri princesses were given in marriages to the rulers of Burma in order to maintain cordial relations between the two countries. But on the whole, the relations between Burma and Manipur was marked by conflicts resulting in the breakout of wars. There was frequent warfare between the king of Manipur and the ruler of Burma. Sometimes the king of Manipur was able to defeat the Burmese forces and annexed its nearby areas. Again the Burmese forces were also able to extend its political control in Manipur by defeating the Manipuri forces. It happened during 1819 to 1826, popularly known as 'Seven Years Devastation' in the political history of Manipur. As a result of this historical background many Manipuris were taken as prisoners of war. These Manipuris in course of time settled in different parts of Burma, protecting their socio-cultural identities, though surrounded by Burmese culture. In some cases, some Manipuris are also assimilated in the Burmese socio-cultural life even by changing their names.

LEP and Manipur

Since the adoption of Look East Policy by the Government of India, there are changes in the relationship between the Manipuris on the Indian side and the Burmese on the other. Moreh, a town in the Indo-Myanmar border has become a centre of trade and business for the

Manipuris as well as Indians. Selling and buying of goods at Moreh, Manipur on one side and Namphalong, on the Burmese side are going on actively as a daily routine. There is also one town called Tamu in Burma, a few kilometres away from Namphalong where people used to go by Taxi for buying valuable goods.

The object of this chapter is to examine the impact of the Look East Policy on the people of Manipur both in the positive as well as in the negative side.

As a result of trade activities at Moreh and Namphalong, people involved in selling and buying of goods came in contact with one another. The Burmese, particularly, womenfolk selling clothes and other essential items learn Manipuri language and can speak nicely. The Manipuris, in order to bargain and buy commodities from the Myanmar shops have picked up their language and know the weight measure system of Myanmar. It may also be mentioned that the Myanmar women selling fishes (both fresh and dry) are very fond of 'Phanek'.[1] Some Burmese women even wear 'Phanek Mapannaiba'.

There are also some cases of intermarriages among the Manipuris and the Myanmarese at the border area, i.e. Moreh and Namphalong. Due to business activities, the people of Manipur and the Myanmarese are becoming closer, exchanging their ideas not only on business, but even touching their personal likes and dislikes.

Different kinds of goods like electronic goods, high quality woods (Teak, etc.), eatable items including rice, fishes, fruits, etc. essential commodities including clothes, groceries, soaps, etc. have been coming from Myanmar through Moreh over the years. The people of Manipur are taking advantages of these opportunities in order to improve their economic status as well as to meet their financial requirements. Many businessmen have emerged dealing with different trade items by running shops in different areas of Manipur, especially in Imphal. Some important places are Singjamei market and Khawairamband, the main market of Manipur. In these two places, there are rows of shops dealing with goods coming from different foreign countries like China, Japan, Thailand, Malaysia, Singapore, Bangladesh, Myanmar, etc. through Moreh. In addition, in every Manipuri family, one can find the use of clothes for daily use, blankets, soaps, eatable items, etc. from Moreh. In every small shops in and around Imphal, there are always Moreh goods available. This shows that Moreh goods coming from Myanmar are always in demand. Manipuri students persuing their studies outside the state always request their parents to send eatable Moreh goods from time to time. One popular item coming from Myanmar is teak woods.[2] Middle class well-to-do families have furnitures made of teak woods in the form of beds, almirahs, sofa sets as well as in making doors, windows in their newly constructed houses. Many firms dealing in teak and other high quality woods coming from Myanmar have emerged in large numbers particularly in Imphal and other adjoining areas.

In cultural fields, there are development of close ties between Manipur and South-East Asian countries. The Government of Manipur sponsored tour programmes periodically to visit different places of Myanmar and other neighbouring areas. There is also one organisation dealing with the periodical visits of the people of Manipur to places of Myanmar.

A team from Manipur went to attend the 5th Surin International Folk Festival at Surindra Rajbhat University, Surin Province, Thailand from 14th to 22nd January, 2010. It was participated by 14 countries. The Manipur team had participated in the indigenous Folk Dance festival, seminars, interaction programme, etc. thereby coming in close socio-cultural contact with the people from different countries including South-East.[3]

On such visits the members of the team came in contact with the people of Myanmar and earn knowledge about their socio-economic and political position and status. The lost link between the people of Manipur and the Manipuris settled in Myanmar (who had been taken as prisoners of war during Pre-British period) has been restored with emotional feelings. In course of time, some of them are also invited to Manipur to attend socio-cultural functions and conferences. The artists from South-East countries are also invited to participate in the festivals organised by government and non-governmental organisations. Recently, the Tourism Department, Government of Manipur organised festival including dance performance by Thai artists. In the exhibition, there were about 15 Thai stalls selling Thai articles. ISKON[4] also organised Dance festival in February this year and artists from South-East Asian countries including Bangladesh had participated.

It may also be noted that the Look East Policy has given negative impact on Manipur. Moreh is said to be the route of drugs, Heroin No. 4 from the Golden Triangle, the main production Centre. As a result, Moreh has become the centre of transporting Heroin No. 4 from Myanmar to Manipur. Some people from Manipur started to deal with drug business smuggling it to Manipur and earning huge profit out of it. There are many persons who became rich within short time due to this drug business. Even politicians including ministers were not free from this business.[5] In course of time the common people were also affected with drugs and many including women and children became HIV positives. At present there are about 30,000 HIV positive persons in Manipur including about 8,000 positive women.[6] In these days of globalisation, the common villagers have started to grow poppy plants in the hills of Manipur, namely Churachandpur, Chandel and Ukhrul districts. There is widespread Poppy cultivation in these areas. The products are smuggled to other states for manufacturing cocaine. The smuggled Poppy products from Manipur have found place in the International cocaine market. The Narcotic and Affairs of Border (NAB), Government of Manipur in collaboration with the Army and Assam Rifles have started to destroy poppy cultivation. And the Narcotic Control Bureau, very recently found that poppy cultivation was already over in the area between Mapithel Hill Range and Wachetkhaibi Hill Range, Ukhrul district. According to the officials, the product may be about 40,000 kgs of opium.[7]

Another negative impact is the processed small packets of eatable items coming through Myanmar to Moreh, Manipur. These products are mainly from China, Thailand, Malaysia, etc. The youth and small children are very fond of these processed items like Tin fishes, Sunflower seeds, Fruits, etc. available even in small shops in the localities. These may affect the health of the children and youth who are the future hopes of our society. The small arms, the bombs and Grenades coming through Myanmar to Moreh, Manipur is also another important thing to take seriously. It is said that these small arms and others are available at Moreh at a cheaper price. There are also many dealers in these items earning good profits. Even women are also involved in this business because of money. Some women are found taking these from Moreh to Imphal.

Immoral trafficking of women is also another negative impact of Look East Policy. Many women became commercial sex workers due to free trade policy. Even women from Myanmar are entering Manipur illegally for this immoral business. Recently two Myanmarese women were arrested on the way to Imphal by Assam Rifles stationed at Tengnoupal.

Concluding Remarks

On the whole we have to balance between the positive and the negative impact of the Look East Policy on the people of Manipur. The government, non-government organisations have to look into these matters seriously. The weak points should be identified and appropriate measures are to be taken up to minimise the negative impact. On the other hand, the benefits and advantages associated with the Look East Policy should be taken by the Government and the people by building up the required infrastructure and providing facilities and opportunities.

NOTES

1. Phanek is the lower garment worn by Meitei woman. And Phanek Mapannaiba is costly one with hand embroidered borders. Now-a-days there are also machine embroidered ones.
2. Teak woods entered Manipur in pieces. There are dealers in teak woods in Moreh, available in a readymade form in pieces and supplied to the firms in and around Imphal.
3. The source of information is Dr. L. Kunjeswori Devi, Associate Prof., History Department, Manipur University, who had attended and presented a paper at the Folk festival.
4. The International Society of Krishna Consciousness in Manipur was established under the leadership of Dr. T.D. Singh (Damudar Maharaja). It organised seminars, conferences, etc. from time to time, attended by foreigners from different countries.
5. One former Finance Minister, Lokhon Singh was arrested with sizeable amount of heroin at Guwahati by the Narcotic Department a few years back.
6. *The Sangai Express*, March 3, 2010.
7. *Poknapham*, March 22, 2010. In the local market one kg. costs between ₹ 30,000 to ₹ 50,000. In the International market one kg. costs about 20 times higher than local price.

17

INDO-MYANMAR BORDER TRADE

L. Seityabati Devi

Introduction

Trade is an engine of economic growth. It is widely acknowledged that low income countries are characterised by smaller sized markets that fail to absorb sufficient volume of output which in turn leads to low incentive for investment. International trade can expand the size of markets leading to an increase in the incentive for investment and promotion of growth of income and savings through more efficient allocation of resources. It also helps to transform the subsistence sector into a monetised sector by providing a market for farm produce and raises the income level and standard of living of people. Higher levels of output and income achieved through international trade can help to break the vicious circle of poverty and promote economic development.

Trade is a natural economic activity, it is transaction of goods/ products or exchange of things for the purpose of earning and meeting needs. Trade is a flow of commodities from producers to consumers. The commodities can flow between persons, human groups and countries. The exchange of things can take place in kind and cash. If such exchange of goods is done on the international boundary line or in the vicinity of it by the people living there it is known as "border Trade".

Trade among the developing countries arises started mainly after the Second World War with the maturity of the concept of import-substitution strategy adopted by the developed countries on the one hand and the prolonged period of economic slow down in the developed countries mainly after the Second World War on the other hand.

During the post-war period a large number of Intra-Bloc. Trade Forums were formed in different parts of the Glob. After the success story of European Union (EU) in the Western world and the Association of South-East Association Nations (ASEAN) in South-East Asia, regional economic cooperation has become a practical proposition today.

Although their survival and success rates are not so impressive, still we are going with the practice through formation of SAARC and its trade counterpart South Asian Free Trade Area (SAFTA). In 1991, a South Asian Preferential Trading Arrangement (SAPTA) amongst the SAARC member countries was set up with the ultimate goal of achieving a South Asian Free Trade Area (SAFTA). Now, India is planning to switch over from SAFTA to SAPTA with the prime objective of economic liberalisation and world/regional/bilateral/unilateral which have direct impact on the economy of India in general, and Manipur in particular.

Indo-Myanmar Trade

Myanmar is a South-East Asian nation, geographically situated as a bridge between South Asia and South-East Asian Regions. To take an active part in a regional cooperation and present globalisation process Myanmar became a member of BIST-EC (an Economic group made up of South-East Asian and South Asian countries). BIST-EC (comprising Bangladesh, India, Sri Lanka and Thailand — Economic Cooperation) was formed on 6th June, 1997. When Myanmar became a member of the BIST-EC group on 22nd December, 1997, the name of the group changed to BIMST-EC.

India-Myanmar share a common border of 1640 km covering three Indian States in the North-Eastern region, viz. Manipur, Mizoram and Nagaland. Myanmar is the largest country on the mainland South-East Asia, with a land area of 6,76,577 sq.km. It has an international border of 5,858 km with India and Bangladesh in the north-west, China on the north-east, and Laos and Thailand on south-east. On the other hand, north-eastern region of India comprises 8 states, viz. Arunachal Pradesh, Assam, Manipur, Meghalaya, Mizoram, Nagaland, Tripura and Sikkim. Located in the North-East most corner of India, this region has a great strategic importance since, it has common border with five foreign countries, namely Bangladesh, Bhutan, China, Myanmar and Nepal.

India's Look East Policy begins with the Bilateral Trade Agreement between Indo-Myanmar Border Trade Agreement, the Trade between two countries took place in both sides, i.e. Moreh (Manipur) in India and Tamu in Myanmar which was signed on 21st January, 1994 at Delhi. (See Agreement in the Annexure-I) with the following four objectives:

1. To exchange the locally produced commodities by people living along both sides of the Indo-Myanmar border.
2. To deal with the foreign trade transactions in freely convertible currencies or in currencies mutually agreed upon by the two countries, including local currencies or through counter-trade agreement.
3. To make the product available cheaper by transporting by land route.
4. To provide schemes for employment generation by creating facilities of manufacturing activities through free trade zones or joint venture establishments on both sides of the border.

With these main objective in mind the Government of India and the Government of Myanmar have agreed to open borders on the following three sectors:

1. Moreh (Manipur) in India and Tamu in Myanmar.
2. Champhai (Mizoram) in India and Hri in Myanmar.
3. Lungwa (Nagaland) in India and in Myanmar.

The actual follow-up action of trade formally opened on 12th April, 1995 by the former Hon'ble Minister of State for Commerce, Government of India, Shri P. Chidambaram along with his Myanmar counterpart Lt. General Tun Kyi, the Minister of trade, Myanmar. Presently, Moreh is the only Land Customs Station side, i.e. Moreh (Manipur) in India and Tamu in Myanmar.

There are 22 items which have been identified and declared as exchangeable items under the Indo-Myanmar Agreement. These items are: 1. Mustered/Rape seeds, 2. Pulses and Beans, 3. Fresh vegetables, 4. Fruits, 5. Garlic, 6. Onions, 7. Chillies, 8. Species excluding Nut-meg, Mace, Cloves, Cassia and Cinnamon, 9. Bamboo, 10. Minor forest produce excluding teak, 11. Betel-Nut and leaves, 12. Fruit items for local consumption, 13. Tobacco, 14. Tomato, 15. Red brooms, 16. Sesame, 17. Resin, 18. Coriander seeds, 19. Soybean, 20. Roasted sunflower, 21. Katha, 22. Ginger and any other commodity as may be mutually agreed upon between the two sides.

Currency unit and existing currency Exchange Rate of Myanmar and India is different.

A. Currency Unit

India (₹)	*Myanmar (kyat)*
100 paisa = ₹ 1	100 pyas = 1 kyat
₹ 1 to ₹ 1000 note	K 1 to K 1000 note
1 paise to ₹ 5 coin	1 ya to 50 pyas coin
₹ 1 to ₹ 1000 note	1 kyat to 1000 kyat note

B. Currency Exchange Rate Mechanism (Base year 2006)

Indian ₹/US $	*Myanmar*
₹ 1 equal to	15.20 kyat (unofficial)
₹ 8 equal to	1 kyat (official)
US $ 1 equal to	6 kyat (official)
US $ 1 equal to	1000 kyat (unofficial)
₹ 48 equal to US $ 1	

Manipur is one of the states in the region that has international boundaries with Myanmar. Connectivity between the region and Myanmar is growing following the improvement in trading relation between India and Myanmar. Moreh is a border town situated in Chandel district of Manipur. It is 109 km. away from Imphal which is capital city of Manipur.

According to census of India 2001, the population of Moreh stood at 14,962. Moreh is inhabited by different groups like Tamils, Punjabi, Marwari, Jain, Meities, Kukis, Muslim, Mizos, etc. It reported that about 2000 people visit the town daily for trading, shopping, etc. Tamu in Myanmar is border town situated on the other side of Moreh. Moreh in India and Tamu in Myanmar are important trade centres for India and Myanmar. The Border area is close to Golden Triangle (Myanmar-Laos-Thailand) where 20 per cent of world's Heroin (so called number four) is reportedly produced. There are large number of illicit drug traffickers, Intra venous Drug Users (IDUS) and sex workers. Because of this situation, people living between the border town are highly vulnerable to Human Immunodeficiency Virus (HIV), Acquired Immuno Deficiency Syndrome (AIDs) and Sexually Transmitted Diseases (STDs). Two other routes between Manipur and Myanmar exist on the eastern border of Ukhrul district. The route connects Kamjong sub-division of Ukhrul district and Somrah area of Myanmar and the other route connects Chingai sub-division of Ukhrul district with Somrh Tract of Myanmar.

India's "Look East Policy" and several new measures taken by both the Central and State Governments to promote enhanced trade link with

South-East Asia provide Manipur based exports in with a highly competitive advantage due to proximity and available of raw materials. In addition to the raw materials available on the Indian side for export units, Myanmar has abundant natural resources including forest, precious stones, livestock and fishery and agricultural products. The items now imported from Myanmar through barter mechanism are Betel Nuts, Turmeric, Red Kidney Beans (Rajma), Kuth Roots, Gram, Resin, Dry Ginger, etc. The forest of Myanmar has teak coverage of about 6.1 million hectares. Major exportable items include cement engineering goods, transport equipments, Motor Cycles, Iron and Steels, Medicine, Chemicals and allied products, Cotton yarn, etc.

Year-wise volume of trade between Moreh (India) and Tamu (Myanmar) are shown in Table 17.1.

Table 17.1: Trade between Moreh in India and Tamu in Myanmar (*Period of April 1995-2005*)

(In rupees)

Sl.No.	*Period*	*Export*	*Import*	*Total*
1.	April, 1995-March, 1996	10,45,27,782	5,38,99,029	15,84,26,811
2.	April, 1996-March, 1997	11,70,51,137	15,17,65,094	46,88,15,231
3.	April, 1997-March, 1998	22,44,72,930	35,08,34,823	87,53,07,753
4.	April, 1998-March, 1999	5,06,09,710	3,74,39,616	8,80,49,326
5.	April, 1999-March, 2000	3,25,65,827	3,67,97,316	6,93,63,143
6.	April, 2000-March, 2001	5,29,17,530	19,38,523	5,48,56,053
7.	April, 2001-March, 2002	1,25,08,345	8,29,71,255	9,54,78,600
8.	April, 2002-March, 2003	3,66,74,503	12,14,60,746	15,81,35,249
9.	April, 2003-March, 2004	8,74,46,759	8,06,26,946	16,80,73,705
10.	April, 2004-March, 2005	5,38,44,825	5,00,81,759	10,39,26,854
	Total	97,26,19,388	96,78,15,067	194,04,34,495

Export : ₹ 97,26,19,388, say ₹ 97.26 crore.
Import : ₹ 96,78,15,007, say ₹ 96.78 crore.

Source: Department of Commerce and Industries, Government of Manipur.

Though the trade between two countries was formally open 15 years back, the full swing of trade is yet to take off owing to lacks of cross border formalisation of currency exchange rate, unable to control the illegal trade and restriction of exchangeable trade items.

Commodity-wise annual data on exports and imports of informal border trade with Myanmar *via* Manipur are given in Tables 17.2 and 17.3.

Table 17.2: Exports and Imports with Myanmar *via* Manipur

Sl.No.	*Name of Item*	*Unit*	*Volume*	*Value (₹ in lakh)*
1.	Jeans, trousers	nos.	127750	383.25
2.	Gents T-shirts	nos.	109500	273.75
3.	Ladies coat	nos.	109500	328.50
4.	Blankets	pieces	18250	182.50
5.	Emergency Lamp	pieces	3650	53.80
6.	Video cassette	pieces	36500	48.80
7.	Supari (Betel nut)	kg.	480	576.00
8.	Fishing Net	pieces	48000	72.00
9.	Heroin (narcotic)	kg.	480	576.00
10.	Ladies T shirts	nos.	91250	228.12
11.	Lip sticks	nos.	127750	63.87
12.	Perfumes	nos.	73000	87.60
13.	Telephone instrument	nos.	18000	270.00
14.	Shoes	pairs	91250	136.88
15.	Toilet soaps	dozens	9125	7.30
16.	Wrist watch	pieces	73000	146.00
17.	Precious stone (gems)	pieces	—	3600.00
18.	Teak wood	truck loads	1825	912.50
19.	T.V.	nos.	400	56.00
20.	V.C.R.	nos.	150	33.00
21.	V.C.P.	nos.	250	22.50
22.	Gas lighter	nos.	400	0.60
23.	Tape recorder	nos.	1000	8.00
24.	Stereo system	nos.	200	16.00
25.	Radio	nos.	500	2.50
26.	Camera	pieces	3650	54.75

Source: Field Survey.

Table 17.3: Exports from India to Myanmar

Sl.No.	*Name of Items*	*Value (₹ in lakh)*
1.	Bicycle	Varies between ₹ 5500.00 and 60000.00
2.	Iron nails	₹ 10,000
3.	Engineering goods (machinery)	₹ 450.00
4.	Paints	₹ 120.00
5.	Medicine	₹ 40.00
6.	Tea/coffee, horlicks and other confectionery items	₹ 258.00

Note: The value of item No. 6 is combined as separate trade data are not available.
Source: Field Survey.

The following goods are also imported from Myanmar to the tune of about 5 to 6 crore per year. This item-wise detailed quantity could not be provided as they are purchased by the traders from across the border as assorted goods. These items are: 1. Pencil Eraser, 2. House knife, 3. Super

Glue, 4. Folding Scissors, 5. Myanmadi Ball pen, 6. Arrow ball pen, 7. Reynolds Ball pen, 8. Caramie pen, 9. Wingsung Fountain pen, 10. Hero Fountain pen, 11. Table Tennis Ball, 12. Table Tennis Bat, 13. Badminton Shuttle, 14. Staple Machine, 15. Staple pin, 16. Cutting knife, 17. Cutting knife (folding), 18. Pencil, 19. Benain Pencil, 20. Measuring Tape, 21. Scale, 22. Gum, 23. Calculator, 24. Colour Envelop, 25. Map Chart, etc. 26. Pencil Box, 27. Umbrella, etc.

On April 28, 2008 "Memorandum of Understanding" was signed between the Indian Trade Delegation represented by Shri Y. Nabachandra, President,National Identity Protection Committee (NIPCO) and the Border Trade Chamber of Commerce (BTCC), Tamu (Myanmar) represented by U. Hla Maung, Chairman, at Monywa, Myanmar.

Whereas, the trade organisations after deliberate discussions decided to lay down the following agreement to strengthen and enhance economic, trade and investment activities for promotion of trade in goods and services as well as create a transparent, liberal and sincere regimes to explore new areas and develop appropriate measures for closer economic cooperation between the parties. The following broad agreements were adopted:

1. That the trading activity between the two sides is limited to 22 numbers and needs to be expanded. Various Myanmar manufactured items such as Mosquito coils, cotton quilts, soaps, candles, garments, fish, etc. may also be considered for inclusion. Both sides agreed to pursue the matter to their respective authorities from their sides.
2. That two trade related authorities both countries will be requested to organise Official Ground Level meetings at least once in a quarter alternatively at Tamu and at Moreh. The traders of both sides shall also be requested to participate meetings. The first meeting may be scheduled preferably in the month of July 2008 at the convenience of both sides.
3. That NIPCO shall extend all assistances/services for pilgrimage of Myanmar citizens up to the Bodh Gaya similar to a Trade Delegation preferably during November 2008 since BTCC extended full cooperation and coordination while arranging a Trade Delegation up to Mandalay by land route *via* Kalemyo, Kalewa and Monywa by NIPCO (25 April - 2 May, 2008).
4. That NIPCO shall pursue for the availability of Raw Wheat to BTCC by requesting all concerned.
5. That for facilitation and promotion of games and sports, a friendly football match shall be arranged at Tamu for the boys and girls of

both sides within the winter season of 2008 subject to approval of Upper Level.

For increasing trade development a join Declaration was signed by Shri Dhiraj Yumnam, Director of Commerce and Industries, Manipur and U. Aung Kyaw Moe, Deputy Director, Directorate of Border Trade, Tamu, Union of Myanmar, for BTCC, U. Hla Maung, President and NIPCO President Y. Nabachandra on 4th September, 2008 at Imphal, India.

1. That the present list of exchangeable item under barter mechanism is restricted to only 22 items and there is dearth of commodities that can be exchanged/bartered. Export through smuggling of goods bear testimony to this. Traders have been persistently requesting for inclusion of more items, even locally manufactured goods in the list of goods and hence, the lists of exchangeable under barter mechanism need to be expanded by increasing the items. These items are smuggled along this Moreh-Tamu sector and this proposal will definitely promote economic activities, curb illegal activities and also capture Government revenues, on the Indian side.

   This list of items that is now freely exchangeable in Myanmar under Myanmar's export-import policy but proposed for inclusion for expansion on Indian side are:

   (i) Parts of bicycle and automobile, (ii) Cotton yarn, (iii) Stainless steel utensils, (iv) Menthol, (v) Suman Rose Pan Masala (non-tobacco), (vi) Red and white sandal woods, (vii) Sanitary items including tools and equipments both for automobiles and carpentry, (viii) Paints and varnishes, (ix) Iron steel rods, (x) Medicines, (xi) Cotton lungies and handloom cloths, (xii) Cosmetics, (xiii) Chemicals (bleaching powder and insecticides), (xiv) Cement, (xv) Sewing and Embroidery machines, (xvi) nails, (xvii) Mosquito coils, (xviii) Fish, (xix) Essence, (xx) Hing, and (xxi) Paraffin wax.

   The two sides of Ground Level Meet agreed to apprise the matter for expansion of exchangeable items to their respective authorities for consideration in the interest of bilateral trade. Further, "Normal Trade" may also be conducted by both sides to carry out Letter of Credit (L/C) system at Moreh-Tamu sector.
2. That the meeting further considered to review the proposal for holding of such Ground Level Meet at least once in a year instead

of on quarterly basis on mutual invitation and acceptance, at the convenience of both sides.

3. That the intention of the NIPCO was in the spirit of promotional activity of tourism. However, the possibility of pilgrimage of Myanmar citizens to Bodh Gaya could only be possible through Kolkata by Air under the existing law of India and not through land-route *via* Moreh-Tamu sector. NIPCO is, however, ready to extend their full cooperation in obtaining visa from Indian authority if the Myanmar pilgrimage happens to possess valid documents.
4. That under the immigration arrangement, traders of Manipur and Myanmar are permitted to travel to Mandalay and Imphal for a period of seven days, with a valid pass. The meeting resolved to request their respective Governments to make the agreement operational to increase trade as well as mutual understanding.
5. That raw wheat is a restricted item under ITC (HS) classification and as such, NIPCO is unable to arrange for export without the licence from Director General of Foreign Trade.
6. That the meeting welcomed the proposal for holding Trade Fairs on both sides to increase trade as well as tourists traffic. The subject will be submitted to the concerned authority of both sides for consideration.
7. That the border trade has not been running smoothly with stability due to lack of facility of transport, banking and other trade related infrastructure. The delegates resolved to pursue their respective Governments for time bound improvements on these vital infrastructures.
8. That the meeting welcomed the proposal for organising a friendly football match at Tamu for the boys and girls of both sides.

Conclusion

The Indo-Myanmar trade pact signed in 1994 was made operational in 1995. The Look East Policy has began to open the investment opportunities for the two countries Moreh in India and Tamu in Myanmar and North-East States.

REFERENCES

Das, Gurudas; N. Bijoy Singh and C.J. Thomas (2005): *Indo-Myanmar Border Trade*, Akanksha Publishing House, New Delhi.

Das, Gurudas and R.K. Purkayastha (2000): *Border Trade: North-East India and Neighbouring Countries*, Akanksha Publishing House, New Delhi.

Director of Commerce and Industries, Government of Manipur, Imphal.

Government of Manipur (1996): *Industrial Policy of Manipur*.

Kathing, J.S.R. (2005): "Indo-Myanmar Border Trade", in Gurudas Das, N. Bijoy Singh and C.J. Thomas (eds.) *Indo-Myanmar Border Trade: Status, Problems and Potentials*, Akanksha Publishing House, New Delhi.

Meinam Binota (2009): "India's Look East" Policy and "Indo-Myanmar Border Trade", in E. Bijoy Kumar Singh and Ksh. Jhaljit Singh (eds.), *Challenges of Economic Policy in Manipur*, Vol. II, Akanksha Publishing House, New Delhi.

Mero, M.K. (2005): "Indo-Myanmar Border Trade in the Light of India's Look East Policy", in Gurudas Das, N. Bijoy Singh and C.J. Thomas (eds.), *Indo-Myanmar Border Trade: Status, Problems and Potentials*, Akanksha Publishing House, New Delhi.

Prasain, G.P. (2000): "Indo-Myanmar Border Trade and Its Impaction Industrialisation and Infrastructurals Development of Manipur", in Gurudas Das and R.K. Purkayastha (eds.), *Border Trade North-East India and Neighbouring Countries*, Akanksha Publishing House, New Delhi.

——— (2004): "Cross-Border Trade Between Manipur and Myanmar: An Assessment of Formal and Informal Trade", Paper presented in the Two-Day Seminar on "Society and Government in Manipur" organised by the School of Social Sciences M.U. under the sponsorship of Omeo Kumar Das Institute of Social Change and Development, Guwahati, on 2-3 June, 2004 at Earth Science Senate Hall, Manipur University.

——— (2005): "Indo-Myanmar Border Trade: Resource Base and Export Potential of North-Eastern Region", in Gurudas Das, N. Bijoy Singh and C.J. Thomas (eds.), *Indo-Myanmar Border Trade: Status, Problems and Potentials*, Akanksha Publishing House, New Delhi.

Singh, E.; Bijoy Kumar and Ksh. Jhaljit Singh (2009): *Challenges of Economic Policy in Manipur*, Akanksha Publishing House, New Delhi.

States Paper and Agreement on Indo-Myanmar Border Trade.

Th. Bharat Singh: *India's Border Trade with Its Neighbouring Countries with Special Reference to Myanmar*, National Council of Applied Economic Research, New Delhi, Sage Publications.

Th. Priyo Kumar Singh (2005): "Informal Trade Along Myanmar-Manipur (India) Border: Magnitude and Composition of Trade Flows", in E. Bijoy Kumar and Ksh. Jhaljit Singh (eds.), *Challenges of Economic Policy in Manipur*, Vol. II, Akanksha Publishing House, New Delhi.

The Sangai Express, Imphal, 1st May, 2004.

Thingnam Singh Kishan (2006): "India's Look East Policy: The North-East: Prospects, Potentials and Implications", *Alternative Frames*, Vol. I issue II, January-March.

This Joint Declaration signed on this 4th day of September, 2008 at the Conference Hall of Manipur State Guest House, Imphal during the visit of Myanmar Trade Delegation to Imphal on 3-7 September, 2008 between the Myanmar Trade Delegation and the National Identity Protection Committee (NIPCO).

This Memorandum of Understanding signed between the Indian Trade Delegation represented by Shri Y. Nabachandra, President, National Identity Protection Committee (NIPCO) and the Border Trade Chamber of Commerce (BTCC), Tamu (Myanmar) represented by U Hla Maung, Chairman, on this 28-4-2008 at Monywa, Myanmar.

18

LOOK EAST POLICY
Trade Facilities in Manipur

K. Kunjani Devi

Introduction

Look East Policy of Government of India was initiated by Former Prime Minister Narasimha Rao in 1991 for bringing good relationship between India and other states of Eastern Asia. Regarding this relationship more emphasis is given among the 10 members of the Association of South-East Asian Nation (ASEAN). The ten members are — Singapore, Malaysia, Indonesia, Brunei, Burma (now Myanmar), Laos, Vietnam, Cambodia, Philippines and Thailand. India has close historical relationship, similarity in culture and religious outlook with the ASEAN states. So, India can easily make new friendship and good relationship with these states because of neighbourhood. Moreover, India Government is trying to bring economic development of the North-East Indian states by linking up with the South-East Asian countries.

Why Trade Facilities in Manipur

The geographical realities in Manipur invites the state to be the trade centre or market place under the Look East Policy of India Government. So far Manipur is not possessing good trade centre because of bad communication system, lack of capital both from the sides of the Government as well as private entrepreneurship, shortage of natural resources and absence of industrial technology with trained and skilled labour. In addition, the insurgency problem, loots, bands and blockades in both the National Highways No. 39 and 53, trade in Manipur is not a success one. In short Manipur needs safe and secular trade routes.

With the introduction of Look East Policy of India Government we can guess that the new plan of constructing the Trans Asian Railway and Trans Asian Highway will bring certain benefits to Manipur for becoming trade centre when they start functioning. For the inter-global Railway and Highway there should be proper security throughout day and night. The Trans-Asian Railway should be very important route in Manipur. This Railway starts from South Korea and runs through North Korea, China, Vietnam, Laos, Cambodia, Thailand, Myanmar, Manipur Valley, Barak valley and enters Bangladesh and finally reaches the centre of India. From India it goes to Pakistan, Iran, Iraq, Turkey, Russia, Finland and lastly connects with the European rail tract. The estimated length of this Railway is 1,40,000 km.

The Trans-Asian Highway is also going to be a very important route in Manipur. One side of the Highway will reach Chitangong, an important port of Bangladesh. This port will be the nearest sea route for the North-East India. It will take only 10 (ten) hours to reach Imphal from the Chittangong Port.

The two international ways will be very valuable and interesting to the people of Manipur. The first rail in Manipur will run through the heart of Manipur valley by fetching the costly and cheapest articles of different varieties with many different sections of people from different parts of the world. The trade centres or markets of Manipur will be piled up with many wonderful trade commodities and different varieties of food items.

The Myanmar Government recently makes a new plan of Kandal Project in the state for a linking route with Mizoram through Manipur. This route will more enrich trade in Manipur. Larg forest products of the North-East India will be easily exported through this route and will improve the economic condition of the area in particular and that of India in general. With the initiation of Look East Policy, Former Indian Prime Minister Manmohan Singh expresses that it is no need for India to go to Western countries for financial help (capital) and industrial technology instead we have to go to Singapore, Thailand, Hong Kong, Tiwan, Korea, Japan, etc.

Analysis of the Policy in Manipur

India Government should have a blue print containing different plans, schemes and policies for Look East Policy. The state keeps this policy in order to bring a good Asian Economic Community. But the policy gives restless to the Manipuries as they do not know the policy clearly. Larger

P.C. of the Manipuries do not want to involve in the process of globalisation. This is the reason why the Manipuries are feeling terror and puzzle to hear the Trans Asian Railway, Trans Asian Highway and Look East Policy. Intellectuals and academicians of Manipur are afraid of the lack of proper infrastructures like capital, good political decision, etc. for the implementation of Look East Policy in the State.

The Government of Manipur should take up proper measures for people's involvement in the policy. The political elites, social elites and economic elites should aware the problems of influxion of foreigners in the state. People from the west and east will visit Manipur daily and a sea deep change will take place in all aspects of life. We should not always be lookers on the changes rather we should change ourselves in constructive way but not in destructive one. The policies and programmes of the Government of Manipur in running public administration should be changed in making good human resources, capital and production by taking aids from both national and international sources without any room of corruption in functioning. Manipur will be the international transit-point of the Western countries, the Middle East and South Asian countries.

Measures to be Taken by the Government of Manipur

For involving in the Look East Policy of India, for a better Manipur, the Government of Manipur should realise the situation in Manipur being the International Transit-Point. By taking the chance of this Transit-Point, Government of Manipur positively has to set-up various attractive markets for: (A) Food stuffs, fruits and medicinal plants totally based on agriculture and good communication system. (B) Handloom and handicrafts totally based on capital and skilled labour in order to get trade facilities in the region.

(A) *Food Stuffs, Fruits and Medicinal Plants*

(i) Market for food stuffs and fruits: Manipur is an agricultural land where 90 per cent of population is cultivators who depend on Monsoon for their occupation. Still Manipur is importing rice from Assam, Bihar, West Bengal, Uttar Pradesh, etc. as she has small areas of cultivable land. Moreover, Government of Manipur is taking up no plan or scheme for double cropping and so on. Consequently, the cultivators spending their time lazily for eight months in a year except June and July (plantation period) and November to December (reaping season). If the Government of Manipur has taken up well plan for agriculture with highly equipped scientific technology, the farmers will work throughout the year as they have the ability to work and desire of earning the whole year. This is known from the National Rural Employment Scheme (NRES) in which the unsalaried people are rushing for getting job.

(ii) The rice of Manipur is noted for good taste. Visitors to Manipur whether male or female are of the opinion that he/she will bring at least 1/2 kg of Manipur rice for his/her husband/wife for its good taste in spite of their heavy luggage. If we have good markets for food stuff people on earth will know the value and taste of Manipuri rice.

(iii) Another variety of rice available in Manipur is Chakhao in Manipur language meaning tasteful rice having good smell, sweet taste and black in colour. This rice is facing world demand and also costly one. Outsiders coming in Manipur favour the Kheer of this rice and the roti/puri made by the flour of this rice because of its good smelling while eating. The Manipuris can pile up the markets of food stuffs with these rice only if our Government arranges for new developments in the agricultural sector of the state.

(iv) Manipuries are facing problems of bad communication system of the area. Out of the nine districts of the state five are in hilly areas where there is rare motorable roads. Many valuable fruits are rotten at the feet of the trees as people cannot bring them for sale because of bad communication system. Only a small cultivable hill areas are reserved for planting pineapples. Pineapple in Manipur is noted for good taste and it is good for health also. It is used as medicine for cancer treatment. We can arrange many trade centres for these fruits and their juice if we have good communication system and modern technology of preparing fruit juice in our state.

(v) Uu-Morok, a capsicum type chilli and a fruit of 2-5 ft. high chilli plant, having good smell and good quality can abundantly be planted in all the districts of Manipur. This chilli can be exported from Manipur if the Government of Manipur gives attention in its plantation. This type of chilli is facing world demand throughout the year both as fresh and dry one.

(vi) Manipur is the single place growing Yongchak (a curry fruit) in India. The flowers are used for salad and fruits are used for curry item as salad, chatney and cooked one. Non-Manipuris living in Manipur are very fond of this fruit as cooked curry. This fruit can also be used throughout the years through ready made process and can be sold throughout the year. Manipur can make a good market for this fruit through good agriculture.

(vii) Manipur is a hilly state having a small area of plain at the very middle of the region. There are many wild grown medicinal plants and husk which can cure many chronic diseases like cancer. Students from several universities of India are coming to Manipur for these medicinal plants and husks for their scientific research work. Manipur can make trade centres for these medicinal items at high cost if the Government takes keen interest in the matter.

(B) *Handloom and Handicrafts*

Mark for Handloom and Handicrafts: In Manipur small industries play an important role in bringing continuous trade through indigenous handloom and handicrafts products of the state. Handloom and handicrafts is a women occupation in which our women have the skill of producing good knitting and embroidery works that can easily attract people to be good buyers. Foreigners are ready to buy these handloom products at the first sight. Government of India and many banks in India are ready to give credit loans for handloom in Manipur.[1] In this connection we can mention examples of some Service Institutes of handloom and handicrafts in Manipur.

1. Ningthibi Collection (at Nagamapal, Imphal): In 1994 Smt. Ng. Bimolata, an excellent knitting and embroidery artist, established knitting and embroidery centre named Bimolata's Creation with a loan of ₹ 95,000 only from Prime Minister Rojana Yoga (PMRY). She gives intensive training to some educated and unemployed girls and women of the society.

Bimolata participated in many exhibitions/melas in different cities of India, i.e. Delhi, Mumbai, Bangalore, Chennai, Pune, Hyderabad, etc. from 2002 October, Imphal Exhibition Bimolata's Creation came to be known as Ningthibi Collection. It is a nice and precious store of knitting and embroidered materials of bridal fineries and home furnishing such as inaphee (Chaddar), bed sheets, mosquito nets, cushion, quilt, pillow with cover, curtains and ready-made items of designed lady blouse, salawar kameez of traditional weaving designs, dupatta, saree, skirts, wrap round and natural grass (Kouna in Manipuri) bags, etc.

Now Ningthibi Collection has employed more than 200 females at different units inside and outside Manipur. The collection is also exporting her goods not only in India, but also to Australia, South Africa, Philippine, etc. In short, Ningthibi Collection has got world recognition through a self-made person. In 2004 she was honoured with National Award 2002 for Small Scale Entrepreneur presented by Dr. Manmohan Singh, then Prime Minister of India at New Delhi in a function organised by Small Industries Development Organisations, Ministry of SSI, Government of India.

In 2005 she was honoured with Excellence and Best Entrepreneur Award by State Bank of India, at New Delhi and also was declared her to sponsor a Design Training Course in Philippine.[2] Bimolata (47 years old) wants to solve the unemployment problem of women and to maintain their livelihood through this organisation. She will able to continue her organisation so long as there is (i) Capital, (ii) Raw materials, (iii) Labour, and (iv) Market.[3]

2. Ketawn (at Yumnam Leikai, Imphal): Handloom and handicrafts work for girls is running from 1981 in Ketawn under the proprietorship of Mrs. Sorojini Devi very smoothly. Two blocks of hostel for Weaving and Embroidery of 50 members each are maintained by paying full salary. It exports handloom and handicrafts products inside and outside India throughout the year.[4]

3. Kasturba Gandhi Institute for Development, Manipur (Kwakeithel Moirangpurel, Imphal): Under the Managing Directorship of Dr. O. Sareeta, this institute had been successfully producing since 2003 handloom and handicraft articles through different three vocational units of crafts, tailoring and embroidery by taking enough fund from the Gandhi Smriti and Darshan Samriti, New Delhi. Girls and women of 15-35 years are getting rotation training for two months in the institute with reasonable stipend. After passing the training they can run the same vocational unit through Self-Help Group of 10 (ten) members and earn soundly. Success reports from New Delhi come for every two (2) months. So long, the fund is available Manipuri women are ready to furnish the handloom and handicraft services.[5]

There are also many embroidery and knitting centres in Manipur producing different designs of traditional dresses to be used only at the time of religious and cultural functions. In hill areas of Manipur also the tribal people (nearly 33 legally recognised ethnic groups) have their own cultural heritage. All the ethnic groups have their own respective traditional dresses and designs. Any outsider wants to purchase the tribal dresses for their attractiveness and comfort. For example, in Manipur, the Muslims, Meiteis and the non-Manipuris use the woollen Naga/Kuki Shawls during winter for getting warmness.

Conclusion

With the success of the Look East Policy of the Government of India Manipuri women will easily able to pile up the markets of Manipur with lungee, woollen shoe, etc. which are highly demanded by the foreigners. Because there are many skilled labourers who can work throughout the year if they get capital, raw materials and markets. The social analysists are of the opinion that the home weaving or cottage industries should be changed into cooperative centres or semi-governmental industrial centres with the help of the Manipur Government. The bureaucrats should not work only on table or paper and ready for cable T.V. or camera. They will go together and work together with the poor, helpless and needy people of the state for bringing good communication system, proper agricultural programme and well sponsorship in handloom and handicrafts centres.

The success and failure of being a goods trade centre or market place in Manipur under the Look East Policy of the Indian Government lies in the sincerity and hardworking of the Government of Manipur along with the help of the people of the region. No outsider will take responsible for bringing civilization of Manipur.

REFERENCES

1. Lanau U. (2010): "Development Handlooms and Handicrafts in a Mini Economic Zone, largely projectised", *Poknapahm*, Local Paper, March 30, 2010, p. 4.
2. Waikhom, Pradeep (2007): "Success Story of Ng. Bimolata Devi: Imphal", p. 2.
3. Interview with Ng. Bimolata Devi, Secretary, Ningthibi Collection, Imphal on March 22, 2010.
4. Interview with Robita Khurkhul, Hostel Warden Knitting Block, Ketawn on March 21, 2010.
5. Interview with Dr. O. Sarita Devi, Managing Director, Kasturba Gandhi Institute for Development, Manipur on March 20, 2010.

19

LOOK EAST POLICY AND MANIPUR
Opium Cultivation and Illicit Trade

T. Ninghorla Zimik

Introduction

Look East Policy (LEP) was first initiated in 1991 with the objective of bringing economic reforms by establishing economic linkages with the countries of the East and South-East Asia and thereby to strengthen our relations and provides India with strategic safety and economic strength. North-East India is surrounded on almost all sides by other foreign countries starting with Myanmar in the east, China and Bhutan in the north and Bangladesh to the south and west. North-East India (NE) is connected with the mainland India's through what is known as the 'chicken neck' —Siliguri corridor. The LEP is expected to provide enormous opportunities and challenges to the nation, especially to the India's North-Eastern region due to its proximity to the countries of the East and South-East Asia. In the national conference on India's Look East Policy held in Guwahati from 7th to 9th October, 2007. The then former Union External Affairs Ministry, Shri Pranab Mukherjee in his key note address said that "we are all aware of the geo-economic potential of the North-East region as gateway to East and South-East Asia. By casually integrating this region through cross border market access, the NE states can become the bridge between the Indian economy and what is beyond doubt the fastest growing dynamic region in the world. NE is one region into whose progress and development we can dovetail over Look East Policy" (*NE Window*, p. 15). The opening of the trade under the policy has started giving great dividends by establishing our trade with the East and South-East Asian countries. In this respect, we need to study the reality of North-East as to how far it had benefited. The harsh reality of LEP was brought out openly by the then DONER, former Minister, Shri Mani Shanker Aiyar in his valedictory address to the Conference. He stated that "the harvest of the initiative (LEP) is so far nil as far as the North-East is concerned. The policy still does not have a document although, it is there for one and a half decades. Nobody has pointed out the true obstacles, NE militancy, violence and lack of security in the implementation of the policy." However, he concluded his speech with a note of optimism that "North-East India if linked to SE Asia and SW China, can magically get transformed. Actually, NE can become the arrowhead of growth and prosperity if plans and strategies are drawn well" (*NE Window*, pp. 16-17).

So far in the nearly two decades of implementation of LEP, no drastic development is visible in North-East except some trade fairs and cultural exchange programmes. Moreover, most of the North-Easterners are not aware of this policy which implies that the project is not yet fully implemented. NE is one of the most underdeveloped and neglected regions of India in spite of its rich natural resources, bio-diversity, unique feature, customs and cultures and geo-political situation. If Government of India has genuine concerns for NE, it should have look NE first and then Look East as opportunity of development. NE India is a big hindrance to the success of LEP. To remove the constraints and make the LEP fully operational, infrastructure must be developed as many foreign countries excepting Thailand are reluctant to invest in NE due to lack of infrastructure. Physical infrastructure particularly power, roads and railways; service infrastructure like customs, rural banking, warehousing, telecom services, etc. are to be made customer friendly. Border management issues have to be reviewed from time to time and tourism has to be geared up and made seamless. Governance issues have to be settled. Apart from developing infrastructure to promote inner connectivity, India is trying to do the same in SE Asia. India has constructed 165 km Tamu-Kalewa-Kalemyo road under the overall supervision of the Union Government with the financial assistance of ₹ 122 crore. Other than this, India is assisting in the construction of the proposed trilateral highway project to connect Moreh in India to Maisot in Thailand *via* Began in Myanmar. The Kaladan Multi-Modal Transit Transport Facility is an ambitious project connecting eastern ports and Sittwe in Myanmar and thereafter through river and road transport to Mizoram will serve as an alternate route for the region. In addition, the project of laying railway lines from Jiribam in Manipur to Hanoi in Vietnam, whose foundation stone was laid on November 19, 2004 by former PM Dr. Manmohan Singh. After the declaration of LEP, Nathu

La Pass was also opened after 44 years of closure for trade with Tibet and China. There is also a strong proposal to reconstruct Stilwell Road to connect Brahmaputra valley with Myanmar and China. The Champhai (Mizoram) Hri (Myanmar) road and a third opening in Nagaland aim at promotion of Indo-Myanmar border trade. Once the proposed Trans-Asian highway and railways network is completed and made functional, it will open up great opportunities for having unprecedented trade and commercial relations with the South-East Asian countries and China. With the aim of creating a big trading block, India is moving towards Comprehensive Economic Cooperation Agreement (CECA) covering Free Trade Agreement (FTA) in goods, services, investments and identification of the areas of economic cooperation. By giving overall improvements in infrastructure, NE states can become significant player in any sub-regional cooperation as it is surrounded on almost all sides by adjoining foreign countries. To obtain the maximum benefit from the policy, the NE region should develop in industry and other sectors which will attract the foreigners. India should be able to produce and supply what the East needs. Thailand has come out with "Look West Policy" keeping track with India's LEP. We have so far discussed on the improvement of infrastructure but the most important factor is how to contain insurgency in the North-East. Until and unless NE is made a peace zone, success of LEP is skeptical. Anyhow, to make the LEP operational and successful, the process of peace and development should go hand in hand as they are like two faces of the same coin.

Manipur: Opium Cultivation and Illicit Trade

North-East India and Myanmar share a common border of 1640 kms covering four states, Arunachal Pradesh, Mizoram, Manipur and Nagaland and out of this Manipur share a common border of 398 kms long porous border. The border trade agreements between Government of India and Myanmar was signed on January 21st, 1994 and trade through Tamu-Moreh route was officially inaugurated at Tamu on April 12th, 1995 by the then Myanmar Trade Minister Lt. Gen. Tunkyi and India's then former Commerce Minister Mr. P. Chidambaram. As the Indian Government has initiated Look East Policy, the Myanmar military regime, the State Peace and Development Council (SPDC) has also been taking keen interest in bilateral trade with India through Moreh, which is India's gateway to the South-East Asian countries. The opening of border trade has paved the way for enhanced tourism, cultural exchange, trade and economic ties.

At the same time it has made NE states a major transit point for drugs originating from Golden Triangle (GT). It has become impossible to check everyone who comes for border trade daily. According to intelligence sources, the opening of the border trade has led to a sharp increase in opium cultivation in Myanmar extending to the border areas of Manipur where poppy cultivation has been extensively cultivated. Fertile soil, vast economic disparity and availability of cheap labour, etc. are mainly the attraction and advantage of investors to encourage poppy cultivation, which is then smuggled out to notorious Golden Triangle through the porous into Myanmar border for producing heroin. The Golden Triangle is an area around 35,000 sq. kms. that overlaps the mountainous region of Myanmar, Laos, Thailand, Vietnam and Yunnan province of China. The GT is one of the most extensive opium producing areas in the world since 1950s. Opium based products from Myanmar, the second largest illicit opium producing in the world after Afghanistan, are merchandised to the rest of the world through Kunming, thus serves as a key destination and transshipment point for the illicit opium trade, whereas Thailand, Cambodia and Vietnam are the main transit corridors from Myanmar to Kunming. After Kumning, it reaches Hong Kong, Macau and then to Taiwan, Indonesia, Malaysia, Singapore, Japan, South Korea, Nigeria, Australia, Europe, North America and so on. The production of opium in the GT has dropped dramatically by 29 per cent in 2006 bringing the total decline in the region since 1998 by 85 per cent. Laos and Thailand are almost free from opium and the GT produces only about 5 per cent of the world opium. Myanmar which remains as the world's second largest opium cultivator, has a decline of its opium cultivation from 165,800 hectares in 1993 to 27,000 hectares in 2007 (*Imphal Free Press*, March 6, 2009 issue).

With the decline in poppy cultivation and production in the GT and Myanmar, poppy cultivation has started booming in NE Manipur and Arunachal Pradesh. During the interview at the State Narcotic Affairs Border Office, with NAB SPS. Amirlal Sharma said that the State's Narcotic Affairs Border Officials in association with the Assam Rifles for the first time destroyed poppy plants cultivated in an around 2 acres of land at Shajik Tampak, Manipur, which is now, the liberated zone from the militants. Moreover, for the first time in the New year 2010, Personnel of NABs, State police department assisted by 7th battalion of Manipur Rifles and 4th IRB destroyed poppy plants worth ₹ 18 lakh being widely grown across the slopes of Nongmeiching hill measuring around 5 acres of land in Senapati district of Manipur from January 18th of 2010 onwards. Cultivation of poppy plants is not allowed in Manipur as per the Narcotic and Psychotropic Substance Act, 1985. Despite the restriction and prohibition, villagers of Terakhong and Heikon have been planting poppy plants as one of their means of livelihood for more than two years. Extract from poppy plants is said to be used in manufacturing not only cocaine but also heroin. The media persons while interacting with Pao, Baite (42), the chief incharge of Terakhong village in Imphal East district disclosed that poppy cultivation was taken up on the side of the hill covering an area of around 6 to 7 sangam (approx. 2 hectares). He further informed the media persons that the cultivation of the last season had been harvested. The yield was around 1 kg of cocaine per sangam and 1 kg of cocaine fetches around ₹ 30,000 in the local market. According to him, the buyers are mostly from state capital Imphal. Heikon villagers are also involved in the poppy cultivation. The Secretary of the village L. Apao while interacting with the media persons expressed that the villager's now realised that poppy cultivation is illegal. However, the villagers are compelled to continue planting as they could not meet their requirement from cultivation of paddy. Acknowledging the grievances being faced by the villagers, All Manipur Anti-Drug Association (AMADA) has started helping the villagers in collaboration with State authorities in creating general awareness on the harmful effects of drugs in Manipur society even by producing courtyard plays based on the theme "Opium war" that took place in China long ago" (*Sangai Express* issue, January 2010, pp. 1-2).

Table 19.1: Destruction of Illicit Poppy/Ganja in Manipur
(*From January to February, 2010*)

Location	*Areas/No. of Plants*	*Approx. Value (in ₹)*
Baruni Hills, Imphal West	6 lakhs/5 acres	18 lakh
Thingthangjang and T. Khunao Village, Churachandpur district	40 acres	1 crore 15 lakh
Tussan Village, Saikul, Churachandpur district	1 lakh 5 thousand plants, 2 acres	4 lakh
Bungpu Hill Range adjoining Tonau Chepaun, Malkot Villages, Ukhrul District	18 acreas and 18,00,000 plants	6 lakh
Ganja: Somdal, Huimi Khanao, Phalee, Tuinem Phungcham, Paoyi and Paorei Villages	14-15 acres	45 lakh
Khongtak Chajol and Thingbajao Villages, Chandel district	235 hectares (poppy)	5 crore 132 lakh

Source: State's Narcotic Affairs Borders Official Records.

According to NCB, Regional Unit Imphal official reports, Poppy plantation started w.e.f. 2009 and the total area under cultivation was 3000 to 9000 acres of land getting crude products of 60,000 to 80,000 kgs of opium. The value of opium in the local market is ₹ 30,000 to ₹ 50,000 per kg and in the international market it ranges from ₹ 3,00,000 to ₹ 5,00,000 per kg. Opium products and other narcotic substances are clandestinely carried out through the unauthorised routes and along the Indo-Myanmar porous border. Ganja (Marijuana) is also smuggled mostly through village routes. The overall seizure of ganja valued by NCB of India (Imphal unit) during the year 2009 April to 2010 March was ₹ 89,20,000 (eight crore nine lakh twenty thousand rupees). As the production is increasing alarmingly, the NCB has redouble its efforts in investigating any laboratory running across the state. According to NCB legal action under the Narcotic Drugs and Psychotropic Substance Act, 1985 (NDPS Act, 1985) the accused or convicted is given a rigorous imprisonment for 5 years with a fine of ₹ 50,000, freeze of the accused/convicted persons movable/immovable properties and Bank accounts, etc. The NCB Intelligence officer R.K. Ibungohal of Imphal unit during the interview informed that the poor tribal villagers living on the Indo-Myanmar border are cultivating poppy on a large scale and for their sustenance, some of them are exchanging the raw products through barter system, e.g. poppy seeds exchanged for rice, etc. Most of the poppy cultivation sites are located in the inaccessible Indo-Myanmar border and giving exact figures and data of its production and area of plantation cannot be ascertained. However, the AMADA along with NAB, after gathering intel inputs visited Thawai village under Senapati district to oversee the plantation areas. But by the time they reached Thawai village all the poppy plants have already been harvested. Meanwhile the AMADA members after reaching the village discovered that, had it not been harvested it would take more than 3 months in scything the poppy plants.

It is also reported in the local dailies that poppy products from Manipur interior areas have direct links with drug/heroin manufacturing units in the Golden Triangle. Apart from local elements, drug mafias from the neighbouring foreign countries such as China, Myanmar, Bangladesh, Nepal are said to have direct contacts in many remote villages of Manipur and investing huge amount of money for the poppy growers. They came as tourist and secretly visited the plantation site to keep their nefarious activities under wrap. The soil texture and weather conditions of Manipur is said to be very suitable in the cultivation of high yielding poppy varieties as well as ganja with the latter narcotic plant well known within and outside the state. As per the NCB report, it is just a matter of an hour or two from the cultivation side to cross the border where the yield consignment could reach clandestine laboratories in GT, where heroin is manufactured with different brand names as 'Tiger' and 'Cobra'. According to NCB source, the Government agencies are put on high alert to curb the illicit activities and plantation. NCB is targeting to completely do away with the poppy plantation in Manipur by 2011. However, in some exceptional cases, growing of poppy plantation is permitted and licitly cultivated in the states of Madhya Pradesh, Rajasthan and Uttar Pradesh under a stringent licensing regime which is operated by Central Bureau of Narcotics. India is the world's sole producer of opium gum for medicinal uses. Diversion of opium illicit crop is one of the sources of opium availability in the illicit market. Afghanistan is the world's largest produce of illicit opium. To eradicate and wipe out poppy plantation completely, the present Afghan government have the portfolio of Anti-drug Minister. They also formed Afghan eradication force and actively doing poppy eradication campaign and destroying opium plants. Afghanistan produces 93 per cent of the world's illicit opium production in the year 2008. Other producers of illicit opium are Myanmar, Laos, Pakistan, etc. Area under illicit opium cultivation was 1,57,000 hectares in Afghanistan followed by Myanmar 28,500 hectares and Laos 1,600 hectares (*NCB Annual Report*, 2008, pp. 3-4.).

The All Manipur Anti-Drug Association (AMADA) has also begun a massive campaign to convince poppy growers to switch over to other alternative plantation like the cereals and vegetables under the objective of sustained campaign to prevent the younger generation from being caught in the drug web and prevent Manipur turning into another like GT of the East. They are very active in anti-drug drive and alcoholism. According to AMADA and NAB information, the raw poppy seeds are boiled and consumed orally which gives the same ecstasy like heroin. Some youngsters directly injected the fluids of the poppy seeds in the vein which resulted in complications of blood flow in the vein. State Narcotic Control SP Mr. Amirlal Singh, and his Myanmar counterpart are meeting after every three months or earlier as to how the opium cultivation could be wiped out from these two areas. For the Myanmar the target year is 2013 and for Manipur is 2011.

Illicit Transit Routes

A flourishig narcotic trade along India's border with Myanmar is helping finance scores of rebel armies to procure arms for their military campaigns, an officials said "In India's North-East, narcotics trade and insurgency are close allies with militants trading in heroin and other forms of drugs to procure arms to continue their secessionist campaigns" (*War on Drugs in Manipur*, p. 8). Poppy grown on the Indian side of the border is transported into Myanmar for refining and the refined heroin either finds its way to Thailand and is routed back into the NE. The lucrativce drugs trade is the primary source of finance for many rebel groups in NE. A number of frontline rebel groups have based inside Myanmar and operate in tandem with some ethnic rebel groups in the Kachin region. With the increased vigilance in the border, drug traffickers are following unconventional methods to smuggle drugs from Myanmar. The drug peddlers use cows and buffaloes by force feeding plastic bags filled with heroin and other synthetic drugs. The drug consignment sealed inside the plastic bags are then collected in the dung or by slaughtering the animals to retrieve the packets. According to police reports there are traffickers using fish apart from cows and buffaloes to conceal packets containing drugs in the daily border trading point (*Ibid.*, pp. 12-13).

China is certainly the main transshipment destination for heroin from Myanmar but is not only the one as NE India also draws some of the traffics. From the poppy fields of North-Eastern Myanmar, opium as well as heroin is transported by road through Bhamo, Lashio and Mandalay to NE India which shares 1,463 km border with Myanmar. Heroin trafficking across the Indo-Myanmar border was first noticed in the early 1990s and 6 heroin laboratories were discovered in western Myanmar in 1992. There are also main trafficking routes leading to western Myanmar to the Indian states of Nagaland, Mizoram and Manipur. The foremost route begins in Mandalay, continuing through Monywa and Kalewa where it splits northward to the Tamu-Moreh border crossing the Indian National Highway No. 39 in Manipur and Southward to Hri-Champhai into Mizoram. Further north, Homalin is reached all the way from Bhamo and serves as springboard into Nagaland from where the heroin goes to Assam and through Dispur, join other shipments bound for Kolkata and the rest of Indian sub-continent (*Ibid.*, p. 26).

With the opening of trade routes under LEP, the diversification of drug trafficking routes increased together with the diversification of illicit drug production. Other than illicit drug trafficking it is also recently discovered that a large quantity of orchids and ginseng roots from Manipur are being smuggled out through the porous Indo-Myanmar border to China which has a high demand. The smuggled orchid varieties are abundantly found in Chandel district. Other than this, rare Ginseng variety and other medicinal plants which are found in Ukhrul district find access to SE-Asian countries too. As far as possible, the forest department authorities should skip smuggling network and entail illicit export of the states rarest asset and products.

Along with other illicit trade, the flesh trade is very active in Moreh town and Tamu. The *Sangai Express* local daily (15th December, 2009) put in the headlines as 'Moreh Turning into Sex Workers Paradise'. Close affinity and proximity of the border towns of Moreh on the Indian side and Tamu of Myanmar as well as easy accessibility into Moreh from other side is creating a big headache to health officers as the influx of health workers pouring into Moreh are on the rise. There is also major danger as most of the sex workers are habitual drug users who indulge in immoral act to earn money. The women's engaged in flesh trade pass through the international border Gate No. 2 posing as domestic helper and once they are inside Moreh, Hotel owners/runners take charge of them. NGOs sources also accounted about 30 sex-workers entering on a daily basis with each of them providing service to about 3/4 customers in a single day. In a significant disclosure the sources insisted that the sex-workers are paying monthly tax of ₹ 500 to the Myanmar army whereas Indian security personnel are said to form a substantial number of customers for the sex-workers. As per record maintained by an NGO run with funding of MACS, Moreh is home to about 260-270 registered sex-workers of whom many of them are young girls. Out of these 160-170 are said to be Myanmarese nationals (*TSE*, 15th December, 2009).

On the security front and other matters related matters, Vice President Dr. Hamid Ansari along with MoS for Defence Mr. Pallam and some journalists visited Mandalay in the month of February 2009 and met Myanmar military Junta General Than Swe and other top military leaders decided to give a fresh impetus to security, trade and economic ties between the two countries. They also agreed on the need for more frequent meetings at the field level to combat the insurgents and maintain peace at the border. General Than Shwe also assured Indian delegation that Myanmar would not allow its territory to be used by the ultras to target India. During his sojourn, the Vice-President also inaugurated Optical fibre link between Moreh Town (India) to Mandalay in Myanmar.

To do away with all the illicit plantation and trade we need to find out the potentials and encourage to develop, and in this respect the sincere initiative from both the State and the Central Governments are highly expected by giving alternative means of livelihood to the common and marginalised people. Though Manipur is an industrially backward state, it has a distinct advantage in the GoI: 'Look East Policy' as it is the gateway to South-East Asia. Manipur being gifted with suitable agro-climatic conditions is producing various food and cash crops, fruits and vegetables which are organic in nature has a great prospects for establishing food processing industries and installing cold storage facilities; establishing of cane and bamboo industry. Opening a high facility plant for meat preservation, cement, chromite, limestone and serpentine plants. Establishment of IT park similar to STPI (Software Tech Park of India) in Manipur due to its high technical manpower can boost skill development and innovation. There is also immense potential for animal hides and skin facility, crafts, pottery, handlooms, etc. In the tourism sector there is scope for large scale development of eco-tourism, adventure tourism, cultural tourism, etc. All the potential areas should be strengthened and make it functional and operational and thereby revolutionise and transform the socio-economic lives of the people. Bringing development in this perspective will enable the people of Manipur in particular and North-East in general to enjoy the dividends of the Look East Policy and make the policy a success.

REFERENCES

Annual Report (2001-02): Narcotic Affairs Bureau, Ministry of Home Affairs.
Annual Report (2008): Narcotic Affairs Bureau, Ministry of Home Affairs.
Janahanbi Barua (2008), *India Vietnam Railway Line Through Manipur.*
North-East Sun, (February 1-5, 2009).
Thabatombi, I.O. (2008): *War on Drugs in Manipur.*
The North-East Window (November 15, 2007).
Thoiba (2005): *Indo-Myanmar Border Trade Through Moreh.*

Newspapers

Imphal Free Press, March 6, 2009.
The Sangai Express, January 19, 2010.
The Sangai Express, February 13, 2010.
The Sangai Express, March 15, 2010.
The Sangai Express, December 30, 2007.

Persons Interviewed

1. R.K. Ibugousana Singh, Intelligence Officer Narcotics Control Bureau, Regional Unit, Imphal.
2. S. Amirlal Sharma, SP, State Narcotics and Affairs of Border, Manipur.
3. Executive Members of AMADA.

20

LOOK EAST POLICY AND ITS IMPACT ON MANIPUR

O. Sareeta Devi

Introduction

India's Look East Policy was major shift of its economic game plan following dramatic fragmentation of the Soviet Union, which happened to be a serious drawback for India particularly for the cordial relation, it had enjoyed with the Soviets. This relationship also caused to be a crucial factor for India's failure to open a good rapport with Asian powerhouses like China, Japan, Korea, etc. In the meantime, the political situation on its own backyard was also not so good as it was either very tricky or never stable till the coming of the Narasimha Rao Government in 1991. These facts could be the reason, which enforced India to look out for a new policy to compensate the loss and also to reconstruct its position interface with the booming economic globalisation.

Thus, Look East Policy of India came into being as an alternative to create a better political and economic connectivity with ASEAN countries, which had been distanced from India due to political reason. The new policy was, therefore, aims towards opening trade and economic partnership with these countries. The policy has got a booster with the visit of the former Indian Prime Minister Narasimha Rao in China, Japan, Korea, Vietnam and Singapore and thenceforth India became a sectorial dialogue partner with ASEAN in 1992, full dialogue partner in 1995, a member ASEAN Regional Forum (ARF) in 1996 and significantly a Summit level partner on par with China, Japan and Korea in 2002. Thereafter, India never looked back and determined to expedite the policy with due care and attention of Ministry of Foreign Affairs, Government of India. Because the Policy itself was very strategic and important as said by the former Prime Minister Manmohan Singh who said "It (the Policy) was also a strategic shift in India's Vision of the world and India's place in the involving global economy".

The first India-ASEAN Business Summit was held in October 2002 at New Delhi and thereafter, it has become an annual feature holding the Summit at Phnom Penh (Cambodia) in 2002, Bali (Indonesia) in 2003, Vietnam (Laos) in 2004, at Kuala Lampur (Malaysia) in 2005 and so on. The following agreements have been entered into by India with the ASEAN:

1. Framework Agreement on Comprehensive Economic Cooperation (for establishing FTA in a time of 10 years) was concluded in Bali in 2003.
2. An ASEAN-India Joint declaration for Cooperation to Combat International Terrorism has been adopted.
3. India has acceded to the Treaty of Amity and Cooperation (TAC) in 2003, on which ASEAN was formed initially in 1967.
4. Agreement on "India-ASEAN Partnership for Peace, Progress and Shared Prosperity" was signed at the 3rd ASEAN-India Summit in November 2004.
5. Setting up of Entrepreneurship Development Centres in ASEAN member states — Cambodia, Myanmar, Laos and Vietnam.

The following proposals were announced by the Prime Minister at the 4th ASEAN-India Summit at Kuala Lampur in 2005:

(i) Setting up centres for English Language Training (ELT) in Cambodia, Laos, Myanmar and Vietnam.
(ii) Setting up a tele-medicine and tele-education network for Cambodia, Myanmar, Laos and Vietnam.
(iii) Organising special training courses for diplomats from ASEAN countries.
(iv) Organising an India-ASEAN Technology Summit in 2006.
(v) Organising education fairs and road shows in ASEAN countries.
(vi) Conducting an India-ASEAN IT Ministerial and Industry Forum in 2006.

Coming a long way from its birth, the Look East India Policy has entered into a new phase today. The policy maker of New Delhi has initiated the idea to facilitate the development of the North-East Region by means of widening its transport and communication networks. The centre had realised the urgent need for establishment of a conducive commercial linkage between these states and the other ASEAN countries so that one may take the advantages of the new policy with a new hope and confidence to the people of NE. LEP also could be a better mechanism to end the stigma of separating the North-East from the Indian mainsteam. Some people may, therefore, rightly consider the policy as a mechanism to appease the North-Eastern Region in view of the air of discontentment and multi-pronged disorders prevailed there. But it should not be taken so lightly. Here, Toki Blah in his article, "India's Eastern Neighbouring (IEN)" challenges in our relationships and the Look East Policy stated that "One recognises the fear of being left behind and its exactly what we should not allow to happen again, simply because we already are the victims of past administrative negligence and political unconcern." The problem of the LEP, therefore, lies not so much from mainland India's overtures to its Eastern neighbours or the so called presumptuous "Keeping with the jones", but from the apathy, ignorance and total indifference of the regions political elite and intelligentsia towards the whole concept of change.

The former Prime Minister of India, Dr. Manmohan Singh in his inaugural address of the Second India-ASEAN Summit meeting on 8 October, 2003 at Bali, had categorically stated "To draw dramatic attention to our geographical proximity we could consider the idea of an India-ASEAN Car Rally a positive routing from Guwahati in North-East India through Myanmar, Thailand and Cambodia to Hanoi in Vietnam." Such a rally would draw in commercial interest in infrastructure along the route. It can promote Tourism and Development. There could be a long-term impact on the Economic Cooperation in the region. The key objective of the Rally was —

1. To demonstrate the promixity of India with the ASEAN countries.
2. To create public awareness of India-ASEAN relations.
3. To promote connectivity, specially road transport.
4. To enhance trade, investment, tourism and people to people links between India-ASEAN countries.

True to the words of the former Prime Minister, the India-ASEAN Car Rally was flagged off by Dr. Manmohan Singh in the afternoon of the 22nd November, 2004 at Guwahati with much fan fare. When the Rally reached Imphal, the capital city of Manipur *en-route* to Thailand *via* Moreh town on the Indo-Myanmar border, it was received by the State with a great enthusiasm. The people were completely enthralled by the very objective of the rally which happened to be a dream come true of the prophetic words, '*Nongpok Thong Hanganiye*' as found in the 16th-17th Century Manuscripts like '*Ningthourol Shingkok*' and more precisely in '*Matam Khonglei Takpa*' (Predicting the course of time) written in ancient Manipuri Archaic script. Significantly, the Manipur Chapter of the said Rally was given the name '*Nongpok Thong Hangba*' meaning the Opening in the eastern gate. But strangely, majority of the people of Manipur particularly, the laymen had no idea about the new Look East Policy till the said Car Rally came to Imphal on the said day. Therefore, the Rally organised in the name of '*Nongpok Thong Hangba*' was precisely a trend setter and sort of inspiration for all parties who had been already engaged in the Indo-Myanmar Border Trade through Moreh town of Manipur which ought to be developed into a potential transit point with necessary infrastructures sooner than later.

LEP and Manipur

It may be pertinent here to point out that the Indo-Myanmar Border was already opened in 1995 subsequent to the Indo-Myanmar Border Trade Agreement between India and Myanmar, which permitted trading of 22 items by the residents of both sides across the border through Moreh. Now, the trade items have been reportedly minimised to 7 only through it was 40 a few years back despite daily transactions in term of crores between borders. Shri O. Ibobi Singh, Chief Minister of Manipur has spoken at length in the Meeting of the Chief Ministers of the North-East States on 'Look East Policy' seated on October 2007 at Delhi. He said, "historically the economy of the North-East Region was very closely interlinked with South-East Asian countries like Myanmar and Bangladesh. The partition of the country in 1947 has dramatically changed their historical links. The opening of the border trade pact in Moreh has begun to restore the bilateral trade between Manipur and Myanmar. Strategically situated in the far-flung corner of this vast Sub-continent, Manipur is a natural corridor to Myanmar and to the rest of South-East Asia. He also pointed out that India's Look East Policy may help to address to the languishing Economic Condition of the State and for which the State Department of Commerce and Industries would have to exercise the responsibilities as the link agent to promote the trade between the two countries. Because out of 1643 kms. long border sharing by the two countries, Manipur alone have 398 kms with Myanmar."

And also the past record shows, there have been long tradition of human links for authorised or unauthorised trading across the border well even before very existence of the new policy and construction of the present market at Namphalong on Myanmar's side. Hundreds and thousands of men and women belonging to both countries are doing small time business as means of livelihood throughout the year by trading garments, electronic goods agricultural products like cereals and pulses, precious and semi-precious stones like ruby, saphire, etc. unmindful of the stress and strains for travelling on the sub-standard Imphal-Moreh roads. A very common sight in this sector is the traditional barter system of common trades within 40 kms. of the international border. One could see every morning at Imphal about hundreds of Tata Sumos and buses ready for departure carrying the petty traders from different parts to Moreh. Likewise hundreds of Myanmaris swarmed to Moreh market from the other side with head loads of items for sale. But surprisingly many of them have no notice of either the very existence of the much-publicised Indo-Myanmar Agreement or any other agreements for which we have been under process of a serious dialogue. But my point for dragging into these simple stories is to demonstrate that many people across the border have found their way in the continuing border trade of domestic products from their own backyards. But still there is a possibility to maximise the export and import condition of both ways by means of improvement of the infrastructural requirements to enhance the productivity both in quality and quantity.

In these circumstances it may rightly presume that the Border trade between Manipur and Myanmar under the shadow of the Indo-Myanmar Border Trade Agreement 1994 could be utilised as an enhancer to gear up the age-old community trade by residents from across the border. They knew well about their business by tradition and apparently need no further rulebooks or the existing State laws to them for the matter of their business. It may, therefore, safely to conclude that the LEP reaches even to the commonest people and help them to their fight for survival, which is more important than the accumulation of huge profits by a few big traders.

Local experts are in a very positive frame of mind and believe that there is no reason to be pessimistic about the Indo-Myanmar Trade in case the provisions of the Agreement are fully implemented. They also pointed out that the entire North-East Region particularly Manipur can be benefited, by taking the advantage of its own geographical location and it can draw major share out of the deal. It is well known that the Border Trade is ought to be operationalised through Moreh in Manipur. In the meantime we are not supposed to contravene the opinion put forwarded by B.K. Sharma and S.N. Goswami that with the liberalisation of the Border Trade, the activities like trade and commerce, banking and insurance services, transport and communication, warehousing, etc. would be increased in the North-East which in turn would accelerate the economic activities of the region. Further, India's determination to expand its business has been proved more than once by number of Agreements and MoUs like — Tripartite Maritime Agreement between India, Thailand and Myanmar, Border Trade Agreement and on Cooperation between Civilian Border Authorities, etc. Further the Indian Companies are physically involved in oil and gas exploration in Myanmar. A feasibility study has also been undertaken for a rail link between India and Myanmar by which Manipur being a border state may avail the consequential advantage.

India had completed the 160 km. long Tamu-Kalewa-Kalemyo highway in 2001 and there is project for construction of a trilateral highway from Moreh in India to Mae Sot in Thailand to Bagan in Myanmar of which, the progress is being reviewed regularly by the Foreign Ministry of the three nations. If it goes on without interruption, there is no reason to disregard the possibilities of route connectivities between border town of Moreh with Thailand, and Myanmar, in near future. Chief Minister of Manipur O. Ibobi Singh also subscribed to the view that Manipur is a natural corridor to Myanmar and the rest of South-East Asia and, so, he categorically stated in the Chief Minister's meeting of NE States on India's Look East Policy held during October 2007 at New Delhi. He proposed some measures to be undertaken as part of the Look East Policy, i.e. (i) to upgradation of Imphal Airport into an International Airport with cold storage facilities, (ii) National Highways No. 39, 53 and 150 across the state to be strengthen to four lane roads for easy flow of heavy vehicles and also to improve the State Highways and Border Roads to meet adequately the Trade and Commercial requirements. (iii) expedite the proposed Trans-Asian-Highway connecting Moreh in Manipur to Mae Sot in Thailand and Bagan in Myanmar (now in progress), (iv) better road connectivity for trading point at Moreh through ASIDE (Assistance to States for Infrastructure Development under the Ministry of Commerce and Industries), (vi) extend rail route from Tupul (now under construction) to Moreh with a hope to reach to Hanoi in Vietnam *via* Moreh, (vi) improve telecom connection between Imphal and Moreh and also to expedite the proposed optical fibre link of 6 kms. between Moreh and Tamu (in Myanmar), (vii) increase the number of tradeable items at the border trade post in Moreh to 44 (now 40 and minimise to

7 reportedly), (viii) credit facilities need to be more easily accessible, and (ix) end the Protected Area Permit in Manipur which happened to be a stumbling block to Tourism Development in the state.

On the other hand, many well known groups and individuals are sceptical about the new Look East Policy. A premier International Trade body of the North-East has decried the lack of benefit to the region from the country's Look East Policy and alleged that the State Governments were responsible for the sad state of affairs. R.C. Agrawal, Chairman of the North-East Federation of International Trade (NEFIT), Guwahati, has expressed displeasure with the progress of the policy saying — "India's policy of strengthening its ties with eastern neighbours has been sadly limited to counter insurgency effort." Sushil Khanna of the Indian Institute of Management has also stated in his article, "Look East, Look South: Backward Border Regions in India and China" that "in contrast to the lukewarm effort for economic integration, the Look East Policy and the concessions and aid are meant to persuade the neighbouring countries to expel insurgent groups seeking shelter in these countries. Frequent visits by the Indian generals and counter insurgency exports meant to pressure these countries to cooperate with the Indian States to crush these movement." At the same length, he further stated that, "The Indian state is suspicious of opening the borders as it fears greater movements of arms and insurgents. Though the land routes of Bangladesh and Myanmar have been opened up the goods that can be traded are confined to local produce as border trade." These viewpoints bear more substance than nuts in view of the frequent diplomatic exercise between the two nations and recent Press Statement of the Home Secretary, Government of India when he visited Imphal on 27 February, 2010 that "the NE insurgents in Myanmar will be flush out soon". These are few instances to be cited as there are many more tales of woos. Despite the signing of the Indo-Myanmar trade way back in 1994 to facilitate a congenial trade practice through Moreh in Manipur, there is no reason to be very happy for the local traders due to multifaceted law and order problems and poor infrastructures and slow progress in development projects already committed by the government authorities.

If one travel by road along the 118 kms. dusty route connecting the state capital with Moreh town, it would be a gruesome experience for everyone. It takes about 4-5 hours to complete the journey. The road condition is never smooth and the passage is fluctuated so often due to frequent security checks and collection of taxes by both authorised and unauthorised parties. Another gruesome sight which have been left scotch free by the successive State Governments for so many years is the collection of sort of illegal taxes by the security forces as a matter of right from petty traders travelling along the Imphal-Moreh road. Still it is going on as a state sponsored trade and it is all in addition to huge taxes imposed by the insurgent groups operating in the region. Against this background, one may ponder whimiscally, whether the Indo-Myanmar trade as part of India's Look East Policy will ever be materialised or is it a boon or bane? Here may I quote Ginsei Lhungdium, the General Secretary of Hills Tribal Council, of Moreh (Manipur) who said, "What we want is that the Government should speed up the process. The Government is always slow but I think and I hope it will get materialise soon." Here the question is naturally on how far the State Government has committed to develop the export-import along this sector like: (i) establishment of trade centre providing facility to traders and entrepreneurs, (ii) improvement of roads, infrastructure under ASID scheme, (iii) setting up Special Economic Zones, and (iv) Introduction of Inland Container and Warehousing facility. The answer would be quite miserable and still the government has failed to provide even the basic facilities like Banking, Postal Service, Power, Water Supply, Good Roadways Communication, adequate security and toiletries along the highway.

Conclusion

Notwithstanding of division of the opinions, the Border Trade across the border is pushing ahead though in a smaller way than expected. A large section of the society still find hopes and inspiration that the Indo-Myanmar Trade could play a pivotal role in promoting the economic condition of the North-East which is exactly the expert vision of the planners. And coming to Manipur once again, it is industrially a backward state and financially not strong either. Border Trade along the Moreh-Tamu sector would be hardly possible to grow by its own without adequate support and encouragement from the government to local traders, entrepreneurs and small-scale units first to generate employment and export avenues. Along with, the State Government should gear up the institutional mechanism to fulfil its promises for the growth of industries and infrastructure developments and check the unauthorised collection of taxes adequately to make the area a free trade zone, whatever status, may be at present. We are bound to accept the ground reality that hundreds and thousands of petty traders and small entrepreneurs find their way under the new Look East Policy and the subsequent

Indo-Myanmar Border Trade across the border as a means of economic empowerment and hence dependable. The commitment to facilitate the export and import along the border should be prioritised to expedite as part of the policy at the earliest or otherwise the jubilation of the '*Nongpok Thong Hangba*' is proned to be remained as a misconception. Here we may cite the Reinvesting Ourselves (*Imphal Free Press*) that, "the moot question is, are we prepared? It would be so self-defeating if we again choose to, or else are forced too, continue with our want of scapegoating history as an excuse for current failures, instead of picking up the courage and calibre to carry on from where history has left us and re-invent ourselves to the needs of the time."

REFERENCES

Border Trade Report (2010): Director of Commerce and Industries, and Informatics Officer, NIC Manipur, January 07.

Dialogue (2007): A *Journal of Astha Bharati*, New Delhi, October-December.

India hoping to take 'Look East Policy' to new level: PM October 23, 2009.

Look East Policy a Failure in NE (2010): *NEFIT Sunday*, January 23.

Nityanand Deva (2005-07): *Look East Policy*, Jaipuria Institute of Management Lucknow.

Record from Manipur State Archives.

Sanjib Baruah (2005): "Gateway to the East" a Symposium on *North-East India and Look East Policy*, June.

Speech of the Chief Minister (2007): Manipur, in the Meeting of Chief Ministers of North-Eastern States on Look East Policy at Hyderabad House, New Delhi, October 31.

State Reception Committee (2004): *India-ASEAN Car Rally*, Government of Manipur.

Sushil Khanna, *Look East, Look South Backward Regions in India and China*, India Institute of Management, Kolkata.

Thiyam Bharat, *Indo-Myanmar Trade and the Economy of Manipur*.

Local Dailies

The Imphal Free Press (English).

The Sangai Express (English and Manipuri).

21

INDIA'S LOOK EAST POLICY AND ITS IMPACTS
An Experience From Manipur

Th. Binarani Devi

Introduction

A new trade policy has ushered in India within the new global economy by giving a sweeping change in the existing trade scenario of the country, mainly after July-August 1991. It embodied elements that are working to alter the very functioning of the economy for good. This new Economic Policy has the clear objective of integrating the Indian economy with the rest of the world. The policy instruments consist of mainly providing all facilities to the private sector for starting new industrial ventures by removing all kinds of government restrictions which had been characteristic features of the Indian Economy from 1950. In other words, most of the trade restrictions had to be liberalised to encourage international trade as one of the policy instruments related to the New Economic Policy. With the absence of a comprehensive policy governing international trade with the eastern neighbours through the North-East India which shares nearly 5,000 kms of border with Bangladesh, China, Myanmar and Bhutan, the Indian Government's Look East Policy (LEP) initiatives, though in its formative stage, generated considerable interest in North-East India in general and Manipur in particular. This priority is to be accorded by all Central agencies concerned and State Governments because, it is in North-East India that South-East Asia begins and, as such, it is for the North-East to be enabled to play the arrowhead role in the further evolution of this Policy. This requires a redefining of the Look East Policy to resolve outstanding issues of trade, transit and investment with the countries neighbouring the region. It also involves promoting Indian investment in infrastructure in partner countries, especially Myanmar, particularly in respect of ports such as Sittawe and international highways to connect the North-East Region to ASEAN. Myanmar shares 1,643 km long border with North-East India (Manipur, Mizoram, Nagaland and Arunachal Pradesh). The Government of India and the Myanmar Government signed a border trade agreement on June 1994 for exchanging locally produced commodities by people living along the border. But on 12th April, 1995 the Indo-Myanmar Cross Border trade was formally opened by P. Chidambaram, the then former Indian Union Minister of Commerce and Myanmar Counterpart Lt. Gen. Tun Kyi, Minister of Trade. Since then the continental trade between the two countries have started formally with the expectation of extending beyond Myanmar to other South-East Asian countries. Indo-Myanmar trade relationship is the stepping stone for promotion of trade between India and other South-East Asian countries. The eventual success of India's Look East Policy will depend on India's ability to control both a maritime and a continental trust in the Look East Policy.

At present two trade centres — one in Manipur at Moreh-Tamu sector, since April 1995, and another in Mizoram at Champhai Rih sector since January 2004 are operating between the two countries. In order to boost border trade, there is a proposal to develop infrastructural and other facilities for the Myanmarese port of Sittawe which is 200 km from the nearest Indian Border in Mizoram. What is, however, discouraging is the tough and inhospitable terrain leading to Zaorkhatwar in Champhai district of Mizoram and Rih in Myanmar and further beyond which by itself is retroactive of the volume of trade. The location of Manipur is with extreme corner of North-East India, which has a long international boundary of 352 km. with Myanmar to the East and South-East. After signing the Indo-Myanmar cross border trade in 1995, Manipur is considered as gateway to South-East Asian countries. So Manipur has a very good experience of both merits and demerits of India's Look East Policy directly.

Trading system between India and Myanmar may be broadly categorised into official or legal and unofficial or illegal. The official or legal multi-lateral or bilateral trade is synonymous with international trade while the unofficial trade is popularly known as smuggling. A major portion of the trade between the two countries is unofficial. Businessmen or trader from Imphal, Kohima, Silchar, Aizawl, Shillong, Guwahati and Kolkata work through the local agents at different trade centres like Moreh, Champhai and Lungmalong on Myanmar Border.

When the border trade was opened in 1995 between India and Myanmar, it covered 22 items as exchangeable items *vide* public notice number 289(PN) dated 10th April, 1995 with effect from 12th April, 1995. But the official legal trade has been dying slowly over the years, while the unofficial trade has been flourishing.

The North-Eastern Region of India is known for its social and economic backwardness as well as never ending story of social and political instability and poor political delivery system. There is a great need for a participatory human development, the investment of human being themselves by means of education and training, i.e. human capital is quite necessary. Again in the pattern of human capital accumulation, youth constitutes the latent resource of human resource development. Today, the trend of unemployment youth stands a major crisis in the human resource development. This crisis, sometimes, responses negative human capital investment. The number of unemployed youth registered in the employment exchange was 5,75,605 in October 2006.[1] The negative responses are made by themselves which directly made erosion in the human capital. Such erosion in the human capital is caused like substance abuse, addiction of alcohol, tobacco and illicit drug and also HIV cases. It set a major social and economic problem as well as waste of human resource development.

Government of India and LEP

India can be regarded as a developed country when the socio-economic and political conditions of all parts/region are developed in an equal way. Mooted as a path breaking initiative to bring development to the North-Eastern Region, India's Look East Policy aims to further the country's buoyant trade with South-East Asia. The present effort in connection with Look East Policy to make the North-Eastern Region a transit point with an attempt to enhance the productive forces of the region for its economic regeneration and development undertaken the utility of the policy. The structure of India's Look East Policy is characterised by free flow of capital, commodities, financial fluidity, deterritorialisation of national political economic frontiers and increasing geographical mobility. The ongoing project of the Government of India for constructing a new rail link between Jiribam-Imphal-Moreh and further linking it to Tamu-Kalay-Segji and Cabinet Committee on Economic Affairs' clearance on the proposal to augment the road network in the North-East, which also includes the connection of the capitals of Nagaland, Meghalaya and Sikkim with the East-West Corridor will enhance the policy.[2] In November 2005 former Prime Minister Dr. Manmohan Singh brought North-East to the centre stage by flagging off at Guwahati the Indo-Asian Car Rally that ended at Batam in Indonesia. This link of the North-East also brought to the fore the diversity of India which is a challenge that the region has to grapple with while trying to solve the problems of its economic backwardness, growing unemployment, militancy, recurring floods and immigration.

Hopes and Aspirations from the LEP

With 96 per cent of the borders of the North-East Region constituting international boundaries, and in explicit recognition of the need to break the fetters of the geo-political isolation of the Region, it is necessary to factor in what the Minister of External Affairs has described as "new inputs" in foreign, defence, internal security and international trade policy. To this end, the immediate priority is to build the required infrastructure right up to the border areas, establishing connectivity and communication links to the cross-border points through which trade and economic exchanges with the countries neighbouring the North-East Region are proposed to be promoted under the 'Look East Policy' (NER Vision 2020).

The proposed Trans Asian Highway from Singapore to Istanbul through India, Myanmar and Thailand will further developed the trade relationship between India and Myanmar and other South-East Asian countries with the introduction of this new highway the most chronic problems of the youth of North-Eastern Region, i.e. the problem of unemployment will solve in somewhat range. They will get job directly as well as indirectly. The location of the region is also more favourable to have a trade relationship with South-East Asian Region as it is even more closer to the market of this region than that of the mainland markets of India like Delhi, Mumbai, Chennai, etc. The originality of the people are also more similar with the people of the South Asian Region than that of the Indian mainland.[3] The rational for a trade led growth strategy for the North-East as integrated to the Look East Policy has been well explained. The landlocked North-East India is ideally placed to link India with ASEAN both in geographical and commercial senses. The North-East also has strong cultural and historical linkages with South and South-East Asia, which could be exploited to forge economic cooperation. Buddhist religious communities of Myanmar, Thailand, etc. want to visit Bodh Gaya, Kusinagar, etc. by crossing North-East India. North-East people like Nagas, Tais, Meiteis, etc. also want to know and exchange their views with the people of their communities who are residing in Thailand, Singapore, Myanmar, etc. Presently in the Western tourist dominated scenario, access to the North-East is seen constraint. While air access will have to be developed as a *sine qua non* for tourism development strategy, fortunately, the Asian Highway Project is looming in the horizon as a great opportunity for the region. The Asian Highway, if properly planned and integrated, can completely change the tourism scenario of the region. It proposes to cover 90,000 km in 25 countries, of which 40,000 km will be international routes and 50,000 km. will be regional routes. ESCAP which is spearheading the project, recognises the excellent tourism potential of the Asian Highways.[4]

The Ambassador of Thailand to India, Krit Kraichitti addressed a press conference at Dimapur, Nagaland on Friday, 6 February, 2010. He expressed about the huge potential to be promoted as a tourism hotspot in North-East India, especially Nagaland. He also mentioned for the promotion of Indo-Thai relationship, particularly in the North-East converge India's Look East and Thailand's Look West policy and establish people to people contract.

There is an ample scope and potential for hydro power resources, oil, gas, eco-tourism, IT, tea, wildlife, herbal medicinal plants, fruits, etc. in North-East India. If all these goods are fully harvested and exported through Myanmar to other South-East Asian countries, it will give direct and indirect job opportunities to the educated and uneducated youth of the region, which will result in the massive growth to the economy of the region.

Manipur After the Look East Policy of India

South Asia's development experience shows that there is a large gap between leading region and lagging region. Poverty is high in lagging regions as compared with leading regions. The spatial distribution of leading and lagging regions shows two features — first, this income gap exists both within countries and between countries, and second, most of the lagging regions are located around the border areas. A key reason why border regions tend to be lagging is lack of connectivity to regional growth centres, lack of infrastructure, political neglect. The location of Manipur is with extreme corner of North-East India bordering with Myanmar on the east. After signing the Indo-Myanmar cross border trade in 1995, Manipur is considered as gateway to South-East Asian countries.

When the border trade was opened in 1995 between India and Myanmar it covered 22 items. But the official legal trade has been dying slowly over the years, while the unofficial trade has been flourishing. Apart from economic and trade-related factors, closer links with Bangladesh and Myanmar are crucial to the issue of controlling insurgency in the North-East Region States. On the other hand, China is an economic hotspot in the world today and needs to be factored into India's economic and foreign policies. Despite improvements in infrastructure linkages at points like Moreh, very little trade benefits seem to accrue to the NER States. This is probably due to the fact that existing trade agreement (like the one with Myanmar) are restrictive towards trade in agricultural products.

Apart from carrying out illegal trade between countries of South Asia through North-East India were losing revenue, from general criminal activities to force inimical to both the countries was taking advantage of the situation. Chief Minister of Manipur, Sri O. Ibobi Sing expressed the need for drawing attention of the Ministry of Home Affairs to the Indo-Myanmar border areas in the Chief Ministers Conference held at Vigyan Bhawan, New Delhi on 7 February, 2010. He clearly mentioned that "It is also known that whenever the army, Assam Rifles and the State Police launch operations, the militant groups seek and find shelter in neighbouring areas of Myanmar."[5] Carrying of arms, ammunitions, taking shelter by the people of underground organisations, etc. are happening in the border areas. Discovering the movement of Myanmarese nationals at Rajai area, Assam Rifles troops launched an operation and apprehended two persons around 7 am of 24 February, 2010.[6] Assam Rifles personnel apprehended two Myanmarese nationals, Khongo (25 years) and Ngapho (30), with 130 kg of materials for making explosives at Ukhrul area of Manipur on Wednesday, 24 Febuary, 2010. Insurgents are moving freely in the border areas and they have their camps there which gave a serious disturbance to the internal security of Manipur especially and North-East India in general. He also mentioned that those arms and ammunitions collected from the insurgents clearly exhibited that they are used weapons from Myanmar. A radio message intercepted by security forces has confirmed the location of Ulfa "Commander in Chief" Paresh Baruah in Myanmar and headquarter of 28th battalion is situated somewhere near the Naga-Myanmarese border.[7] The alleged involvement of leaders from different angles — politicians, underground organisations, intelligence, bureaucrats, etc. are also coming up in the ongoing scenario of the Indian border issues. In an interrogation report of Hafizur Rahman clearly shows the ISI-Ulfa-Tarique nexus. Hafizur admitted that some National Security Intelligence (NSI), Directorate General of Forces Intelligence (DGFI) and Chittagong Urea Fertilizer Company Ltd. (CUFCL) officials were in the attempt to smuggle 10 truck loads of arms on April 2 in 2004. "Hafizur Rahman (the Accused) has confessed before the Magistrate (Bangladesh court) that he had met Tarique (Former Bangladeshi Prime Minister Khaleda Zia's son) at Hawa Bhaban along with Ulfa leader Paresh Baruah on April 1, 2004.[8] The message which was intercepted on Friday, 5 February, 2010 which being relayed between the respective operators of Baruah and Ulfa central executive committee member Jiban Moran, was about a charge of alleged sexual harassment brought by a women militant against two of her seniors. Human movements are not envisaged as a means of addressing some of the tangled ethnic and identity problems that the north-eastern region has been facing in the wake of Independence and reorganisation of India's borders with the neighbouring countries. These movements are seen as only secondary to trade, tourism and usual cultural exchange activities. Look East Policy is never seen as offering any opportunity to the region for solving its complex problems generated from alarming immigration from across the borders. Much of it occurs independently of so-called trade, tourism and cultural exchange activities.[9] Such investment might also be encouraged where required for transit between the Region and the rest of India, as also for trade with the neighbourhood and beyond. However, in such a process, we recognise that it is critical to address the challenges of border management, especially with regard to cross border migration, terrorism, drugs and arms supply and other forms of non-conventional security threats for ensuring the rights and traditions of local indigenous ethic groups comprehensively in the context of global forces of change, internal and external threat, etc.

The increase in illegal trade specially of drug trafficking is largely responsible for the fast degeneration of social environment in Myanmar bordering states of North-East India such as Manipur, Mizoram, Nagaland and Arunachal Pradesh. North-East region is in the most critical heroin trafficking route of India. Different chemicals which are used in producing heroin No. 4 from raw opium are smuggled from Kolkata and other parts of the country to Tamu, Mandalay, then to the north-eastern part of the Shan States. After refining, Heroin No. 4 is smuggled to North-East India then into the world market.[10] India is sandwiched between the Golden Triangle — Burma, Thailand and Laos in the east and the Golden Crescent — Pakistan, Afghanistan and Iran in the west. In the north

Nepal is a major source of supply of Marijuana and hashish in the world market. The Golden Triangle and the Golden Crescent are the main producer and supplier of opium and opium drug, morphine, brown sugar and heroin to the West.[11] Located on the massive chuck of hilly areas of four South-East Asian countries — Thailand, Myanmar (Burma), Laos and Vietnam — the Golden Triangle is one of Asia's two major opium producing areas. Drug mafias from China, Myanmar, Bangladesh and Nepal invest in such plantation in remote places including, Manipur, engaging local villagers. It is just a matter of an hour to two from the cultivation site to cross the border from where the same could be easily reached the clandestine laboratories in the Golden Triangle from where heroin is manufactured with different brand names. The value of one kg. of heroin in the local market is ₹ 10 lakh and it shoots upto ₹ 1 crore in the international market. Under Section 48 of the Narcotic Drugs and Psychotropic Substance (NDPS) Act, the NCB (Narcotic Control Bureau) is empowered to attach and destroy illegal cultivation of poppy plants among other narcotic substance.[12] But in connection with the problem, surprise information is security personnels are directly and indirectly involved in this trade. Among the security personnels, the Myanmarese army, the Indian Customs Department, the BSF, etc. are focused in the media. Keeping this fact in view, any sort of free trade between India and South-East Asia entails the risk of opening a floodgate of immigrants and with it hordes of heroin smugglers from across the border.[13] With the opening of more roads, railways through Myanmar are sure to bring drugs and infectious diseases. The impact of the golden triangle is badly felt particularly in Manipur and other North-East States and India in general where the number of drug addicts are increasing. As a result, the number of drug addicts in Manipur is increasing day by day. Manipur AIDS Control Society checked 1,65,747 (3,38,203) samples. Out of those persons, 24,198 (33,408) found HIV positive in 2009.[14] Consequently, the HIV positive cases are also increasing day by day. Not only the local people, the armed security personnels who are posted in the border areas are also suffering from this case. Inspector General, BSF, Assam, Nagaland, Meghalaya, Manipur, Joyti Prasad Sinha expressed to the UNI, Shillong that six jawana in BSF are found HIV positive in North-East India. And 94 persons are found in the BSF in India as a whole.[15] The figure of the HIV affected persons is increasing so quickly in the state of Manipur when it compared with the All India figure. The rich middle class people from other parts of India and abroad rushed towards this region for the business of this high value low weight items. But their business gives direct impetus to the youth of the region so badly.

For total reaping of the benefits of India's Look East Policy, industrialisation of the state is quite necessary for the state of Manipur. But, more than a decade after the initiation of India's Look East Policy, there has been no serious introspective effort on the part of the state to change the infrastructure and industrial structure of the region. Despite its comparative advantage in this region, tourism, cultural and its allied industries are not perceived as an important economic activity. The lack of infrastructure and the issues of the Protected Areas Permit System, the frequent administrative changes, unstable governments and transfer of staffs, etc. hamper the natural growth in these areas. There is little to cheer about industrial growth in the region even though the states concerned had formed a joint front to put up in vein a credible image to the perspective investors to alloy their apprehensions about security and sustainability. The North-Eastern Industrial Development Policy (NEIDP) launched in 1997 and later extended to other special category states provided for incentives to entrepreneurs in the form of transport subsidy and tax exemptions and it could attract no more than ₹ 1,268 crore in the region in course of seven years as compared to Himachal Pradesh which draws ₹ 7,010 in just one year. The policy having proved to be a damp squib for the North-East during its life span of ten years, the states of the region are now engaged in an all out offensive in favour of an alternative package with additional incentives exclusively for the region. Little wonder than that the Council's (North-Eastern Council) residue in February 2006 to accord due importance to industrial pace through launching of innovation schemes was too convincing to create any flutter among the investors.[16]

As a part of infrastructural development Government spend crores of rupees on building markets, dams, bridges and roads but everything exists on papers. The availability of huge consumer goods and items brought from other parts with the full operationalisation of Look East Policy may usher the economically weaker sections of our society into retreated behaviour. The practice of consumerism, a Look East Policy phenomenon, will endanger the North-East by exposing it to a situation where there is tension in the wants, which in order to balance global consumer tastes, images, needs and meanings, consequently compels it to desire things which are actually absent. The easy and abundant availability of consumerist items and goods in the region is more or less certain which would in most cases serve the interest of the multinational companies. Local farmers sell their products on nominal rates which are bought by middlemen who hoard it. This artificially increases the prices.

Those poor local farmers buy their basic necessity produced manufactured goods from the middlemen at high prices again. Government makes different policies, programmes, etc. in connection with the infrastructural development of the state of Manipur. But, the implementation of those policies and programmes are always with question marks. As for instance, Manipur connects with the Indian mainland by only two national highways, i.e. NH-39 and 53. The responsibility for repairing work for only a distance of 23 km of road from Maram to Mao at NH-39 was given to BRTF in 1976 which was not completed in the given period. Then the Manipur State Government requested the Central Government for handling the responsibility of repairing whole Highway (from Maram to North AOC) to BRO. But unluckily, the activities of the BRO were also not satisfactory. So, eventually the work for repairing and construction on NH-39 was taken over by the State Government. The point I want to emphasise here is this the repairing of only 2 km road could not be completed, despite all the so called efforts, within 34 years what will be the condition of the overall infrastructural development of the State.

With the opening of new trade routes in the region with a liberalised economy, the forceful flow of massive migrant population has led to serious complications in the fragile economic, political and cultural life of the indigenous people. The presence of mainland immigrants and illegal foreigners is not only a threat to the indigenous population of the region but also a security risk for the country as a whole. Immigration on a large-scale has created an environment conducive for the emergence of communal and linguistic problems. The emergence of collusive networks of smugglers organised criminal gangs and religious extremist groups operating in the North-Eastern greatly accentuated the problems of illegal immigration. Apart from the problems of drug smuggling, human trafficking, gun running, etc. generally associated with cross-border immigration, another security concern is the infiltration of foreign intelligence agencies along with the hordes of espionage and other clandestine operating.[17]

The states of North-Eastern Region are popularly known for their poor and backwardness. Parents of poor children want to give higher education and good proper jobs for their children. Children and women of North-East region are trafficking to other states of India and neighbouring countries. Hundreds of children are reported missing from north-eastern region every year and traffickers are increasing targeting children who are either poor or are victims of domestic violence. In many cases, the traffickers lure parents with promises of good education and food for their wards, and then take the children away to work in other states under inhuman conditions. From the source of local papers (*Poknapham*, Imphal local daily, 30-1-2010) we come to now how much children are trafficked, when and where.

Table 21.1: Number of Children Trafficked During the Last Three Years

Year	*No. of Children*	*Destination*
2007	5	Singapore
2008	22	Chennai
2009	16	Chennai
2010 (January)	54	Tamil Nadu

Source: Poknapham, Imphal Local Daily, January 30, 2010.

The benefits of free trade should reach to the people of North-East rather than going to the business houses in big cities. The Look East Policy of India should not only be a tool to use North-East as a corridor for free trade with neighbours. The overall situations of region are also need to take into account. One important constraint, at present, is regional conflict that has made South Asia one of the least integrated regions of the world. Capital flows through legal channels are negligible, transit arrangements are cumbersome and expensive, and physical connectivity is limited. If a person wants to go to Myanmar, he needs to collect passport from Kolkata. Under drawn to dusk entry pass system the Indians have to pay ₹ 10 or 30 Kyat to the Myanmar authority as entry fee for every individual while crossing border but for Myanmarese no entry fee is charged. Additionally, lack of effective cooperation has constrained progressed on a range of public goods involving climate change, water management, HIV/AIDS and other disaster management. Indeed, in an environment of regional peace and better economic cooperation, the biggest gainers will likely be the poor. A careful look at South Asia's geography shows that the border areas tend to be generally underdeveloped due to poor connectivity, lack of investments, and political neglects. In most cases, economic activities in border areas are constrained by poor connectivity with the regional growth centres and by lack of access to international trade outlets. When we are going to Moreh from Imphal, that is a distance of only 107 km from Imphal, it takes nearly four hours. It also became a gamble in the hands of some local groups and businessmen by calling *bandhs* and strikes for many days. The knowledge of trade with full technical infrastructure is quite necessary, over and above, there is a need for more universities and technical institutes for the youth of the region. Introduction of new and relevant courses in the Universities would help talented students to pursue courses of their choice. But due to the lack of this opportunities minimum expenditure of the region are going out in connection with the education of the youth. The number of higher and technical educational institutions is very low in this region while it is compared with other parts of the country. The following figures show the minimal infrastructure of North-East India in the field of technical and non-technical education.[18]

Table 21.2: Number of Universities and Engineering Institutes in North-East India and some Major States of India

State	*Universities*	*State*	*Engineering Institutes*
North-East	15	North-East	10
Delhi	17	Madhya Pradesh	61
Maharashtra	42	Gujarat	37
Karnataka	23	West Bengal	54
Tamil Nadu	35	Uttar Pradesh	89
Uttar Pradesh	34	Punjab	45
Bihar	14	Maharashtra	155
Rajasthan	20	Karnataka	118
Gujarat	17	Andhra Pradesh	236
West Bengal	20	Tamil Nadu	254

Without the proper knowledge to trade system and technical know how, the chances and fruits of the Government of India's Look East Policy will snatch away automatically from the hands of the local people. Consequently, these will create a lot of unwanted situations in the region.

From the above few points and others, it is very clear that after nineteen years of India's liberalised economic policy and after sixteen years of signing of free trade with the neighbouring countries, one question is still with us — will it be boon or curse to the younger generation of North-Eastern Region generally, and Manipur particularly? Here I would like to draw the attention of the Central and State Governments, if the governments are not taking proper steps in time it will create total chaos and confusion in the region instead of development. Only making policy and programme is not enough for development. Already we have certain loophole from the side of the government that the long cherished dreams of the Look East Policy are yet to be fulfilled. For achieving the real fruits of the India's LEP, I want to mention few suggestions:

(i) To control illegal trade along the 1,640 km. long border with Myanmar and increase the number of official trade items like bicycle, fertilizers, medicine, etc.

(ii) To improve the insufficient infrastructural facilities such as road, transport and communication, banking, insurance, constancy services, warehouse, hotel facilities, etc.

(iii) To find out the measures for improving the present law and order situation of the North-Eastern States in general and bordering states of Manipur and Nagaland in particular which have cause the slow pace of development indirectly and disrupt the normal volume of trade due to frequent bandh, economic blockade and distortions, etc.

(iv) Removal of ignorance of procedures to be followed in the international trade like commercial documents, letter of credit, regulatory documents and export assistance documents by the traders on both sides.

(v) Government might to facilitate certain programmes to encourage the involvement of local people to the infrastructural and trade development.

(vi) Opening of new secondary and tertiary sectoral industry in the area which will give more job facilities to the youths of the region.

REFERENCES

1. *The Sangai Express*, Imphal, November 15, 2006, p. 2.
2. *The Hindu*, October 24, 2005.
3. Th. Binarani Devi (2008): "India's Look East Policy and Youths of Manipur", in B.J. Deb, K. Sengupta and B. Dutta Ray (eds.), *Globalization and North-East India*, Concept Publishing Company Pvt. Ltd., New Delhi, p. 322.
4. Elangbam Nixon Sing (2008): "Tourism in North-East India: Exploring the Paradise", in Asok Kumar Ray and Satyabrata Chakraborty (eds.), *Society, Politics and Development in North-East India*, Concept Publishing Company Pvt. Ltd., New Delhi, pp. 253-54.
5. *The Times of India*, February 8, 2010, p. 4.
6. *The Times of India*, February 26, 2010, p. 4.
7. *The Times of India*, February 7, 2010, p. 3.
8. *The Times of India*, February 9, 2010, p. 1.
9. Das Sameer Kumar (2008): "Between South and South-East Asia: Recasting India's North-East in the Age of Globalization", in Asok Kumar Ray and Satyabrata Chakraborty (eds.), *Society, Politics and Development in North-East India*, Concept Publishing Company Pvt. Ltd., New Delhi, p. 153.
10. *Eastern Frontier*, A Monthly News Magazine, Bikay Loitongbam, Kwakeithel Thiyam Leikai, Imphal, Manipur, Vol. I, Issue No. 6, June 2006, p. 7.
11. Y. Indira Leima (2010): *Nishagi Mishirakta Manipur*, Indira and Co-Publishing House, Paona Bazar, p. 75.
12. *The Times of India*, February 13, 2010, p. 4.

13. "Alternative Frames", *Economy, Polity, History and Culture*, Vol. I, Issue II, June-March, 2006, p. 42.
14. *Manipur Aids Control Society Record.*
15. *Poknapham* (2008): Manipur local daily paper, November 29, 2006.
16. Deb, B.J. (2008): "North-East India and Its Council for Development", in B.J. Deb, K. Sengupta and B. Dutta Ray (eds.), *Globalization and North-East India*, Concept Publishing Company Pvt. Ltd., New Delhi, p. 13.
17. *Alternative Frames, op. cit.*, p. 32.
18. *The Times of India*, November 6, 2006, p. 3.

INDEX